GRACIOUS GOODNESS

A PEACH OF A COOKBOOK

by
The Junior League
of
Macon, Georgia

Printed in the USA by

WIMMER
The Wimmer Companies, Inc.
Memphis • Dallas

ISBN 0-941162-15-X

COOKBOOK COMMITTEES
*Mrs. Rufus Dorsey Sams, III
Chairman
*Mrs. William W. Williams
Vice Chairman • Recipe Chairman
*Mrs. Alex R. Mitchell
Marketing Chairman

*Mrs. V. J. Adams, Jr.
Mrs. Clark Ballard
Mrs. John Barrow
*Mrs. Oliver C. Bateman
*Mrs. William W. Baxley, Jr.
*Mrs. James A. Berg, Jr.
*Mrs. Madge Birdsey
*Mrs. Miles A. Brewer
*Mrs. Derry Burns, Jr.
Mrs. Frank Butler
Mrs. R. William Buzzell
*Mrs. Charles J. Cartwright
*Mrs. Charles F. Causey
Mrs. R. Douglas Cole
Mrs. Joseph S. Costanzo
*Mrs. E. Max Crook
Mrs. L. Rodney Crutchfield
Mrs. John A. Draughon
*Mrs. Guy B. Eberhardt
*Mrs. Gary Ertel
Mrs. Donald C. Eubanks
Mrs. J. Everett Flournoy
Mrs. Benjamin M. Garland
Mrs. Lyn M. Gilbert
Mrs. Warren C. Grice
Mrs. William A. Gudenrath
*Mrs. F. Kennedy Hall
Mrs. William M. Hall
*Mrs. Albert S. Hatcher, III
Mrs. John F. Head, III
*Mrs. Thomas C. Kendrick-Holmes

Mrs. William W. Kidd
Mrs. Allen King
Mrs. Marion H. Liles, Jr.
Mrs. Edgar Young Mallary, III
Mrs. Bert Maxwell, III
*Mrs. R. John McNeill, III
Mrs. Sidney E. Middlebrooks
Mrs. Douglas Noble
Katherine C. Oliver
Miss Marguerite Pellett
Mrs. Daniel L. Pike
Mrs. Calder Pinkston
Mrs. John H. Puryear
Mrs. William H. Rankin
Mrs. Donald K. Ream, III
Mrs. Warren Reid
*Mrs. Donald W. Rhame
Mrs. Ronald E. Robeson
Mrs. John F. Rogers, Jr.
*Mrs. Monty W. Rogers
Mrs. G. Boone Smith, III
*Mrs. Grady A. Smith
Eden P. Solomon
Mrs. James Linton Solomon
*Mrs. H. Jerome Strickland
Mrs. G. Phelps Wade
Mrs. Steve L. Wilson
Mrs. John R. Woodford
Mrs. George Youmans
*Mrs. Andrew W. Young
Mrs. Robert M. Young

*This symbol denotes that the league member has served more than one year on the cookbook committee.

Recipes appearing in this cookbook without names are cookbook committee recipes obtained from friends and other sources.

My heartfelt thanks to all of you who were generous enough to share your favorite recipes and interested enough in this effort to see the Macon Junior League cookbook become a reality. With your help a common task has come aglow and has become exciting. Our cookbook committees for the past few years have aimed for excellence and have worked diligently to achieve that goal. I appreciate the invaluable assistance of interested sustainers: Mrs. Thomas McKelvey, Mrs. Flew Murphey, Mrs. Donald Rhame, Mrs. Wilbur I. Tucker and Mrs. Frank Walthall; of interested fans who typed and met our deadline: Patsy Gardin, Cindy Johnston, and Sandra Tucker; of our art director, Pat Quinn, a special talent who has become a very special friend; and of our printers who have assisted and advised along the way. To each of you, to my husband for the many constructive suggestions he offered, and to God who has walked with me through this venture and who has brightened every circumstance, I offer my deepest appreciation. This book is dedicated to all of you, your husbands, and your families who have been patient with the launching of *Gracious Goodness*.

Sidney Tucker Sams
(Mrs. Rufus Dorsey Sams, III)

Cookbook Chairman

TABLE OF CONTENTS

RECIPES

INTRODUCTION

"Gracious Goodness" is an outstanding collection of recipes. For over two years, our league collected the time-tested recipes of the cooks of Middle Georgia who have made our region's version of the Southern cuisine so delicious.

Located in the Piedmont Plateau in the exact center of Georgia, Macon enjoys a delightfully mild climate. Crisp falls, mild winters and cool flowering springs combine to offer Middle Georgia one of the longest growing seasons on our continent. In this sweet gentle air roses bloom in December, vegetables grow in profusion and our famous Georgia peaches set their buds. Our climate is said to be ideal for producing this beautiful fruit, the Peach, from the very early varieties shipped to the Eastern markets, to the succulent yellow Elbertas harvested in July.

Commercial cultivation of peaches in the Middle Georgia area had its beginnings as early as 1878 when our peaches were first shipped in refrigerated chests to the Northern markets. Peaches from Georgia reached these markets before any other state had mature peaches to ship. By 1904 the world's largest peach orchard was flourishing in Middle Georgia. During this period of "Peach History" three million peach trees were planted each year in the fertile sandy loam along the fall line of the Piedmont Plateau and the Coastal Plains.

From the treasured collections of families who have grown peaches for a hundred years, our peach recipes are so superb that we have given them a special section. You will treasure them all!

Our collection runs the gamut from the very formal and sophisticated to the 'quick and easy' recipes that today's busy women often need.

We can vouch for the goodness of each recipe. We've tried each recipe in a loving spirit as our families and friends joined in the fellowship at a series of "Tasting Parties". Luncheons, teas, dinners and children's parties were used in testing submitted recipes.

"Gracious Goodness" will be at home in the kitchen of brides, career girls, and the bachelor cook as well as in the kitchen of the experienced cook.

With over 700 of Macon's best recipes included in our collection, we know you will be delighted with every one you try. "Gracious Goodness" is going to be your favorite cookbook.

Mrs. Thomas H. McKelvey
(Rosemary Fanguy)

APPETIZERS
AND
BEVERAGES

ANTIPASTO

¾ cup wine vinegar
½ cup oil
2 tablespoons sugar
1 teaspoon salt
½ teaspoon oregano
¼ teaspoon pepper
¼ cup water

2 carrots, sliced
2 ribs celery, sliced
1 green pepper, cut in strips
1 (3 ounce) jar green olives,
  drained
1 cauliflower, cut in small
  pieces

In large skillet combine all ingredients and bring to a boil. Stir occasionally. Simmer covered for 5 minutes. Cool. Refrigerate at least 24 hours. Drain well. Serve with Ritz crackers. Serves 6.

Mrs. Wallace Miller, III
(Jane Oliver)

ARTICHOKES AND BACON
Very Good

1 (12 ounce) package sliced
  bacon

2 (6 ounce) jars marinated
  artichoke hearts

Cut bacon strips in thirds. Cut artichoke hearts in halves or thirds depending on size. Wrap pieces of artichoke hearts with 1 strip bacon each and secure with toothpick. Broil on both sides. Yields 40-50.

Mrs. C. Emory Johnson
(Wendy Bernhardt)

AGNES' CHAFING DISH ARTICHOKE HEARTS

½ cup butter
4 ounces bleu cheese

3 (14½ ounce) cans artichoke
  hearts, drained, sliced

Heat butter and bleu cheese in saucepan over medium heat, stirring until melted. Transfer to hot chafing dish and mix in artichoke hearts. Spear with toothpicks. Serves 10-15.

Mrs. R. William Buzzell, II
(Virginia Beasley)

ASPARAGUS FOLDOVERS

1 loaf bread, crusts removed
Hollandaise sauce
grated Parmesan cheese

1 (14½ ounce) can asparagus
½ cup butter, melted

Trim crusts from bread; roll flat. Spread with Hollandaise sauce; sprinkle with Parmesan cheese. Fold each bread slice over canned drained asparagus spear; insert pick. Brush melted butter on rolled bread and sprinkle with more Parmesan. Bake at 400° for 12 minutes. Serve hot.

Mrs. Carr G. Dodson
(Katherine Pilcher)

CANDIED BACON

1½ cups brown sugar
2 teaspoons dry mustard

1 pound thick-sliced bacon

Mix brown sugar with mustard. Put thick-sliced bacon flat on broiler pan with small amount of water underneath. Sprinkle sugar-mustard mixture on top of bacon slices. Bake 325° for 1 hour.

Mrs. Joseph G. Merritt
(Fannie Smart)

CAVIAR PIE
Make ahead

7 hard-boiled eggs, sieved
3 spring onions, finely chopped
salt and pepper to taste

2-4 tablespoons mayonnaise
1 (8 ounce) carton sour cream
1 (2 ounce) jar black caviar

Add onions, salt and pepper, mayonnaise (enough for spreading consistency), to eggs. Spread on bottom of pie plate (egg mixture serves as pie shell). Spread a layer of sour cream on top of egg mixture. Spread caviar on top of sour cream just before serving. Serve on rye crisp crackers or party rye. Serves 6-8.

Mrs. William W. Williams
(Ann Warlick)

BLEU CHEESE BALL
Freeze

2 (3 ounce) packages cream
  cheese
4 ounces bleu cheese
4 ounces mild Cheddar cheese
1 tablespoon Worcestershire
  sauce

1 small clove garlic, chopped
  very fine
½ cup chopped nuts, divided
hot sauce to taste

Have cheeses at room temperature. Blend all ingredients, reserving half the nuts. Shape mixture into ball. Chill overnight in bowl lined with waxed paper. Roll ball in reserved nuts before serving.

Mrs. Benjamin M. Garland
(Carol Adams)

VARIATION: BRANDIED BLEU CHEESE BALL: Add ½ teaspoon sherry, ½ teaspoon brandy extract, 1 teaspoon McCormick's Salad Supreme seasoning, and chopped ripe olives to cheese mixture. Mold into a ball.

Mrs. Bruce J. Bishop
(Eleanor Richardson)

CHEESE CAKES
Surprise Flavor

1 cup butter or margarine
½ pound sharp cheese
2 cups flour

salt and cayenne pepper to
  taste
confectioners' sugar

Soften butter and cheese in mixer and blend thoroughly. Add remaining ingredients and mix well. Drop by teaspoonfuls onto cookie sheet. Bake in a moderate 325° oven for about 15 minutes. When cool, dust with confectioners' sugar. Yields 100 quarter size cakes.

A quick, easy and delicious alternative to cheese straws.

Mrs. Charles M. Cook
(Emily Chase)

HINTS

Marinate pineapple strips in Grand Marnier for appetizer.

CHEESE CUBES
Make ahead and freeze

1 loaf bread, unsliced
½ cup margarine
1 (3 ounce) package cream
  cheese

4 ounces extra sharp cheese
2 egg whites, stiffly beaten

Remove crusts from bread, cut in bite-size cubes, set aside. In double boiler, melt margarine, cream cheese, and sharp cheese until mixture is rubbery. Beat 2 egg whites stiff; fold whites into cheese mixture. With tongs, dip cubes into mixture, covering entire cube. Place on ungreased cookie sheet. Refrigerate several hours. Cook at 400° until brown, serve hot. Yields 3 dozen.

Mrs. William W. Williams
(Ann Warlick)

CHEESE STRAWS

3 cups sifted flour
1 pound New York sharp
  cheese

1 cup margarine
1 teaspoon salt
½-¾ teaspoon cayenne pepper

Allow cheese and margarine to reach room temperature or become soft. Grate the cheese. Mix all the ingredients together. Fill a cookie press with the dough. Line cookie sheets with waxed paper. Using press, put the dough onto cookie sheet and cut into the desired length. Cook in 325° oven for approximately 15 minutes or until slightly brown. Allow to cool on brown paper. Serves 150.

Mrs. Lee P. Oliver
(Katherine Carmichael)

CHEESE FONDUE
Wonderful!

2 cups grated Gruyère cheese
2 cups grated Cheddar cheese
3 tablespoons flour
1 garlic clove, cut

2 cups dry white wine
3 tablespoons light rum
1 tablespoon lemon juice

Combine cheeses together with flour. Rub fondue pot with garlic; add wine and heat until bubbly. Slowly stir in cheese mixture and cook until melted. Stir in rum and lemon juice. Serve in fondue pot with cubes of French bread.

CAMEMBERT CROQUETTES

2 packages Camembert cheese
   rounds, chilled and cut in
   wedges

2 eggs, well beaten
⅔ cup bread crumbs

Cut 2 packages chilled Camembert wedges in half. In small bowl, beat eggs well. Measure bread crumbs into a shallow dish. Dip cheese in eggs; cover completely. Roll in crumbs. Repeat dipping and rolling. Cover and chill thoroughly. Just before frying, place cheese in freezer for 10 minutes. Heat 1 inch of oil to 375°. Fry wedges about 15 seconds on each side until lightly browned. Drain. Serve hot as hors d'oeuvres or as a dessert with fruit and wine. Serves 12.

CURRIED CHEESE BALL

¾ cup chopped almonds
½ cup chutney
½ teaspoon dry mustard

2 teaspoons curry powder
2 (8 ounce) packages cream
   cheese, softened

Toast almonds on ungreased cookie sheet until lightly browned for about 5-7 minutes in a 350° oven. Chop almonds fine, add chutney, dry mustard, and curry powder and mix well. Add cream cheese and mix well with hands. Chill until firm. Shape into ball and serve with crackers. Serves 8-10.

Mrs. William M. Matthews
(Fran Flournoy)

CHEESE BALL

2 (8 ounce) packages cream
   cheese
2 tablespoons chopped onion
1 (8 ounce) can crushed
   pineapple, drained well

1 large bell pepper, chopped
   (less, to taste)
1½ cups chopped pecans

Combine all ingredients, except pecans. Form into a ball and roll in chopped pecans. Serves 15.

Mrs. Charles F. Rehberg, Jr.
(Nancy Rowland)

"PLAINS SPECIAL" CHEESE RING

1 pound grated Cheddar
  cheese
1 cup chopped nuts
1 cup mayonnaise
1 small onion, grated

black pepper to taste
dash of cayenne
garlic salt to taste
strawberry preserves

Mix all ingredients except preserves; mold with hands into desired shape. (A large Tupperware mold with lid can be used). Place in refrigerator until chilled. Serve with strawberry preserves and Escort crackers. If a ring mold is used, unmold cheese and serve with center of mold filled with strawberry preserves.

Mrs. Girard Jones
(Susan Smith)

HERBED BOURSIN
Can be made in food processor

1 (8 ounce) package cream
  cheese, softened
1 clove garlic, crushed
1 teaspoon caraway seed

1 teaspoon basil
1 teaspoon dill weed
1 teaspoon chives
lemon pepper

Mix first 6 ingredients. Roll in a ball and cover with lemon pepper. Serve with crackers. Serves 4-6.

Mrs. W. Tyler Evans, Jr.
(Sarah Halliburton)

CHEESE COOKIES
Different

½ cup butter
½ pound New York Extra Sharp
  cheese, grated
1 cup flour

½ teaspoon salt
¼ teaspoon cayenne pepper
2 teaspoons onion soup mix
pecans to garnish

Mix butter and cheese together well. Add remaining ingredients. Roll dough on floured board and cut with small cutter. Bake at 350° for 20-25 minutes or until golden. Yields 6 dozen.

COQ AU VIN

5-6 boned chicken breast
  halves
seasoning salt
4 slices bacon, fried and diced
¼ cup butter
2 cloves garlic
24 pearl onions, frozen
3-4 (2 ounce) cans button
  mushrooms
¼ cup brandy
1½ cups red wine

1 rib celery, diced
¼ cup chopped parsley
½ teaspoon thyme
1 bay leaf
1 teaspoon salt
½ teaspoon pepper
2 tablespoons flour
2 tablespoons butter
1 (10½ ounce) can condensed
  consommé

White sauce:
4 tablespoons butter
4 tablespoons flour

2 cups milk

Cut chicken breasts into bite-size pieces and pat dry. Salt generously with seasoning salt. In heavy saucepan, fry bacon until crisp then remove and set aside. Add butter and crushed garlic and sauté for a few minutes. Have butter and bacon drippings hot. Brown chicken pieces, quickly. In saucepan, combine chicken, bacon, onion and mushrooms. Heat brandy briefly and pour over chicken. Ignite and let burn off. Pour in wine and all seasonings. Mix butter, flour and consommé together and add to saucepan. Bring all to a simmer and cook, covered, for 30 minutes. Remove chicken, onions and mushrooms and set aside. Bring sauce to boil and boil rapidly until sauce is reduced by half. The sauce will thicken and lightly coat spoon. Make white sauce from butter, flour and milk. Add chicken and some sauce to white sauce. Add mushrooms and onions to mixture and mix well. Serve in chafing dish with toothpicks. Serves 24.

Mrs. William W. Williams
(Ann Warlick)

CUCUMBER BALLS

1 (8 ounce) package cream
  cheese
1 teaspoon grated onion

2 teaspoons grated cucumber
chopped pecans
parsley

Combine cream cheese, onion and cucumber. Form into marble-size balls and roll in pecans. Decorate with parsley. Chill. Serves 12.

Dr. Robert H. Jones

PATÉ OF CHICKEN LIVERS

1 pound chicken livers
3 spring onions, chopped
½ cup butter
1½ tablespoons sherry
1½ tablespoons brandy or to taste

2 teaspoons salt
¼ teaspoon nutmeg
¼ teaspoon pepper
pinch thyme, basil, marjoram
parsley to garnish

Sauté livers and onions in butter for 4-5 minutes until browned but pink in the middle. Transfer to a bowl. Stir sherry and brandy into butter remaining in pan, then pour over livers. Add spices and mix well. Purée one-third at a time in blender until very smooth. Chill in a buttered loaf pan and surround with parsley and melba rounds. Serves 10-12.

Mrs. Edgar Y. Mallary, III
(Lloyd Washington)

OPEN-FACED MINI-REUBENS

½ cup Thousand Island Dressing
24 slices party rye bread
1½ cups well-drained chopped sauerkraut

½ pound thinly sliced corned beef
¼ pound sliced Swiss cheese

Spread ½ teaspoon dressing on slice of bread. Place 1 slice corned beef on each slice of bread, and top with sauerkraut. Cut cheese the size of bread, and place over sauerkraut. Arrange sandwiches on a baking sheet; bake at 400° for ten minutes or until cheese melts. Serves 2 dozen.

HINTS

To make crystallized grapes:
    1 pound green grapes
    ½ cup water
    1 cup sugar
Boil water and sugar. Cool and dip grapes into syrup. Sprinkle grapes with granulated sugar. Chill. Serve with cheese and crackers.

Spread softened cream cheese on ham slices. Place 1 piece drained pickled okra on each slice, roll up ham. Refrigerate to set up. Slice into 1-inch slices before serving.

INDIAN CHICKEN BALLS

¼ pound cream cheese, room
    temperature
2 tablespoons mayonnaise
1 cup chopped pecans

1 cup chopped chicken
1 tablespoon chopped chutney
1 teaspoon curry powder
1 cup grated coconut

Mix all ingredients except coconut. Shape into small balls, roll in coconut. Place on tray and chill in refrigerator. Serve with toothpicks. Serves 30.

Mrs. Harold E. Causey
(June Farmer)

CURRIED EGG SALAD SPREAD

8 water chestnuts, finely
    chopped
6 hard-boiled eggs, chopped
¼-½ cup mayonnaise
2 green onions, finely chopped
1 teaspoon curry powder
    (or to taste)

½ teaspoon Worcestershire
    sauce
salt and freshly ground pepper

Combine all ingredients and blend well. Cover and chill until ready to serve. Serve with white melba rounds.

Mrs. John Marbut, Jr.
(Katie Dickey)

LAYERED CAVIAR COCKTAIL MOLD

3 envelopes unflavored
    gelatin
2 cups canned chicken broth

1 (2 ounce) jar black caviar
1 (2 ounce) jar red caviar
2 hard-cooked eggs, sieved

Soften gelatin in chicken broth in 1 quart saucepan. Heat and stir until gelatin dissolves. Chill until partially set. Divide gelatin into 3 portions of ⅔ cup each. Into one portion, fold black caviar, into one fold red caviar, into one fold eggs. Turn the red caviar mixture into a 3-cup mold. Chill until set. Add egg mixture and chill until set. Add black caviar mixture and chill until firm. Unmold and serve with melba rounds or any thin bland cracker. Serves 4-6.

CAPONATA
Cold Eggplant Spread

1 pound eggplant, peeled and cut in ½ inch cubes (about 4 cups)
½ cup olive oil, divided
1 cup finely chopped celery
½ cup finely chopped onion
¾ cup tomato purée
¼ cup tomato paste
½ cup water or wine vinegar
1 teaspoon salt
⅛ teaspoon pepper or to taste
1½ teaspoons sugar
½ cup thinly sliced green olives
1 tablespoon capers, washed and drained

Sprinkle eggplant cubes with salt, let drain 30 minutes, wipe off. Using half the oil, sauté eggplant for 8-10 minutes. Remove eggplant. Add remaining oil to pan, add celery and sauté for a few minutes; add onions and sauté another 8-10 minutes. Return eggplant to pan, along with remaining ingredients, and add tomato purée, tomato paste, salt, pepper, sugar, olives and capers. Stir gently, simmer, stirring often for 20-30 minutes or until thickened. Taste and correct seasonings. Serve warm or store in refrigerator and serve chilled on crackers. Keeps in refrigerator for 1-2 weeks. Makes about 4 cups.

Mrs. Flew Murphy
(Valeria McCullough)

HAM BALLS

⅓ cup dry bread crumbs
¼ cup milk
¼ cup catsup
¼ cup chopped onion
1 egg
¼ teaspoon salt
pepper to taste
1 pound ground ham
1 pound ground pork

SAUCE:
1 cup apricot preserves
¼ cup water
1 tablespoon Worcestershire sauce
2 tablespoons catsup
2 tablespoons vinegar
1 tablespoon prepared mustard

Mix first 9 ingredients together and form into balls. Place balls on cookie sheet and bake for 25-30 minutes at 350°. Drain balls on absorbent paper. Cool. They may be frozen at this stage.
For sauce: Combine all ingredients and add meat balls to coat. Convert to chafing dish or other heated container for serving. Serves 25-30.

MUSHROOM CROUSTADES

CROUSTADES:
24 slices fresh white bread

2 tablespoons butter, melted

MUSHROOM FILLING:
4 tablespoons butter
3 tablespoons finely chopped
  shallots
½ pound mushrooms, finely
  chopped
2 level tablespoons flour
1 cup heavy cream
½ teaspoon salt
⅛ teaspoon cayenne

1 tablespoon finely chopped
  parsley
1½ tablespoons chopped
  chives
½ teaspoon lemon juice
2 teaspoons grated Parmesan
  cheese
butter

Croustades: Cut bread with 3-inch glass or cutter. With pastry brush, coat inside of muffin tins (small size) with the melted butter. Fit round of bread into tin. Preheat oven to 400°. Bake for 10 minutes or until lightly browned on edges. Remove and let cool.

Filling: Chop shallots and mushrooms very fine. In heavy skillet, slowly melt 4 tablespoons butter and before foam subsides, add shallots. Stir almost constantly over moderate heat for about 4 minutes without letting them brown. Stir in mushrooms. Mix well into butter and see that they are thoroughly coated. Leave on their own. In a few minutes they will begin to give off a good deal of moisture. Stir them from time to time and continue to cook until all moisture has evaporated (about 10-15 minutes). Remove pan from heat. Sprinkle 2 tablespoons flour over mushrooms and stir thoroughly until no trace of flour is visible. Immediately pour in heavy cream to simmer and cook 1-2 minutes longer. Remove quickly from heat and stir in seasonings and herbs. Fill croustades and mound filling slightly. Sprinkle with Parmesan cheese, dot with butter and arrange on cookie sheet. Preheat oven to 350° about 10 minutes before you serve. Heat for 10 minutes in oven, then briefly under broiler. Watch them carefully as they will burn easily. Serves 8 or more.

May prepare ahead and refrigerate or may freeze with or without filling.

Mrs. William B. Dasher, Jr.
(Eloise Wilson)

HINTS

Marinate honeydew balls in sherry and apricot brandy.

MARINATED ARTICHOKES AND MUSHROOMS

2 pounds fresh mushrooms
1 cup vinegar
½ cup oil
1 clove garlic
1½ tablespoons salt
1 teaspoon freshly ground
   pepper

2 (7 ounce) cans artichokes,
   drained
½ teaspoon thyme
½ teaspoon oregano
1 tablespoon dried parsley
1 onion, sliced in rings

Wash and drain fresh mushrooms. Combine all other ingredients in bowl. Mix well; add drained artichokes and mushrooms. Marinate overnight in refrigerator. Serve on platter lined with fresh spinach leaves. Serves 6.

Mrs. E. Baxter Evans
(Maida Ragan)

VARIATION: Add 1 tablespoon Worcestershire sauce, ½ teaspoon dry mustard, and cooked shrimp.

Mrs. J. Terrell Pope
(Lynn Warren)

STUFFED MUSHROOMS

2 dozen large mushroom caps,
   preferably fresh
stems of mushrooms, finely
   chopped
2 cups chopped pecans
½ cup chopped parsley
½ cup softened butter

2 cloves garlic, crushed
½ teaspoon thyme leaves
1 teaspoon each salt and
   pepper
1 cup heavy cream

Mix togther all ingredients except mushroom caps and cream. Fill caps with mixture. Pour cream over and bake at 350° about 20 minutes. Baste 2-3 times. Recipe may be halved or doubled easily. Serves 8.

Mrs. Gary C. Ertel
(Holly Akre)

HINTS

Cover large stuffed olives with cream cheese and roll in chopped salted nuts.

MUSHROOM TURNOVER

PASTRY:
1 (3 ounce) package cream
  cheese, softened
1½ cups flour
½ cup butter, softened

FILLING:
1 onion, minced
3 tablespoons butter
½ pound fresh mushrooms,
  minced
¼ teaspoon thyme
½ teaspoon salt
pepper to taste
2 tablespoons flour
¼ cup sour cream

Pastry: Mix cheese and butter. Stir in flour and blend. Chill.
Filling: Sauté onion in butter until golden. Add mushrooms and cook 3 minutes. Add seasonings and sprinkle flour over mixture. Add sour cream and cook until thickened. Roll chilled dough very thin and cut out 3-inch rounds. Place 1 teaspoon filling on each round; fold edges over and press together. Prick with fork and bake at 450° for 15 minutes on ungreased cookie sheet. Serves 25.

Can be frozen before baking.

Mrs. Donald C. Eubanks
(Martha McKay)

FRIED MUSHROOMS
Simply Delicious

1 cup beer, chilled
1½ cups self-rising flour
1 pound fresh mushrooms

Mix beer and flour together. Dip mushrooms into batter and fry in deep fat until golden brown (about 5 minutes). For a variation, fry broccoli and cauliflower. Serves 8.

Mrs. John A. Draughon
(Sally Hines)

HINTS

Bake cubes of Italian sausage, drain well and serve in a chafing dish in 2 inches of warmed white wine.

Spread halves of jumbo pecans with Roquefort and cream cheese.

SAUSAGE-STUFFED MUSHROOMS

30-40 large fresh mushrooms,
   stemmed
3 tablespoons butter, melted
1 pound bulk sausage, cooked
   and drained

½ cup toasted bread crumbs
½ cup pizza or spaghetti sauce
1 egg
Mozzarella cheese

Dip mushrooms in butter. Stuff with mixture of sausage, bread crumbs, sauce and egg. Top with a 1-inch square of sliced Mozzarella cheese. Bake at 425° for 15 minutes. Serve at once.

Mrs. Bert Maxwell, III
(Mardi Barnes)

SAUSAGE PINWHEELS

2 cups Bisquick
½ cup liquid (¼ cup water and
   ¼ scant cup Wesson Oil

1 pound hot or mild sausage

Mix and knead the Bisquick and the liquid. Divide into 2 equal amounts and roll out. It is much easier to roll out between waxed paper. It is also easier to let the sausage come to room temperature before making the pinwheels. Divide the softened sausage into 2 equal amounts and then spread in a thin layer over the Bisquick pastry. Roll up, wrap in foil and freeze. Slice while frozen. Bake about 20 minutes at 400°. Serves 10.

Mrs. George Youmans
(Ann Dunlap)

HOT SAUSAGE BALLS IN SOUR CREAM

2 pounds hot pork sausage
1 (9 ounce) jar Major Grey's
   chutney, chopped fine

9 ounces sherry (or less to
   taste)
1 (8 ounce) carton sour cream

Roll sausage into bite-size balls; place in shallow pan and bake in preheated 300° oven 45-55 minutes until done but not crisp. Drain off grease after 30 minutes and continue cooking. Drain thoroughly. Put chutney, sherry, and sour cream into a pan and cook gently for a few minutes. When ready to serve, place sausage balls in a chafing dish and cover with sauce.

Mrs. Don B. Benton
(Pat Mock)

CHAFING DISH SAUSAGE

4 pounds hot bulk sausage,
  cooked and drained
4 cups sour cream
1 cup milk

½ cup flour
3-4 (4 ounce) cans sliced
  mushrooms, drained
toast points

Brown sausage and drain. Add sour cream, mixing well. Add mushrooms and return to low heat. Mix flour and milk, and pour over sausage mixture; heat slightly and continuously roll mixture with spoon until meat mixture becomes somewhat coated and thickens. (Do not overheat as grease will drain out of sausage.) Best reheated in double boiler. Serve in chafing dish using toast points to dip mixture. May be served over rice or noodles as a main dish but recommend using mild sausage.

Mrs. William S. Lamb
(Josephine Barker)

CHAFING DISH TERIYAKI

1½ pounds tenderloin, sliced
  ⅛ inch thick

Sauce:
1 cup mild hickory barbecue
  sauce

½ cup sherry
1 jigger vermouth

Slice meat ⅛ inch thick, 1 inch long, ½ inch wide. Flatten meat. Marinate overnight in sauce made from mixing barbecue sauce, sherry and vermouth. Drain meat, reserving sauce. Grill meat until browned. Place meat in chafing dish and cover with reserved sauce. Serve with toothpicks. Serves 12.

STEAK BITS

4 or 5 pounds sirloin or beef
  tenderloin
salt, pepper, flour

loaf of French bread
melted butter
2 tablespoons lemon juice

Cut beef in small cubes; season with salt, pepper and flour. Run under broiler. Serve in hollowed out loaf of French bread with butter and lemon juice on top of beef as a sauce.

Mrs. Leo A. Erbele
(Josephine Phelps)

CRANBERRY MEATBALLS

2 pounds ground beef
1 cup packaged corn flake
 crumbs
1/3 cup dried parsley
2 eggs
2 tablespoons soy sauce

1/4 teaspoon pepper
1/2 teaspoon garlic powder
1/3 cup catsup
2 tablespoons instant minced
 onion

SAUCE:
1 can jellied cranberry sauce
1 (12 ounce) bottle chili sauce
2 tablespoons firmly packed
 dark brown sugar

1 tablespoon bottled lemon
 juice

Heat oven to 350°. In large bowl, combine beef, flake crumbs, parsley flakes, eggs, soy sauce, pepper, garlic powder, catsup, and onion and blend well. Form into small walnut-sized meatballs. Arrange in 15 x 10 x 1-inch pan. Set aside and make sauce. For sauce, combine cranberry sauce, chili sauce, brown sugar, and lemon juice in a saucepan. Cook over moderate heat (250°) stirring occasionally, until mixture is smooth and cranberry sauce is melted. Pour over meatballs in pan. Bake uncovered for 30 minutes. Pour mixture into a chafing dish and serve with toothpicks. Makes 60 meatballs.

You may make meatballs ahead of time and freeze.

Mrs. John C. Walker, III
(Kathy Kidd)

MARINATED EYE OF ROUND

3-4 pound eye of round roast
lemon pepper, to taste
Worcestershire sauce, to taste

soy sauce
dash lemon juice

Rub roast generously with lemon pepper. Add Worcestershire generously and add some soy sauce and lemon juice. Place in glass pan or plastic bag and roll roast every 7-8 hours for 3 days. Cook at 350° for 1 hour. Let completely cool (best overnight) and return roast to grocer and have it shaved. Serve with rolls as appetizer or may be used for meal or sandwiches. Serve Tiger's horseradish sauce as condiment.

Mrs. Frank Hall
(Marion Gwaltney)

CURRIED MEAT TURNOVERS

FILLING:

2 tablespoons butter or
   margarine
1 medium onion, chopped
¼ pound fresh mushrooms,
   chopped
1½ cups coarsely ground pork
   (leftover pork roast is fine;
   any cooked meat or poultry
   may be used)

1 tablespoon sherry
1 tablespoon soy sauce
½ teaspoon sugar
½ teaspoon curry powder
   (or more, to taste)
2-3 tablespoons sweet or sour
   cream

PASTRY:

1 (8 ounce) package cream
   cheese, softened
½ cup butter or margarine
   softened

2 cups sifted flour
½ teaspoon salt

Filling: Heat butter in skillet; add onion and mushrooms and sauté until onion is transparent. With slotted spoon remove to bowl. Add pork to skillet and heat, stirring 1-2 minutes. Add sherry, soy sauce, sugar, and curry powder. Mix well and cook over low heat for 2-3 minutes. Combine with mushrooms and onions, mix well, then add enough cream to moisten mixture. Allow to cool before using.

Pastry: Mix pastry ingredients together. Roll dough as thin as possible (about ⅛ inch thick) on a lightly floured board. Cut into 3-inch circles. Place scant teaspoon filling on one side of circle; moisten edge of circle with water, fold dough over, moisten top edge with water, then press edges with fork to seal. Prick top with fork; place on ungreased baking sheet and bake at 400° for about 15 minutes or until lightly browned. Serves 40 turnovers.

Mrs. Donald K. Ream, III
(Liz Daves)

HINTS

Sprinkle bacon with a little flour or run it under cold water before frying to prevent curling.

The flavors garlic, pepper, and cloves get stronger when frozen. The flavors of salt, onion, or sage get milder when frozen.

VIDALIA ONION DIP
Men love this!

5 or 6* Vidalia onions, sliced
1 cup sugar
½ cup white vinegar
2 cups water
½ cup mayonnaise
1 teaspoon celery salt

Slice the onions thin and soak from 2 to 4 hours in sugar, vinegar and water. Drain well; and toss with mayonnaise and celery salt. Serve on saltine crackers.
*This is a famous sweet onion grown in Vidalia, Georgia—so tasty and mild they are considered a real delicacy. Serves 8.

Mrs. Andrew Young
(Pam Watkins)

SWISS ARTICHOKE DIP

1 (14 ounce) can artichoke
    hearts
8 ounces Swiss cheese, grated
1 cup Hellmann's mayonnaise

Quarter artichoke hearts. Mix grated cheese and artichoke hearts with mayonnaise. Pour mixture into 1 or 1½ quart baking dish. Cook covered at 350° for 15 minutes, uncover and continue cooking for 15 minutes or until mixture bubbles and cheese is melted evenly. Serve with Triscuit crackers.

Mrs. D. Clark Ballard
(Nancy Johnson)

GINGER DIP

1 cup mayonnaise
1 (8 ounce) carton sour cream
3 tablespoons grated onion
¼ cup minced parsley
1 (8 ounce) can water
    chestnuts, finely chopped
3 tablespoons (or more)
    chopped candied ginger
1 tablespoon soy sauce
dash Tabasco

Combine all ingredients and serve with crackers or chips. Makes 3 cups.

Mrs. Donald M. Johnson
(Elizabeth Jones)

MEXICAN CHEESE DIP

1 (16 ounce) can tomatoes
1 (10) ounce can Ro-Tel
  tomatoes with chiles
¾ cup water
¾ ounce chili powder
  (Half of 1½ ounce can)

¾ ounce cumin
  (Half of 1½ ounce can)
2 cloves garlic
2 pounds Velveeta cheese
½ pound sharp Cracker Barrel
  Cheddar cheese

Mix first 6 ingredients. Use a garlic press for garlic, and add to tomato mixture. Simmer 1 hour. Add cheeses and stir until melted. Serve hot with large Fritos. Serves 30.

CURRY DIP FOR VEGETABLES
Quick and easy

1 cup canned pineapple
  chunks, drained
1 (8 ounce) package
  cream cheese
2 tablespoons chopped
  chutney

1 cup mayonnaise
1 tablespoon finely chopped
  onion
1 tablespoon curry powder

Mix all ingredients in a blender. Serve with assorted raw vegetables.

Mrs. V. J. Adams, Jr.
(Angela Gaultney)

ESCARGOTS

3 green onions, chopped
1 cup white wine, divided
1 (4½ ounce) can large snails
snail shells

½ cup softened butter
2 tablespoons minced parsley
2 teaspoons garlic salt
bread crumbs

Chop onions and sauté in ¾ cup wine for 5-8 minutes. Rinse snails and split to make 24. Put onions in snail shell; top with snail. Combine butter, parsley and garlic salt. Put shells in snail pan. Add 1 tablespoon wine to each pan and sprinkle shells with crumbs. Bake at 400° for 10 minutes. Serves 4.

HINTS

Garlic cloves will not dry out if stored in a bottle of cooking oil.

SEA ISLAND DIP
Delicious!

1 (8½ ounce) can artichokes, drained, minced
1 cup mayonnaise
2 cup fresh Parmesan cheese

garlic salt (use sparingly)
½ onion, chopped
1½ teaspoons lemon juice

Mix all ingredients together and bake at 375° for 15-20 minutes until bubbly and slightly browned. Serve with crackers. Serves 6-8.

Mrs. George Youmans
(Ann Dunlap)

QUICK SPINACH DIP

1 (16 ounce) package frozen chopped spinach, thawed and well drained (uncooked)
1 (8 ounce) carton sour cream

1 tablespoon mayonnaise
1 tablespoon minced onion
1 (0.4 ounce) package ranch style buttermilk dressing

Mix all ingredients. Chill, serve with corn chips. Serves 4-6.

Mrs. W. Tyler Evans, Jr.
(Sarah Halliburton)

SEAFARER DIP

1 pound fresh mushrooms, sliced
¼ cup butter
2 (10¾ ounce) cans cream of mushroom soup
1 (10¾ ounce) can cream of shrimp soup
1 (8 ounce) package cream cheese
1 pound shrimp, boiled and peeled and cut into bite-size pieces

2 (8 ounce) cans water chestnuts, sliced
1 pound lump crab meat
1 teaspoon Tabasco
2 teaspoons dry mustard
2 teaspoons curry powder
4 tablespoons Worcestershire sauce
salt and cayenne pepper to taste

Sauté mushrooms in butter. Heat soups, add cream cheese, and stir until cream cheese is melted. Add remaining ingredients and serve hot from a chafing dish on melba rounds.

Mrs. William W. Baxley, Jr.
(Charlene Carpenter)

HOT CLAM DIP
Good, easy, and inexpensive

1 (8 ounce) package cream
   cheese
1 (10½ ounce) can minced
   clams, drained, reserving
   liquid
1 tablespoon lemon juice

2 tablespoons clam broth
1 tablespoon prepared mustard
2 teaspoons Worcestershire
   sauce
⅛ teaspoon garlic powder
dash cayenne pepper

Bring cheese to room temperature. Drain clams and reserve liquid. Combine cheese, lemon juice, clam broth and seasonings. Blend in clams. Heat before serving. Serves 25-30.

Can be made ahead and refrigerated. May seem thick when taken from refrigerator but heating will bring to proper temperature and consistency. Serve with dip size corn chips. For a party of 75 to 100, triple the recipe and serve from a chafing dish.

Mrs. Donald W. Rhame
(Alacia Lee)

BRAUNSCHWEIGER IN GELATIN
Can be made a day ahead

1 envelope unflavored gelatin
½ cup cold water
1 (10½ ounce) can condensed
   consommé
½ pound Braunschweiger

1 tablespoon wine vinegar
3½ tablespoons mayonnaise
1 teaspoon poppy seed
   (optional)
¼ teaspoon dry mustard

Soften gelatin in cold water. Heat consommé to boiling. Remove from heat, add gelatin and stir until dissolved. Pour into a lightly greased 2-cup mold. Chill until firm. Mix remaining ingredients. Take top of gelatin mixture and scoop out enough to put Braunschweiger mixture into mold. Be sure to leave enough gelatin on bottom and sides. Fill center with Braunschweiger mixture, making certain mound of mixture is ¼-½ inch below top of mold. Heat the gelatin that has been scooped out until melted. Pour melted gelatin over top of mold. Chill until firm. Unmold and serve with crackers. Serves 6.

Mrs. H. M. Comer Train
(Anne Bush)

HOT CRAB SPREAD

1 (8 ounce) package cream
   cheese
2 tablespoons milk
1 cup crab meat

2 tablespoons chopped onion
½ teaspoon horseradish
salt and pepper
2 ounces slivered almonds

Blend cream cheese, milk, crab meat, onion, and horseradish. Add salt and pepper. Place in shallow baking dish. Sprinkle almonds on top and bake at 350° for 20 minutes. Serve hot as a dip.

Mrs. Thomas H. Hall, III
(Sara Jennings)

PEPPY PARTY OYSTERS

1 medium onion, chopped
1 cup chopped celery
3 cloves garlic, chopped
½ cup butter
1 pound fresh mushrooms,
   sliced (or 6 ounce can,
   drained)
1½ quart oysters, chopped
1 teaspoon salt
½ teaspoon mustard
cayenne pepper, black pepper

1 tablespoon Worcestershire
   sauce
¼ teaspoon mace
2 tablespoons lemon juice
1 loaf French or Italian bread
   (about 2-3 cups crumbs)
2 eggs, beaten slightly
½ cup sherry
½ cup chopped parsley
½ cup diced green onion tops

Sauté first 3 ingredients in butter in large pan until tender. Add mushrooms and sauté a few minutes longer. Chop oysters, drain, (save juice), and add to above mixture. Add salt, mustard, mace, Worcestershire, pepper, and lemon juice to mixture, bring to a boil, then remove from heat, and allow to cool. Toast slices of bread and roll into crumbs. Add 2 cups to oyster mix. Beat eggs and sherry together and add to mixture and stir well. If mixture is too moist, add more crumbs; and if too dry, add oyster liquid. If serving as a casserole, butter dish, top with crumbs, dot with butter and bake for ½ hour at 350 to 375°. To serve in individual ramekins, heat for 20 minutes in oven at 375°-400°. (Serve this as an hors d'oeuvre in the chafing dish with a variety of crackers. Recipe doubles easily. If you want to serve as a side dish use ½ the amount of oysters and 2-3 diced, sautéed eggplant. Serves 30 or more as hors d'oeuvres on crackers. Serves 8-10 as a main dish—either in individual ramekins or a large casserole.)

Mrs. Flew Murphey
(Valeria McCullough)

OYSTERS AND ARTICHOKES

6 artichokes
¼ cup butter or bacon grease
4 tablespoons flour
⅓ cup minced green onions
1 large clove garlic, minced
½ cup minced parsley
3 dozen oysters, liquid
¾ teaspoon salt

½ teaspoon pepper
½ teaspoon thyme
¼ teaspoon marjoram
pinch of cayenne pepper
½ cup dry white wine
1 (4 ounce) can sliced
   mushrooms
5-6 thin sliced rounds of lemon

Steam artichokes until tender. Remove leaves and scrape meat. Reserve. Slice and mash hearts. Make a roux with the butter and flour, by first melting butter in iron skillet over medium heat. Then add flour stirring until mixture is a true caramel color. (This takes a while but is the real secret!) Add onion and garlic to the roux and stir continuously until soft. Add oyster liquid, salt, pepper, thyme, marjoram, parsley, artichoke mixture and simmer 20 minutes. (Should become the consistency of a thick sauce). Add wine, mushrooms, and oysters and cook 4-5 minutes until edges of oysters begin to curl. Pour into buttered ramekins and top with lemon rounds. Refrigerate overnight for best flavor. Heat in 350° oven until heated through and serve. Serves 6.

Mrs. Chris Sheridan, Jr.
(Beth Childress)

OYSTERS ROCKEFELLER DIP

2 (10 ounce) packages frozen
   chopped spinach
4 tablespoons butter
2 tablespoons flour
½ cup milk
½ cup spinach liquid
1 (6 ounce) roll jalapeño cheese
1 teaspoon Worcestershire
   sauce

pinch of nutmeg
¾ teaspoon celery salt
¾ teaspoon garlic salt
½ teaspoon salt
½ teaspoon pepper
2 (8 ounce) cans oysters,
   drained

Cook spinach and drain, reserving liquid. Make a cream sauce with butter, flour, milk, and spinach liquid. Add cheese and all seasonings. Mix spinach into sauce and heat. Add oysters and heat. Serve from chafing dish. Make 2 hours in advance. Can be put into oyster shells and served on a bed of rock salt. Also can be run under the broiler with bread crumbs on top. Serves 8.

BLEU CHEESE CRAB MEAT

2 tablespoons butter
⅔ cup finely chopped onion
½ cup finely chopped bell
  pepper
1 cup diced celery
1 cup milk
1 cup light cream
6 ounces bleu cheese,
  crumbled

1 cup sliced pitted ripe olives
4 (6 ounce) packages frozen
  crab meat, drained
2 teaspoons paprika
2 tablespoons parsley
toast points

Sauté onion; celery, and bell pepper in butter. In the meantime, in double boiler, combine milk, cream and bleu cheese. Heat until bleu cheese is melted and mixture is smooth. Add ripe olives and crab meat. Fold in sautéed mixture; stir 20 minutes to blend well. Sprinkle with paprika and parsley. Serve in chafing dish with toast points.

GUACAMOLE MOUSSE

1 envelope unflavored
  gelatin
1 cup cold water
1 chicken bouillon cube,
  crumbled
¼ teaspoon salt

1½ cups sieved avocado
½ cup sour cream
3 tablespoons finely chopped
  green onion
2 tablespoons lemon juice
½ teaspoon hot sauce

Soften gelatin in cold water in a small saucepan. Add bouillon cube and salt. Heat, stirring constantly, until gelatin and bouillon are dissolved; cool slightly. Combine avocado, sour cream, green onion, lemon juice, and hot sauce; stir in gelatin mixture. Pour into a 3-cup mold and refrigerate until firm. Unmold and garnish as desired. Serve with crackers. Makes about 2⅔ cups.

Mrs. William M. Gibson
(Bonny D. Denton)

HINTS

When substituting dried herbs for fresh, be sure to use only ⅓ as much.

Fill avocado halves with cocktail sauce surrounded by shrimp as a dip.

CRAB-SWISS BITES

1 (7 ounce) can crab meat,
  drained and flaked
1 tablespoon sliced green
  onion
4 ounces Swiss cheese,
  shredded (1 cup)
½ cup mayonnaise

1 teaspoon lemon juice
¼ teaspoon curry powder
1 package flaky style rolls (12
  rolls)
1 (5 ounce) can water
  chestnuts, sliced

Combine the crab meat, green onion, Swiss cheese, mayonnaise, lemon juice, and curry powder. Mix well. Separate rolls. (Separate each roll into three layers). Place rolls on ungreased baking sheet. Spoon on crab meat mixture. Top with slice of water chestnut. Bake in preheated 400° oven for 10-12 minutes. Serve hot. Makes 36.

Mrs. Ronald E. Robeson
(Carol Clark)

RIPE OLIVE QUICHE
Make ahead and freeze

6 eggs
1½ cups slivered ripe olives
1 pint sour cream
1½ teaspoons oregano
1½ cups shredded Swiss
  cheese

2 tablespoons chives
¾ teaspoon salt
dash cayenne
dash lemon pepper
dash Worcestershire sauce
pastry for pie crusts

Beat eggs with spoon. Add all remaining ingredients and mix well. Fill uncooked pie shells with mixture (mixture will be slightly thick). Bake at 425° for 15 minutes. Reduce temperature to 375° and continue baking for 25 minutes or until filling is set. Makes 2 pies.

Great. Can be done in cookie sheet and arrange bought pie shells to fit bottom of pan. Double filling recipe and cut in squares. Can be sliced in squares and frozen.

HINTS

To preserve flavor of fresh herbs, chop then place in paper towel and squeeze under running water.

SHRIMP MOLD

1 (10¾ ounce) can condensed
   tomato soup
1 envelope unflavored gelatin
3 (3 ounce) packages cream
   cheese, softened
¼ cup cold water

1 cup mayonnaise
¾ cup chopped celery
½ cup chopped onion
1½ cups chopped shrimp
lemon juice

Heat tomato soup and add gelatin which has been softened in cold water. Combine soup mixture with all the remaining ingredients and pour into a greased mold. Chill to set mold. Serve unmolded with cracker as an appetizer. Yields 5 cups.

Mrs. William W. Chichester
(Eleanor Tarr)

SHRIMP COCKTAIL A L'ORANGE

8 large oranges
48 cooked, peeled shrimp
1½ cups heavy cream
¾ cup catsup

3 tablespoons tomato paste
3 tablespoons Scotch whiskey
lettuce, shredded

Cut tops off oranges and reserve. Hollow out pulp, reserve shells, and dice oranges. Dice shrimp and combine with diced oranges. Combine cream, catsup, tomato paste, and scotch and beat until it thickens. Combine sauce with shrimp and oranges. Line orange shells with thin layer of shredded lettuce. Pour in shrimp mixture. Top with lid. Serve on crushed ice, if desired. Serves 8.

Dr. Robert H. Jones

MINIATURE SHRIMP QUICHES

24 tiny tart shells
3 tablespoons grated Parmesan
   cheese
½ cup chopped, cooked shrimp
½ cup grated Swiss cheese

3 egg yolks
¾ cup light cream
dash Tabasco
½ teaspoon salt

Divide Parmesan cheese, chopped shrimp and Swiss cheese among tart shells. Place in bottom of each tart shell. Mix egg yolks, cream, Tabasco and salt and fill tart shells with mixture. Bake in 325° oven for 15 minutes. Yields 24 miniature quiches.

Mrs. Robert J. Adams
(Madge Webb)

CURRIED SHRIMP MOUSSE

1 medium onion, chopped
2 tablespoons mild Indian curry
1 (14 ounce) can peeled
  tomatoes
1 chicken bouillon cube
1 cup mayonnaise

1 envelope unflavored gelatin
2 tablespoons cold water
¾ pound small shrimp, cooked
6 hard-boiled eggs
2 tablespoons apricot jam
  (optional)

Sauté onion in a little oil. Add curry, tomatoes, and bouillon cube and simmer 20 minutes. Cool slightly and add mayonnaise. Place gelatin in 2 tablespoons cold water, then dissolve over low heat. Add cooked shrimp, chopped eggs and gelatin to onion mixture and stir. Pour into a mold and chill thoroughly. Serve unmolded on a bed of lettuce topped with apricot jam, if desired. Serves 6 as first course.

Mrs. Hubert C. Lovein, Jr.
(Ann Elliott)

HOT CRAB DIP

1 pound fresh crab meat or 3
  (6 ounce) packages frozen
  Wakefield crab meat
1 tablespoon horseradish
2 tablespoons capers
1 teaspoon grated lemon rind
juice of ½ lemon
½ teaspoon Ac'cent

2 cups Hellmann's mayonnaise
dash of Worcestershire sauce
garlic salt to taste
oregano to taste
parsley to taste
basil to taste
¾ cup grated sharp cheese

Mix all the above ingredients and seasonings except the cheese, and put in a 1½ quart casserole. Top with grated cheese. Bake 20-25 minutes at 350°. Serve with crackers. (Sociables are great with this dip). Serves approximately 25-40.

Mrs. Donald W. Rhame
(Alacia Lee)

HINTS

Over an 8 ounce block of cream cheese, pour a 5 ounce bottle of Pickapeppa sauce. Serve as a spread with Ritz crackers.

SHRIMP CRAB COCKTAIL MOUND

1 (8 ounce) package whipped
   cream cheese
1 (6 ounce) package frozen
   crab meat
1 pound fresh shrimp, boiled,
   peeled and deveined

onion juice, salt, pepper,
   Tabasco, Worcestershire
   sauce to taste
small amount mayonnaise

SAUCE:
⅓ cup chili sauce
¼ cup catsup
4-5 teaspoons horseradish
Worcestershire sauce to taste

salt to taste
1½ tablespoons lemon juice
dash pepper
few drops Tabasco

Mix first 3 ingredients, seasonings and mayonnaise together and form into oval mound. Refrigerate until firm. Mix sauce ingredients and chill. At serving time cover mound with sauce made by mixing ingredients together. Garnish with parsley and serve with rye crackers or some other tasty cracker.

Mrs. Timothy K. Adams
(Julie Bearden)

SPINACH BALLS
Can be frozen

1 (10 ounce) package frozen
   chopped spinach
1 cup herb-seasoned stuffing
   mix
¼ cup imported fresh
   Parmesan cheese, grated
½ small onion, grated

3 eggs, beaten
6 tablespoons butter, softened
lemon juice to taste
¼ teaspoon garlic powder
Season-All, Ac'cent, pepper to
   taste

Cook spinach and drain very well, chop spinach and add herb stuffing and grated Parmesan cheese. Stir until mixture has a fine texture. Add beaten eggs and all other ingredients. Mix. Roll into balls. Place on cookie sheet and bake at 325° for 10 minutes. Serves 8.

Mrs. William J. Buzzell
(Claude Burns)

HINTS

White pepper is stronger than black pepper.

SHRIMP SPREAD
Great!

½ cup margarine or butter, softened
1 (8 ounce) package cream cheese, softened
2 teaspoons mayonnaise
dash of garlic salt
⅛ teaspoon pepper

⅛ teaspoon Worcestershire sauce
2 teaspoons lemon juice
1 small onion, finely chopped
½ cup finely chopped celery
2 (4½ ounce) cans small shrimp, drained

Combine butter, cream cheese, mayonnaise, garlic salt, pepper, Worcestershire sauce and lemon juice; mix well. Stir in onion, celery and shrimp. Yields 2¼ cups.

Mrs. Derry Burns, Jr.
(Juliette Smith)

CRAB MEAT RING

1 teaspoon unflavored gelatin
¼ cup cold water
2 (8 ounce) packages cream cheese, softened
2 tablespoons cooking sherry
¾ teaspoon seasoned salt
1 (2 ounce) jar pimientos, drained, chopped

2 (6 ounce) packages frozen King crab meat, thawed, drained, cut up
⅛ teaspoon ground black pepper
¼ cup snipped parsley, divided

Sprinkle gelatin over water to soften; stir over hot water until dissolved. Beat into cream cheese until smooth. Stir in next 5 ingredients and 2 tablespoons parsley. Pour into a 3-cup ring mold. Refrigerate at least 4 hours or until set. To serve, turn out on plate; garnish with remaining parsley. Place parsley sprigs in center. Serve with crackers. Yields 3 cups.

Mrs. Robert L. Dickey, III
(Cynde Martin)

HINTS

Caviar should be added to a recipe lastly. The oil discolors the other ingredients.

SHRIMP REMOULADE

¼ cup horseradish
¼ cup Dijon mustard
⅓ cup wine vinegar
2 cloves garlic, chopped
6 tablespoons catsup

2 tablespoons paprika
1 teaspoon salt
½ cup olive oil
½ cup chopped green onions
1 pound peeled, cooked shrimp

Combine all ingredients and refrigerate. Toss occasionally. Marinate shrimp overnight for best flavor.

Mrs. Jerome Strickland
(Joyce Henderson)

CRAB DIP IN CABBAGE

1 medium cabbage
1 medium onion
1 (8 ounce) package cream
  cheese
1 (6 ounce) can crab meat,
  drained well
¾ teaspoon salt

dash of cayenne pepper
1 teaspoon Worcestershire
  sauce
1 teaspoon black pepper
¾ teaspoon horseradish
¾ cup mayonnaise

Hollow cabbage from the top making the shell into a bowl to use as server. Grate the cabbage you scooped out and the onion in the blender. Mix cream cheese and crab meat. Add all other ingredients, including cabbage and onion. Fill the cabbage shell and serve with assorted crackers. Serves 40.

Mrs. Rick W. Griffin
(Sally Roberts)

STRAWBERRIES IN MAY WINE

1 cup May wine or dry Rhine
  wine
juice of 1 medium orange
½ cup firmly packed brown
  sugar

½ teaspoon almond extract
3 pints fresh strawberries,
  washed and hulled

Combine wine, orange juice, sugar, and almond extract. Pour over strawberries and marinate, chilled at least 2 to 3 hours. Serve strawberries in marinade. Serves 8.

Mrs. Stuart C. Davis III
(Kay Lamar)

ALMOND-FLAVORED FRUIT PUNCH

2 cups sugar
1 quart water
1 quart orange juice
1 quart pineapple juice

1 pint jar of Realemon juice
1 tablespoon almond extract
2 teaspoons vanilla extract
2 quarts ginger ale

Dissolve the sugar in the water. Add the remaining ingredients to the sugar-water mixture, except the ginger ale. This punch may be made, minus the ginger ale and stored, refrigerated for 2-3 weeks in a 1 gallon glass jar. Add cold ginger ale prior to serving (2 parts punch to 1 part ginger ale approximately). Serves 20.

Mrs. William C. Boswell, Jr.
(Margaret Wilson)

RASPBERRY PUNCH

1 (46 ounce) can unsweetened
   pineapple juice
1 (40 ounce) jar unsweetened
   apple juice
1 (6 ounce) can frozen
   lemonade, reconstituted

1 (6 ounce) can frozen limeade,
   reconstituted
1 teaspoon almond extract
½ gallon raspberry sherbet

Mix all juices. Blend and allow to stand several hours - overnight is preferable. At serving time, pour into punch bowl and add sherbet, cut into small pieces. Serves 40 generously (4 ounce cups).

For 125 servings, use 3 recipes and 2 gallons sherbet. This is a beautiful and delicious punch, especially appropriate for bridal teas.

Mrs. V. J. Adams, Jr.
(Angela Gaultney)

HINTS

To hot chocolate, add 1 cup of strong coffee. Top with whipped cream flavored with almond extract.

ICED TEA PUNCH

3 quarts water
8 tea bags, regular size
½ cup sugar

1 (12 ounce) can frozen
   lemonade concentrate
1 (1 liter) bottle ginger ale

Bring water to a boil; add tea bags, cover and allow to stand for 5 minutes. Remove tea bags; stir in sugar. Add thawed lemonade concentrate. Set aside to cool. Chill ginger ale. When ready to serve stir in chilled ginger ale. Pour over ice to serve. Yield: 4½ quarts.

MOCHA PUNCH

1 (2 ounce) jar instant coffee
1 (16 ounce) can Hershey's
   chocolate syrup

3 quarts milk
2 pints vanilla ice cream

Dissolve coffee in one pint very hot water. Add syrup and milk. Refrigerate for several hours. At serving time, pour liquid over large scoops of ice cream in a punch bowl. Top with sweetened whipped cream. Serves 20.

Mrs. W. T. Moody, III
(Mary MacGregor)

CHRISTMAS PUNCH

8 tablespoons Soochong tea
2 quarts boiling water
1 cup sugar
1 (6 ounce) can frozen orange
juice
1 (6 ounce) can frozen
lemonade
1 fifth cognac

1 gallon California Chablis
wine
grenadine syrup, (optional)
1 (8 ounce) jar red maraschino
cherries
1 (8 ounce) jar green
maraschino cherries
4 quarts soda

Measure the tea into a large teapot and pour fresh boiling water over it. Cover and brew for 10 minutes. Strain into a large pitcher and stir in the sugar. When sugar dissolves, add the orange juice and lemonade. Divide the entire mixture between gallon jugs, and add half the cognac and wine to each. If you would like the punch bright red, add a little grenadine syrup to each bottle. Cap and store in refrigerator. Ice blocks: Freeze a ¼ inch layer of water in the bottom of 2 bread loaf pans. Cut the green cherries in quarters and lay them, smooth side down on the ice to look like wreaths. Cut the red cherries into eights and fashion a red "bow" on each wreath. Pour in just enough water to cover the cherries. Freeze firm. Pour in another 2 inches water and freeze very hard. Prior to serving, unmold a block of ice by putting it in a punch bowl and covering it with a hot towel. Pour half the contents of one of the gallon jugs over the ice and add 1 quart of soda water. Replenish punch bowl with the other ice block and additional punch as needed. Serves 50 liberally.

The color of the punch without red and green is a pleasant weak tea color and in no way detracted from the spirit of Christmas. The most compliments were from the men - All good Irish drinkers. I considered it a great success!

Mrs. George R. Barfield, III
(Patricia Sheridan)

CHAMPAGNE PUNCH
Easy and Refreshing

2 fifths Chablis white wine
1 fifth champagne

1 pint strawberries, washed
and stemmed

Marinate strawberries in white wine 12 hours. Add champagne just before serving. Serve in stemmed wine glasses. Serves 16-20.

BANANA PUNCH

3 cups sugar
6 cups water
3 cups unsweetened pineapple
 juice

2 cups orange juice
¼ cup lemon juice
3 large bananas, blended
2 quarts lemon-lime soda

Mix all ingredients, except lemon-lime soda, together and freeze in gallon container. One hour before serving, remove from freezer. Mix 2 quarts of lemon-lime soda with frozen mixture and serve from a punch bowl. Yields 1½ gallons.

Mrs. Bruce J. Bishop
(Eleanor Richardson)

FRUIT JUICE PUNCH WITH SHERBET

2 (32 ounce) cans frozen orange
 juice
4 (18 ounce) cans frozen
 lemonade

4 (6 ounce) cans frozen
 pineapple juice
1 gallon pineapple sherbet

Add water to juice concentrates according to the directions on the cans. Chill juices and pour over sherbet just before serving. Serves 50.

Mrs. Robert L. Dickey, III
(Cynde Martin)

WASSAIL PUNCH

1 gallon apple cider
1 tablespoon whole cloves
1 tablespoon whole allspice
2 sticks cinnamon
¼ teaspoon powdered mace

¼ teaspoon grated nutmeg
¼ teaspoon salt
1 cup light brown sugar
2 lemons, thinly sliced
3 oranges, thinly sliced

Pour cider into large kettle. Add spices, salt, sugar, and fruit. Bring to hard boil. Cover and simmer 15 minutes. Remove from stove, cool, and then strain. Serve hot.

Mrs. Neil A. Struby
(Hazel Burns)

PINK SPARKLE PUNCH

2 cups boiling water
2 (3 ounce) packages
  strawberry gelatin
½ cup sugar
1 (46 ounce) can pineapple
  juice

1 (6 ounce) can frozen orange
  juice, thawed
1 (6 ounce) can frozen
  lemonade, thawed
6 cups cold water
1 quart ginger ale, chilled

Combine boiling water, gelatin, and sugar. Stir until gelatin and sugar are dissolved. Add fruit juices and cold water; chill. Just before serving add ginger ale. Garnish with lemon slices, orange slices or ice ring with fruit.

ORANGE SHERBET PUNCH

1 quart lemon ice milk
2 cups vanilla ice milk
2 cups orange sherbet

2-3 (28 ounce) bottles collins
  mixer

Put ice milks and sherbet in punch bowl. Add collins mixer a few minutes before serving. Serves 20.

COFFEE PUNCH
A New Orleans favorite

1 gallon very strong coffee (like
  French Market Coffee)
3 tablespoons vanilla extract
2 pints half-and-half

sugar to taste
1 gallon vanilla ice cream,
  softened

Add vanilla extract to coffee and refrigerate until well chilled. Add half-and-half and sugar to taste. Combine coffee mixture and ice cream in punch bowl just before serving. Serves 15.

Mrs. Chris R. Sheridan, Jr.
(Beth Childress)

VERY GOOD PUNCH

1 (3½ ounce) package lime
    gelatin
1 (3½ ounce) package lemon
    gelatin
2 cups water

2 cups sugar
1 large can pineapple juice
2 lemons
32 ounces ginger ale

Dissolve flavored gelatin in 2 cups boiling water. Add sugar and stir to dissolve. Add pineapple juice, juice of 2 lemons and enough water to make 1 gallon. Just before serving add 1 quart of ginger ale.

ORANGE BLUSH PUNCH

2 (6 ounce) cans frozen orange
    juice, thawed
2 cups cranberry juice

½ cup sugar
1 quart club soda
ice ring with orange slices

Combine thawed orange concentrate, cranberry juice and sugar; mix well. Chill. When ready to serve, pour in punch bowl and add soda. Freeze water with orange slices and mint leaves in ring mold. Float ice ring in punch bowl.

LEMON SLUSH
A light, refreshing dessert, too

1 (12 ounce) can frozen pink
    lemonade

1½ cups sherry
6 ounces water

Blend the lemonade with sherry and water. Put in freezer. Before serving, thaw to slush. Serve in wine or champagne glass. Serves 4.

Mrs. Hudnall G. Weaver
(Margaret Smith)

FRUIT PUNCH

1 gallon water
5 cups sugar
2 (46 ounce) cans pineapple
   juice
1 (1 ounce) bottle almond
   flavoring

1 (16 ounce) bottle
   reconstituted lemon juice
2 (28 ounce) bottles ginger ale
food coloring (optional)

Mix water and sugar; stir until dissolved. Add pineapple juice, almond flavoring and lemon juice; chill. When ready to serve add ginger ale and food coloring if desired. Yield: 50 to 60 servings.

WEDDING PUNCH

4 cups sugar
4 cups water
2 (3 ounce) packages orange
   flavored gelatin
1 (3 ounce) package lemon
   flavored gelatin

9 cups boiling water
2 (46 ounce) cans pineapple
   juice
2 (16 ounce) bottles lemon
   juice
2 (1 liter) bottle ginger ale

Bring 4 cups of water to a boil. Add sugar; set aside to cool. Dissolve orange and lemon flavored gelatin in 9 cups of boiling water; cool. Combine cooled sugar and gelatin with pineapple and lemon juice; mix well. Pour into empty milk cartons or other large container; freeze. Remove from freezer about 4 hours before serving to allow punch to thaw to a slushy stage. Place in punch bowl and add ginger ale. Serves 75.

SANGRIA

1 (1 pint 7 ounces) bottle red
   wine
2 tablespoons sugar
1 lemon, sliced
½ orange, sliced

2 ounces Cointreau
2 ounces brandy
12 ounces club soda
24 ice cubes

Combine wine, sugar, lemon slices, and orange slices. Stir until sugar dissolves. Stir in remaining ingredients. Let stand 15 to 20 minutes. Serve in 4 tall glasses.

Mrs. John W. Collier
(Lynn Loessner)

CRAN-LEMON COOLER

2 cups water
½ cup sugar
2 cups cranberry juice cocktail

½ cup lemon juice
ice cubes
lemon slices

Combine water and sugar. Stir until sugar is dissolved. Add cranberry juice cocktail and lemon juice. Chill thoroughly. At serving time, pour over ice cubes and garnish glasses with lemon slices. Serves 6.

Mrs. James F. Carson, Jr.
(Beth Hodges)

LEMON SANGRIA

3½ cups dry white wine,
   chilled
3 unpeeled lemons, sliced
1 unpeeled orange, sliced
1 green apple, peeled, cored
   and cut into wedges

small bunch green grapes
½ cup cognac
¼ cup sugar
1 (10 ounce) bottle club soda,
   chilled
ice cubes

Combine all ingredients, except soda and ice cubes in large pitcher and chill overnight. Just before serving, add soda and ice cubes and stir lightly. Pour into glasses and add fruit as desired. Add ½ cup more cognac for potency. Yields 1½ quarts.

Mrs. Rufus Dorsey Sams, III
(Sidney Tucker)

PINEAPPLE FLOAT
Refreshing

2½ cups pineapple sherbet
1 cup dry white wine

1 cup ginger ale

Combine all ingredients and stir slightly. Serve in tall glasses. Serves 4.

VARIATION: For punch, mix 1 quart club soda, 1 quart pineapple sherbet, 3 cups apricot nectar and 1 (46 ounce) can pineapple juice.

MOCK COCKTAIL

2 cups white grape juice
1 cup pineapple juice
1½ cups lime juice

green food coloring
1 quart ginger ale

Combine fruit juices. Add green food coloring to juices for desired color. Store in refrigerator. Just before serving, add ginger ale and garnish with mint. Serve over crushed ice. Serves 12.

Mrs. Robert M. Young
(Katie McNamara)

GOLDEN COOLER

1¼ cups water
¾ cup sugar
3 cups orange juice

3 cups pineapple juice
¾ cup lemon juice
1 (1 liter) bottle ginger ale

Bring water to a boil and add sugar; stir until dissolved. Add fruit juices and mix well. Pour into a gallon milk carton or large freezer container; freeze. Remove from freezer several hours before serving time to allow the mixture to thaw to a slushy stage. Add ginger ale, stir and serve. Makes 3 quarts.

HINTS

If chocolate is served with dessert wines, the quality of wine is lost.

STRAWBERRY SLUSH

2 ounces unsweetened
  pineapple juice
1½ ounces coconut cream

3 to 4 medium strawberries or
  2 ounces of frozen berries

Place strawberries, pineapple juice and coconut cream in a blender. Add equal amount of ice cubes. Blend about 1 minute or until smooth and creamy.

MOCK PINK CHAMPAGNE

½ cup sugar
1 cup water
1 (6 ounce) can frozen orange
  juice concentrate

1 (6 ounce) can frozen
  grapefruit juice concentrate
1 (28 ounce) bottle ginger ale
⅓ cup grenadine syrup

Mix sugar and water in saucepan; boil for 5 minutes. Cool. Add frozen concentrates; refrigerate. Chill for several hours. At serving time add ginger ale and grenadine syrup.

TANGY TOMATO COCKTAIL

1 gallon tomato juice
2 teaspoons celery salt
4 teaspoons salt
1 teaspoon onion salt

½ teaspoon Tabasco sauce
½ teaspoon Worcestershire
  sauce
½ cup sugar

Combine all the ingredients and bring to a boil. Remove from heat; chill. Yield: 4 quarts.

FROZEN FRUIT DRINK

1½ ounces unsweetened
   pineapple juice
1 ounce coconut cream

2 ounces frozen strawberries
   or 3 medium fresh ones
⅓ medium ripe banana
ice

Place all the ingredients in a blender; add equal amount of small ice cubes. Blend until smooth and creamy. Yield: 1 (12 ounce) drink.

LIME JULEP

1 cup lime juice
1 cup sugar

4 cups unsweetened pineapple
   juice
1 quart ginger ale

Combine lime juice and sugar in saucepan. Heat until sugar is dissolved. Add pineapple juice, stir well and set aside to cool. At serving time add ginger ale and pour over crushed ice. Serve with a slice of lime on glass. Yield: 12 servings.

FROSTED ORANGE
Childrens' Delight

1 (6 ounce) can frozen orange
   juice
1 cup water

½ cup sugar
1 cup milk
½ teaspoon vanilla

Place all the ingredients into a blender. Fill the remainder of blender with ice. Blend until ice is crushed and drink is smooth and frothy. Yield: 5 servings.

QUICK DRINK

1 quart apple juice, chilled   **1 quart ginger ale, chilled**

Mix chilled juice and ginger ale and serve over ice. So simple yet so refreshing.

LEMONADE-BANANA SHAKE

2 cups cold milk   **3 medium bananas, sliced**
1 (6 ounce) can frozen   **1 pint vanilla ice cream,**
** lemonade concentrate,**   ** softened**
** thawed**

Place milk, lemonade concentrate and sliced bananas in a blender. Blend until smooth. Add ice cream and blend again. Yield: 4 (10 ounce) servings.

ICE RING

Boil water for a clear ice ring, set aside to cool. Pour small amount of water into ring; freeze. Place fruit on ice and freeze. Add water a little at a time freezing after each addition, so fruit will not float and move in ring.

CHRISTMAS EGGNOG

6 eggs, separated
1½ cups sugar, divided
¼ teaspoon salt
6 cups milk

2 cups whipping cream
2 teaspoons vanilla
Ground nutmeg

Beat egg yolks. Gradually add 1 cup of the sugar and the salt, beating constantly. Gradually add milk and cream. Cook in a double boiler over hot water. Stir constantly until mixture thickens and coats the spoon. Cool and add vanilla; chill. When ready to serve beat egg whites until foamy. Gradually beat in remaining ½ cup sugar; fold into chilled custard. Spoon into chilled punch bowl and sprinkle with nutmeg. Yield: 16 servings.

HOT COFFEE EGGNOG

⅓ cup instant coffee
2 cups water
2 quarts canned eggnog

whipped cream and cinnamon
to garnish

In large saucepan, combine instant coffee, water and eggnog. Heat thoroughly but do not boil. Serve in mugs. Garnish with whipped cream and sprinkle with cinnamon. Yields 20 (½ cup) servings.

SMELL OF CHRISTMAS
Not for Consumption

1 quart water
1 quart apple cider
1 quart pineapple juice
4-6 pieces ginger

1 teaspoon allspice
2 teaspoons pickling spice
3 sticks cinnamon
14-15 whole cloves

Combine all ingredients in a saucepan and bring to a boil. Boil 5-8 minutes, then reduce heat to simmering. The aroma is wonderful and Christmasy!

HINTS

Iced tea requires half as much sugar if sweetened hot rather than cold.

RUSSIAN TEA
Sweet

8 cups water
1 heaping teaspoon whole
    cloves
1½ cinnamon sticks
4 tea bags

1 cup sugar
1½ cups orange juice
½ cup pineapple juice
¼ cup lemon juice

In a large pot place 8 cups of water. Bring water to a boil. Shortly before the water boils, add cloves and cinnamon sticks. Continue boiling for 1 minute. Remove from heat, add tea bags and steep for 5 minutes. Remove tea bags and add sugar and juices. Serve hot. Yields 15 servings.

Mrs. F. Kennedy Hall
(Ann Kite)

BRAZILIAN COFFEE

⅓ cup cocoa
1 teaspoon ground cinnamon
½ teaspoon salt
1 (14 ounce) can sweetened
    condensed milk
4 cups water

1½ cups strong coffee
cinnamon sticks
ground nutmeg
½ cup brandy (optional)
¼ cup light rum (optional)

Combine cocoa, cinnamon, and salt in a 3 quart saucepan. Add sweetened condensed milk, stirring until smooth. Place pan over medium heat; gradually stir in water and coffee. Heat thoroughly but do not boil. Garnish each cup with a cinnamon stick and sprinkle with nutmeg. Add ½ cup brandy and ¼ cup light rum along with the coffee and water, if desired. Leftovers can be refrigerated. Yields 7 cups.

Mrs. William M. Gibson
(Bonny D. Denton)

HINTS

For delicious iced coffee, freeze extra strong coffee in ice cube trays. To serve, put in a tall glass. Pour warm milk over and top with 1 tablespoon whipped cream.

HOT RUSSIAN TEA MIX

2 cups instant tea
2 cups Tang powdered orange
   concentrate
1 teaspoon cloves

2½ cups sugar
2 (.22 ounce) packages
   Kool-Aid lemonade mix
2 teaspoons cinnamon

Mix all ingredients together in very large bowl or jar. Store in covered container. Makes 1 quart. Use 2 teaspoonfuls of mixture to 1 cup hot water when serving.

Mrs. John C. Walker, III
(Kathy Kidd)

HOT CHOCOLATE MIX
Great Christmas Gift

1 (2 pound) box Nestles Quick
1 (1 pound) box confectioners'
   sugar

1 (11 ounce) jar Coffee-mate
1 (8 quart) box powdered milk

Mix ingredients together. Store in a gallon jar. To serve, fill cup half full with chocolate mix and add boiling water.

Mrs. Andrew W. Young
(Pamela Watkins)

HINTS

A pinch of salt added to overperked coffee will eliminate bitter taste.

CITRUS TEA

6 whole cloves
2 cups water
8 tea bags, regular size
6 cups water

1½ cups sugar
⅔ cup orange juice
½ cup lemon juice

Bring 2 cups water to a boil; add cloves; remove from heat, and allow to stand for 1 hour. Bring 6 cups of water to a boil. Add tea bags, remove from heat, cover and allow to stand 5 minutes. Remove tea bags. Add sugar; stir until dissolved. Strain clove mixture. Combine tea, clove mixture, and fruit juices. Stir well. Serve hot or cold. Yield: 9 to 10 servings.

HOT SPICED TEA

2 gallons water
1 tablespoon whole cloves
4 pieces stick cinnamon
6 regular tea bags
2 cups sugar

1 (6 ounce) can frozen
  lemonade
1 (12 ounce) can frozen orange
  juice

Place spices in a tea ball or tie in a piece of cheesecloth. Place in boiling water and simmer for 20 minutes. Remove from heat. Remove spice bag; add tea bags. Steep for 15 minutes; remove tea bags. Add sugar and juices; stir well. Let stand overnight. Serve hot. Yield: 2½ gallons.

PERCOLATOR PUNCH

1¾ cups cold water
2 cups cranberry juice
2½ cups unsweetened
  pineapple juice
3 cinnamon sticks

1 tablespoon whole cloves
½ tablespoon whole allspice
¼ teaspoon salt
½ cup brown sugar

Pour juices and water into an 8-cup percolator. Break cinnamon sticks and place with remaining ingredients in percolator basket. Perk through a cycle. Serve hot. Serves 8 to 10.

INSTANT CAFÉ CAPPUCINO

½ cup instant coffee
½ cup powdered chocolate
   drink mix

1 cup powdered coffee
   creamer
¼ cup orange-flavored
   breakfast drink

Place all ingredients in blender or processor. Process on high until particles are very fine. Store in an air tight jar or tin. Use 3 rounded teaspoons to a cup of hot water. Yield: 12 to 14 servings.

SOUTHERN MINT JULEP

1½ teaspoons confectioners'
   sugar
6 fresh mint leaves, plus 2-3
   sprigs fresh mint
dash cold water
1½ cups shaved ice

4 ounces bourbon
2 slices lemon
¼ teaspoon confectioners'
   sugar
2-3 drops brandy

Place 1½ teaspoons sugar, mint and water in a glass. Crush mint until bruised. Fill glass almost to the top with shaved ice, packing down firmly. Pour in bourbon and with a long spoon, mix with ice. Put glass in refrigerator for 1 hour or in freezer for ½ hour. The glass should be thoroughly frosted. Remove glass from refrigerator. Garnish drink with lemon and mint which has been sprinkled with ¼ teaspoon confectioners' sugar. Put the drops of brandy on top and serve with a straw. Serves 1 drink.

HINTS

A fifth of champagne yields 6 servings.

BREADS

BLINTZES

2 cups flour
1 cup sugar
5 large eggs
¾ cup half-and-half

2 cups milk
2 tablespoons brandy
3 tablespoons butter, melted

FILLING:
1 pound cottage cheese,
  drained
1 egg

2 tablespoons sugar
1 tablespoon heavy cream
2 teaspoons lemon juice

Sift together flour and sugar. Beat eggs and add to sugar mixture. Add remaining ingredients and beat until mixture is smooth. Let stand at room temperature. Make thin cakes on lightly buttered griddle. Use ¼ cup batter per blintz.

Filling: Mix filling ingredients together. Fill each cake and roll up. Serve with sour cream and apricot preserves.

GRANOLA

1 cup sesame seeds, unsalted
1 cup pumpkin seeds, unsalted
1 cup sunflower seeds,
  unsalted
1 cup whole or sliced almonds,
  unsalted
1 cup soy granules, unsalted
1 cup cashew pieces, unsalted

1 cup raw wheat germ
5 cups old-fashioned rolled
  oats
1 cup powdered milk
1 cup honey
1 cup Safflower oil
1 cup chopped dates (optional)

Mix dry ingredients. Mix honey and oil and blend into dry ingredients. Bake at 300° for 45 to 60 minutes in a shallow baking dish. Cook half of recipe at a time in 13 x 9 x 2-inch pan. Turn with spatula every 10 minutes. Cool on brown paper. Add dates if desired after cooled. Store in airtight container. Makes 4 quarts.

The first time you might want to half the recipe since it makes a lot. Very good - and good for you! Will need to get most of ingredients at health food store.

Mrs. E. Baxter Evans
(Maida Ragan)

HERBED TOAST POINTS

½ cup margarine, softened
¾ teaspoon parsley flakes
¾ teaspoon oregano
¾ teaspoon marjoram
¾ teaspoon thyme

¾ teaspoon basil
¾ teaspoon herb-seasoned salt
16 slices thin white bread,
  crusts removed

Combine margarine and seasonings; stir well. Spread herbed margarine over bread slices; cut each slice into 4 triangles. Bake at 250° for 35 minutes. Yields 5⅓ dozen.

Mrs. William M. Gibson
(Bonny D. Denton)

FRENCH TOAST
Make ahead

2 eggs
¼ cup sugar
½ teaspoon grated lemon rind
1 cup milk

1 teaspoon vanilla extract
8 slices 1-inch thick day old
  French bread
2 tablespoons butter

Beat eggs with sugar in shallow dish. Stir in rind, milk and vanilla extract to blend. Dip bread slices on one side to coat, then turn and soak 30 minutes or covered overnight in refrigerator. Preheat large skillet or grill to medium heat. Add butter and heat to sizzling point. Fry bread until brown (6 minutes on each side). Sprinkle with confectioners' sugar or nutmeg, if desired. Serve with preserves or syrup. This toast is similar to old fashioned bread pudding. Serves 8.

Mrs. Betty Moseley Ramsbottom
(Betty Moseley)

ORANGE FRENCH TOAST

1 egg, beaten
½ cup orange juice
5 slices raisin bread

¾ cup crushed graham
  crackers
1 tablespoon butter

Combine egg and orange juice. Dip bread in mixture then in crumbs. Fry in 1 tablespoon butter until brown. Serves 2.

BUTTERMILK WAFFLES

1 egg
1½ cups buttermilk
1½ cups flour
3 teaspoons baking powder
1 tablespoon sugar (optional)

¾ teaspoon salt
½ teaspoon (scant) soda
2 large mixing spoons melted
   fat or oil

Beat egg into buttermilk. Sift dry ingredients and add to egg-buttermilk mixture. Add fat. Pour batter onto a heated waffle iron. Makes about 6 waffles. Serve with melted butter and syrup. Serves 2-4.

Mrs. George G. Felton
(Anne Corn)

OATMEAL PANCAKES
Wheatgerm gives pancakes nutty flavor

1 egg
3 tablespoons oil
1½ cups buttermilk
¼ cup skim milk
⅔ cup rolled oats
⅔ cup flour

¼ cup wheat germ
2 tablespoons dry skim milk
½ teaspoon soda
½ teaspoon salt
2 teaspoons sugar

Beat first 4 ingredients. Add remaining ingredients and stir until moist. Batter will be lumpy. Use electric fry pan at top heat. Grease pan and drop batter by teaspoonfuls onto skillet. Makes 6-8 pancakes.

POPOVERS

1 cup sifted flour
½ teaspoon salt
2 eggs

1 cup milk
1 tablespoon melted butter

Mix all ingredients well, and bake in greased custard cups filled two-thirds full on cookie sheet (not too close together). Preheat oven and bake 30-45 minutes at 425°. Yields 5 custard cups.

Mrs. Elder Barnes
(Nancy Elder)

SOUR CREAM COFFEE CAKE

1 cup butter
1½ cups sugar
3 eggs
2½ cups unsifted flour
1 teaspoon baking powder
1 teaspoon soda

¼ teaspoon salt
1 cup sour cream
1 teaspoon almond extract
1 cup brown sugar
2 teaspoons cinnamon
1 cup chopped nuts

Grease and flour 2 layer cake pans. Cream butter with sugar. Add eggs, sift flour, baking powder, soda and salt. Add alternately with sour cream. Add extract. Put layer of batter in cake pans. Sprinkle with mixture of brown sugar, cinnamon and chopped nuts. Add batter on top of mixture. Sprinkle top with remaining sugar, cinnamon and nuts. Repeat. Bake at 350° for 25 minutes. Yields 2 coffee cakes.

Miss Helen Gibson

SARAH'S CINNAMON PUFFS

2 packages dry yeast
½ cup warm (not hot) water
¾ cup lukewarm milk
¼ cup sugar
1 teaspoon salt

½ cup shortening
2 eggs
3¼ cups sifted flour
1 tablespoon vanilla extract

COATING MIXTURE:
½ cup melted butter
1 tablespoon cinnamon

1 cup sugar

Combine yeast and water; let stand 5 minutes. In large mixing bowl combine milk, sugar, salt, shortening, eggs, yeast mixture and half of the flour. Beat 2 minutes with electric mixer or by hand until smooth. Add remaining flour and vanilla extract. Beat 2 more minutes. Drop 1 tablespoon batter into well-greased muffin cups. Place in warm draft-free place (80-85°) and let rise until doubled in bulk and they reach top of muffin pans (30-40 minutes). Bake at 375° for 18 to 20 minutes, or until golden brown. Remove from pans and dip top and sides in melted butter and into cinnamon and sugar coating mixture. Yields 2½ dozen.

Mrs. Waddell Barnes
(Martha Davis)

HINTS

A little sugar in pancake batter makes pancakes brown more easily.

DELICIOUS CORN MEAL MUFFINS

1 cup self-rising cornmeal   ½ cup oil
1 (8 ounce) carton sour cream   2 eggs
1 (8 ounce) can creamed corn   1 teaspoon baking powder

Grease muffin tins and put pan into oven while oven preheats to
375°. Mix all ingredients together in mixing bowl and pour into hot
muffin tins. Bake at 375° for 35 minutes. Can be kept in freezer.
Yields 12 large or 24 small muffins.

Mrs. Hugh Moss Comer
(Virginia Bateman)

AUNT ANNE'S FRIED HOECAKES
Good with vegetable soup

1 cup self-rising cornmeal   enough ice cold water to make
salt to taste (about ¾ teaspoon)   mixture VERY "pour-able!"
½ to ¾ cup bacon grease

Pour bacon grease into heavy iron skillet. Heat to medium. Place a
tablespoonful of meal mixture carefully in skillet, one at a time,
being careful not to place them too close together. Turn with
pancake turner once while frying. When brown and crisp, remove to
paper towels for grease to absorb. Serve hot, either with or without
butter. Serves 2-3.

Mrs. Samuel W. Popejoy
(Helen Farmer)

VIRGINIA SPOON BREAD

1½ cups milk   pinch of salt
½ cup cornmeal   dash of sugar, if desired
1 egg   1 teaspoon baking powder
2 tablespoons shortening

Boil milk and meal, stirring constantly 5 to 10 minutes until fairly
thick. Add egg, shortening, salt, sugar and baking powder. Pour
mixture into a baking dish and bake in a preheated 375° oven for 30
minutes.

Mrs. Elder Barnes
(Nancy Elder)

SARA'S JALAPĒNO CORN BREAD

2½ cups plain meal
2 tablespoons sugar
4 teaspoons baking powder
1 cup flour
1 tablespoon salt
3 eggs
1½ cups milk

½ cup cooking oil
1 (1 pound) can cream-style corn
6-10 minced jalapēno peppers plus seeds
2 cups grated sharp cheese
2 cups finely chopped onions

In a bowl, sift dry ingredients. In separate bowl, beat eggs lightly and stir in milk and oil. Add liquid mixture to dry mixture. Stir in cream-style corn. Add minced peppers, grated cheese and chopped onion. Use electric mixer to blend peppers through bread. Pour batter into 2 well-oiled pre-heated 9 x 11-inch pans. Bake at 425° for 30 minutes or until done.

SOUR CREAM MUFFINS
Melt in your mouth

½ cup margarine
½ cup sour cream

1 cup self-rising flour

Melt margarine. Stir in sour cream and flour. Spoon into miniature muffin tins. Bake at 350-375° oven for 25-30 minutes. Yields 18 small muffins.

Mrs. Robert F. Fincher, Jr.
(Jeanne Wiggins)

FOOLPROOF CORN BREAD MUFFINS

1 egg
1½ cups milk (if you prefer buttermilk, add ½ teaspoon soda and delete baking powder)
3 tablespoons flour

1½ cups white or stone ground meal
1½ teaspoons baking powder
1 teaspoon salt
2-3 tablespoons shortening or oil, melted and hot

Beat egg until light; add a little of liquid; mix this with flour and meal which has been sifted with baking powder and salt. Add melted shortening or oil and sufficient liquid to make smooth batter and beat well. Have pan sizzling hot when batter is poured. Bake in preheated oven at 450° for 20 minutes. Yields 16 medium-size muffins.

Mrs. E. Max Crook
(Susan McNeill)

BLUEBERRY MUFFINS
Different

1 cup shortening
2 cups sugar
3½ cups self-rising flour
1⅓ cups milk
6 tablespoons boiling water
6 eggs

2 teaspoons vanilla extract
1 teaspoon almond extract
2 (16 ounce) cans blueberries,
  drained *or*
2 pints fresh blueberries

Cream shortening and sugar. Blend in flour, milk and boiling water and beat for 2 minutes. Add eggs, vanilla and almond extract. Beat 2 more minutes. Fold in blueberries and spoon into greased regular-size muffin tins lined with muffin cups. Bake at 375° for 20-25 minutes. If using fresh blueberries, sift small amount of flour over blueberries and coat well before adding to batter to prevent the berries from settling to bottom. Yields 48 muffins.

Mrs. Rufus Dorsey Sams, III
(Sidney Tucker)

OATMEAL-RAISIN MUFFINS
Good breakfast treat

1 cup sifted flour
3 teaspoons baking powder
½ teaspoon salt
¼ cup shortening
1 cup quick-cooking rolled oats
1 egg

1 cup milk
½ cup brown sugar
½ cup raisins
¼ cup sugar
¼ teaspoon cinnamon

Sift together flour, baking powder and ½ teaspoon salt. Cut in shortening until crumbly. Stir in oats. Combine egg, milk and brown sugar and beat well. Stir into dry ingredients; add raisins. Spoon into paper baking cups in muffin pans. Combine sugar and cinnamon; sprinkle over batter. Bake in 425° oven for 15-20 minutes. Yields 12 muffins.

Mrs. Andrew W. Young
(Pamela Watkins)

HINTS

Place a small dish of water in the oven while bread is baking to keep the crust from getting too hard.

PATTY'S BROWN SUGAR MUFFINS
Good with ham

1 cup brown sugar
½ cup soft or melted margarine
1 egg
1 teaspoon vanilla extract

1 cup milk
2 cups flour
¼ teaspoon salt
1 teaspoon baking soda

Cream sugar and margarine. Add egg, vanilla extract, and milk and stir. Add flour, salt, and baking soda and mix well by hand. Pour into greased muffin tins and bake at 375° about 20 minutes. Serve hot from oven. Yields about 18 large or 36 small muffins.

Mrs. N. Tyrus Ivey
(Cathy Ewing)

APPLE MUFFINS

2 cups flour
½ teaspoon salt
2 teaspoons baking powder
½ cup sugar
¾ teaspoon cinnamon

¼ teaspoon nutmeg
1 egg, beaten
1 cup milk
⅓ cup melted shortening
¾ cup chopped apples

Sift dry ingredients. Mix and add egg, milk and shortening. Stir until ingredients are just moistened. Add apples. Fill greased muffin tins two-thirds full. Bake at 400° for 25 minutes. Yields 12 muffins.

CARAWAY CHEESE MUFFINS

2 cups flour
1 tablespoon baking powder
½ teaspoon salt
¼ cup sugar
⅔ cup butter, softened

3 ounces grated sharp cheese
2 teaspoons caraway seeds
1 egg
1 cup milk

Combine dry ingredients. Cut in butter. Your dough will be coarse. Add cheese and caraway seeds. Combine egg and milk to moisten and add to cheese dough. Fill greased muffin tins two-thirds full. Bake at 400° for 25 minutes. Yields 12 muffins.

Mrs. Rufus Dorsey Sams, III
(Sidney Tucker)

CHEESE MUFFINS
Light!

3 cups coarsely grated Cheddar
  cheese
1⅓ cups flour
2½ teaspoons baking powder
1 tablespoon sugar

½ teaspoon salt
1 egg
1 cup milk
4 tablespoons butter, melted

Sift dry ingredients. Stir cheese into dry ingredients until well coated. Beat egg with milk and stir into flour mixture until just blended. Add butter. Bake in greased miniature muffin pans at 350° for 20 minutes.

Mrs. Robert M. Young
(Katie McNamara)

AUNT MAE'S REFRIGERATOR ROLLS

1 cup water
½ cup margarine
½ cup shortening
¾ cup sugar
1½ teaspoons salt

1 cup warm water (105°-115°)
2 packages dry yeast
2 eggs, slightly beaten
6 cups flour

Boil 1 cup water in saucepan. Set off stove. Add margarine and shortening and stir until melted. Add sugar and salt. Cool to luke-warm. In large bowl, put 1 cup warm water. Sprinkle yeast over and stir to dissolve. Add butter, sugar, shortening mixture and eggs to dissolved yeast. Add flour, enough to make thick dough, and mix thoroughly. Cover and refrigerate overnight. About 2-2½ hours before serving rolls, turn dough out on floured board, roll to desired thickness of about ⅓ to ¼ inch, cut with round biscuit cutter and fold in half. Place on greased pan. Let rise about 1½-2 hours. Bake at 400° for 12-15 minutes until well browned. Yields 4 dozen.

It is not necessary to use all the dough. Make out as many rolls as you need, cover the remaining dough and keep refrigerated. Dough will keep for several days.

Mrs. Deming Jones
(Doris Chandler)

Similar recipe submitted by:
Mrs. E. Max Crook
(Susan McNeill)

CRESCENT BUTTER ROLLS
The Best

4 cups soft wheat flour (White Lily, Pillsbury is a hard wheat)
½ teaspoon salt
1 tablespoon sugar
1 package dry yeast
¾ cup lukewarm water
¾ cup undiluted evaporated milk (no substitute)
1 cup butter, room temperature

Sift flour, salt and sugar. Dissolve yeast in lukewarm water. Add to dry ingredients with milk. Mix well. Turn out and knead until smooth and elastic on lightly floured board. Roll into strip 10 x 24 inches. Divide butter into 5 equal portions. On bottom half of rectangle, spread 1 portion of butter evenly. Fold over remaining half rectangle and press down. Wrap in waxed paper. Let chill 7 minutes in freezer. Repeat rolling, butter spreading, folding and chilling four times. After last chilling, wrap in waxed paper and place in refrigerator overnight. Next morning, cut dough in 4 portions. Roll each portion the size of dinner plate. Cut in 8 pie-shaped wedges. Roll up from wide end and shape into crescents. Chill 1 hour. Remove from refrigerator and glaze with 2 teaspoons melted butter mixed with 2 teaspoons milk. Bake in 400° oven, at once, 12-15 minutes. Yields 32 rolls.

Mrs. Rufus Dorsey Sams, III
(Sidney Tucker)

WHOLE WHEAT ROLLS

1¾ cups lukewarm water
1 package yeast
1 egg
½ cup sugar
1 teaspoon salt
3 cups sifted flour
3-4 tablespoons oil
2½-3 cups unsifted whole wheat flour

Using a large mix master bowl, blend water, yeast, egg, sugar, and salt. Add the 3 cups sifted flour by degrees. Then add the oil. Next add the whole wheat flour. Grease top and let rise in a warm draft-free area about 2 hours or until doubled in bulk. Place in a greased covered bowl in refrigerator. Pinch off dough and place in muffin tins. Let rise about 2 hours. Bake at 450° for about 10 minutes or until brown. Yields 36 rolls.

Mrs. Joe E. Timberlake, Jr.
(Elizabeth Durant)

POTATO ROLLS
Crusty and Delicious

1 package dry yeast
½ cup warm water
pinch of sugar
⅔ cup Crisco
1 cup mashed potatoes (with salt)

½ cup sugar
1 teaspoon salt
2 eggs
1 cup scalded milk
6 cups flour

Add yeast to warm water and sugar. Let stand. Mix Crisco, mashed potatoes, sugar and salt. Add eggs and beat well. Add scalded milk. When dough is warm (not hot), add yeast mixture. Stir in 3 cups flour and mix well. Then add remaining flour and mix well. Cover and let rise in a warm draft-free area until doubled in bulk. Push down, cover well, and store in refrigerator. Take out about 2 hours before baking. Shape as desired (I cut round and fold over), and let rise. Bake at 425° for about 20 minutes.

Mrs. J. Wilbur Coggins, Jr.
(Sue Moss)

RUM ROLLS

3¼ cups flour
1 package yeast
1 cup milk
6 tablespoons margarine
⅓ cup sugar
½ teaspoon salt
1 egg

2 tablespoons butter, melted
1 cup brown sugar
1 cup raisins
1¼ cups confectioners' sugar, sifted
1½ teaspoons rum extract
1½-2 tablespoons hot water

Mix 2 cups flour and yeast together with hands. Heat milk, margarine, sugar and salt until warm, stirring constantly, until margarine melts. Add to dry mixture in bowl and beat 3 minutes. Add egg and beat for 1 more minute. Stir in remaining flour to make soft dough. Turn out and knead 5 minutes. Cover in bowl and let rise 1 hour in a warm draft-free area until doubled in bulk. Turn out and shape into 2 balls. Cover and let rest 5 minutes. Roll into 2 rectangles; brush with butter. Combine brown sugar and raisins and sprinkle over dough; roll up jelly roll fashion and cut in ¾ inch slices. Place in 24 muffin tins. Let rise 45 minutes. Bake at 375° for 20 minutes. Remove rolls from pan and spoon on frosting made of confectioners' sugar, rum extract and hot water. This recipe can be frozen. Yields 2 dozen.

ORANGE ROLLS

*½ recipe of Refrigerator Roll
dough
6-8 tablespoons butter, softened
½ cup sugar

1½ teaspoons grated orange
rind
2 cups confectioners' sugar
3-4 tablespoons orange juice

Make up recipe of roll dough. Use only half for orange rolls. Divide this amount into half again. Roll each portion, on lightly floured boards, into a 12 x 8-inch rectangle. Stir together the butter, sugar (granulated), and orange rind. Spread half of this mixture over each rectangle, like a jelly roll, beginning with long side. Slice into 18 equal slices. Place rolls in cupcake papers in muffin pans (this helps hold glaze) or use 3 greased 8-inch or 9-inch square baking pans. Let rolls rise about 1½ hours. Bake at 375° for 15 minutes or until lightly browned. Combine confectioners' sugar and orange juice. Drizzle over warm rolls to glaze. Yields 36 rolls.

*For refrigerator roll dough, see Aunt Mae's Refrigerator Rolls.

Mrs. E. Max Crook
(Susan McNeill)

ALL-BRAN REFRIGERATOR ROLLS

1 cup shortening
¾ cup sugar
1½ teaspoons salt
1 cup boiling water
1 cup bran

2 packages dry yeast
1 cup lukewarm water
2 eggs
6 cups flour

Combine shortening, sugar, salt and boiling water. Add bran. Dissolve yeast in lukewarm water. Add eggs and yeast mixture to flour mixture. Mix in flour. Place in bowl, leave room for rising, cover and refrigerate dough overnight. To make rolls, remove dough from refrigerator. On floured board, knead dough until smooth and not sticky, roll out, and cut with small biscuit cutter. Let rise 2½ to 3 hours. Bake on greased cookie sheet at 450° about 15 minutes or until brown. This recipe can be halved. Yields 5-6 dozen.

Mrs. William E. Hollis
(Allee Gardiner)

HINTS

To keep rolls warm longer, put piece of foil under napkin in serving basket.

YORKSHIRE PUDDING
Delicious with beef gravy

2 cups flour
1 teaspoon salt
2 cups milk

4 eggs
rendered beef suet (½ cup*)

Sift together flour and salt. Stir in 2 cups milk, beating with a whisk until smooth. Add eggs, one at a time. Beat for 1 minute after each egg. Cover bowl with dry towel and chill mixture for at least 2 hours. Put ½ cup rendered fat in 9 x 13-inch pan and bake at 450° until drippings are sizzling. Beat chilled batter vigorously. Pour this batter in hot drippings and bake for 15 minutes at 450°. When risen, reduce temperature to 350° and bake 10-15 minutes more until brown.

Rendered fat - put suet in pan in a hot oven and bake until you have ½ cup drippings.

Mrs. William W. Williams
(Ann Warlick)

PUFF SHELLS

1 cup water
½ cup butter
¼ teaspoon salt

1 cup sifted flour
4 eggs

In a heavy saucepan, boil water, butter and salt. Reduce heat to low. Add flour at once. Stir briskly until mixture leaves side of pan and forms ball. Remove from heat and cool slightly. Add eggs one at a time. Beat after each addition until smooth and glossy. Grated cheese may be added if desired. Drop by teaspoonfuls onto greased cookie sheet. Bake at 400° for 30 minutes. Cool on racks. Cut off tops and fill with chicken salad or other spread. Yields 40 shells.

These may also be frozen after cooling. Delicious as dessert puffs, adding 1 teaspoon sugar.

Mrs. Steve L. Wilson
(Gena Ware)

HINTS

Porous yeast bread can be caused by over rising or cooking at too low a temperature.

CHARLEY'S FAVORITE BISCUITS

2 cups self-rising flour   ½ cup Crisco shortening
½ teaspoon cream of tartar   ⅔ cup milk
2 teaspoons sugar

Mix together the flour, cream of tartar, and sugar. Cut in ½ cup shortening. Add the milk. Quickly mix together and then pat out the dough on a well-floured board for about 30 seconds. Do not pat down too hard!! Cut out biscuits and bake at 450° on cookie sheet for about 10 minutes. If regular flour is used, add 4 teaspoons baking powder and ½ teaspoon salt. Yields 6 large biscuits or 12 small biscuits.

Mrs. Charles F. Causey
(Alice Jackson)

FANNY'S ANGEL FLAKE BISCUITS

2 packages yeast   1¾ cups buttermilk
⅓ cup warm water   1 teaspoon baking soda
5 cups self-rising flour   3 teaspoons sugar
1 cup Wesson oil

Dissolve yeast in warm water; add remaining ingredients. Mix by hand. Dough will be wet and sticky. Pinch off half of dough and knead in more flour. Roll out dough and cut in circles. Coat both sides in oil. Fold biscuits in half. Other portion may be made up or refrigerated for a week. Bake 12 minutes at 475°. Yields 3-4 dozen.

Mrs. William M. Flatau
(Nellie Dean Mason)

CHEESE BREAD

2½ cups Bisquick   1 beaten egg
½ pound New York sharp   1 cup milk
   cheese

Grate half the cheese and dice the other half. Mix Bisquick, cheese, egg and milk to blend. Do not use an electric beater. Pour mixture into a loaf pan and bake 50-55 minutes at 350°.

Mrs. Milton Heard, Jr.
(Kathryn Moate)

CINNAMON BREAD

2 cups warm water
¼ cup honey
2 packages dry yeast
1 tablespoon salt
½ cup oil

6 cups unbleached flour,
  divided
4 tablespoons cinnamon
1½ cups light brown sugar

Mix first 3 ingredients and let stand about 10 minutes or until foamy. Add salt, oil, and 3 cups flour and beat at highest speed for 8 minutes. Stir in remaining 3 cups of flour. Cover and let rise in a warm, draft-free area about 3 hours. Divide dough in half, knead, and roll out on well-floured board. Spread ½ cup sugar and cinnamon mixture over the dough and roll up, being sure to pinch seam and ends closed. Repeat process with remaining dough. Place loaves in greased bread pans and let rise for 1 hour. Brush top with oil or egg white. Bake at 350° for 20 minutes. Reduce heat to 300° and cook 40 minutes longer. Remove from pans and cool on rack. Yields 2 loaves.

If you have a food processor large enough for 6 cups of flour, allow the processor to do all the work for you.

Mrs. Timothy K. Adams
(Julie Bearden)

BANANA NUT BREAD
Lemon and sour cream make this special

1½ cups flour
½ teaspoon baking powder
½ teaspoon baking soda
¼ teaspoon salt
½ cup butter
1 cup sugar

2 eggs
1 teaspoon vanilla extract
grated rind of ½ lemon
¾ cup mashed ripe bananas
2 tablespoons sour cream
1 cup chopped nuts

Sift together flour, baking powder, soda, and salt. Set aside. Cream butter, gradually add sugar. Beat in eggs one at a time, add vanilla extract, lemon rind, and bananas. Stir in flour, alternately with sour cream. Fold in nuts. Pour into a greased loaf pan or 3 small loaf pans and bake at 350° for 1 hour. Less for small pans—about 35 minutes. Test with toothpick.

Mrs. Robert T. Thetford
(Elizabeth Goodwyn)

BLUEBERRY LOAF

3 cups flour
2 teaspoons baking powder
1 teaspoon baking soda
½ teaspoon salt
⅔ cup corn oil
1⅓ cups sugar
4 eggs

½ cup milk
1½ teaspoons lemon juice
1 cup crushed pineapple, drained
2 cups canned blueberries, drained
1 cup chopped pecans

Sift flour with baking powder, soda and salt; set aside. In large bowl, combine oil, sugar, eggs, milk, lemon juice and pineapple. Mix well. Add dry ingredients and mix well. Fold in drained blueberries and pecans. Pour mixture into 2 greased and floured loaf pans. Bake at 350° for 40-45 minutes. Yields 2 loaves.

CREAM CHEESE RIBBONED NUT BREAD
Good enough for company

FILLING:
1 (8 ounce) package cream cheese, softened
1 cup sugar

¼ cup flour
1 egg

GLAZE:
1½ cups confectioners' sugar

1-2 tablespoons milk

BREAD:
3 cups flour
½ cup sugar
1½ teaspoons salt
1½ teaspoons soda
¾ cup oil

¾ cup milk
½ cup honey
2 eggs
1½ cups chopped nuts

Preheat oven to 350°. Generously grease using 1 tablespoon solid shortening, a 12-cup fluted tube pan. In small bowl, blend all filling ingredients until smooth; set aside. In large bowl, combine all bread ingredients except nuts; blend until just moistened. Stir in nuts. Spread one third of batter (1⅔ cups) in greased pan. Pour filling evenly over batter. Carefully spoon on remaining bread batter. Bake 55-65 minutes until toothpick inserted in center comes out clean. Cool upright in pan 15 minutes; remove from pan. Cool. To make glaze, combine confectioners' sugar and milk until smooth and spoon over bread.

PUMPKIN BREAD

1 cup salad oil
3 cups sugar
1 teaspoon vanilla extract
4 eggs
2 cups pumpkin (fresh or
  canned)
3½ cups sifted flour

1½ teaspoons salt
2 teaspoons baking soda
1 teaspoon cinnamon
1 teaspoon nutmeg
½ teaspoon baking powder
⅔ cup water
½ cup chopped nuts

Mix at low speed on mixer salad oil, sugar, vanilla extract and eggs. Stir in pumpkin. Sift together flour, salt, baking soda, cinnamon, nutmeg and baking powder. Fold dry mix into egg mixture. Add water and nuts. Mix again. Pour into 2 ungreased loaf pans. Bake 1 hour at 350°. Yields 2 loaves.

Mrs. Crawford B. Edwards
(Mildred Taylor)

VARIATION: In addition to ingredients listed, add ½ teaspoon ginger, ¼ teaspoon cloves and ⅔ cup white raisins.

ORANGE-CRANBERRY BREAD

2¼ cups Pillsbury flour (or
  other hard wheat flour)
1 cup sugar
2 teaspoons baking powder
½ teaspoon baking soda
½ teaspoon salt
1 cup coarsely ground
  cranberries, measured after
  grinding

1 heaping tablespoon freshly
  grated orange peel
½ cup pecans
1 egg
⅔ cup fresh or diluted frozen
  orange juice
2 tablespoons melted butter or
  margarine

Sift together flour, sugar, baking powder, soda and salt. Stir ingredients into ground cranberries. Add orange peel and pecans. Combine egg, orange juice and butter. Blend together all mixtures. Place waxed paper on bottom of 2 greased 8 x 4-inch loaf pans. Divide batter between pans and bake at 350° for about 50 minutes. Yields 2 loaves.

Mrs. Warren H. Thorpe
(Margaret Stum)

WHOLE WHEAT LOAF BREAD

5 or 6 cups flour (½ whole
  wheat, ½ unbleached)
2 packages yeast
2 cups milk

½ cup oil
½ cup honey
1 tablespoon salt
2 eggs

Put 2 cups flour and yeast in bowl and blend with electric mixer. Put milk, oil, honey and salt in boiler; heat a little hotter than lukewarm. When mixture is hot (not scalded or boiling), turn on mixer and pour mixture, all at once, into flour with dough hook, or by hand. Add two eggs and beat briefly, add flour slowly beating constantly. Let rise in a warm, draftfree area until doubled in bulk (in bowl covered with cloth). Shape into two loaves and let rise again. Bake at 325° for ½ hour. Cool on cake racks.

Mrs. Mallory C. Atkinson, Jr.
(Maysie Cobb)

CHALLAH BREAD

2 packages yeast
2½ cups warm water
6 tablespoons sugar
2 teaspoons salt
⅓ cup salad oil

4 eggs
8⅔ cups flour
1 egg yolk mixed with 1
  teaspoon cold water
4 teaspoons poppy seeds

Dissolve yeast in warm water in a large bowl. Add sugar, salt, oil, eggs, and 6 cups of the flour. Beat thoroughly. Gradually add more flour until dough is too stiff to beat with a spoon. Place remaining flour on a pastry board, turn dough out on top of it, and knead until the dough is smooth and all the flour is absorbed. Add a little more flour if dough is still sticky. Place dough in a very large greased bowl, cover, and let rise in a warm, draft-free place for about 1½ hours or until triple in bulk. Punch dough down and divide into 12 portions. Shape each portion into a rope about 1 inch in diameter. Braid 3 ropes together. Tuck under ends and place in a well-greased 5 x 9-inch loaf pan. Repeat for other loaves. Let rise ¾ hour until triple in bulk. Brush tops with egg wash and sprinkle with poppy seeds. Bake in preheated 375° oven for 30 minutes. Remove to cool on racks. Yields 4 loaves.

Mrs. Robert T. Thetford
(Elizabeth Goodwyn)

HINTS

In making yeast bread that has to be refrigerated, cover the top by rubbing oil on it. This will prevent a hard crust.

BRAIDED ONION BREAD

1 package yeast
¼ cup warm water
1 (8 ounce) carton sour cream
1 envelope Swiss onion soup
   mix
¼ teaspoon baking soda
2 tablespoons sugar

2 teaspoons salt
2 tablespoons butter, softened
3 eggs, beaten
1 cup warm water
6½ to 6¾ cups sifted flour
sesame seeds

Sprinkle yeast into ¼ cup warm water to soften. In large mixer bowl, combine sour cream, onion soup mix, baking soda, sugar, salt, butter, 2 beaten eggs and 1 cup warm water; stir in softened yeast until smooth. Gradually add enough flour to form a stiff dough. Knead dough on floured board until smooth, about 5 minutes. Then cover with towel and allow to rise in warm place until doubled. Punch dough down. Divide half of it into thirds. Roll each strip into parts about 15 inches long. Braid 3 strips together, sealing ends. Repeat with remaining dough. Place braids on a lightly greased cookie sheet side by side. Let rise in warm place until light. Meanwhile, preheat oven to 350°. Brush braids with beaten egg; sprinkle with sesame seeds. Bake 40-45 minutes or until golden and firm. Cool on a wire rack and serve or freezer wrap cooled braids. To serve, refrigerate fully wrapped frozen braids. Before serving, heat them wrapped in foil in 400° oven about 30 minutes. Unwrap and cut into slices. Yields 2 loaves.

Mrs. Edmund E. Olson
(Beverly Knight)

CARROT BREAD

1½ cups flour
1 teaspoon baking powder
1 teaspoon soda
1 teaspoon cinnamon
½ teaspoon salt

¾ cup oil
1 cup sugar
2 eggs, beaten
1 cup grated carrots
¼ cup chopped walnuts

Mix dry ingredients together. Combine oil and sugar. Beat in eggs. Add dry ingredients and beat until smooth. Stir in carrots and walnuts. Pour in a greased and floured loaf pan. Bake at 350° for 55-60 minutes. Yields 1 loaf bread.

HINTS

When freezing party sandwiches, spread bread with butter, not mayonnaise.

APPLE BUTTER BRAN BREAD

1 cup All-Bran
1½ cups apple butter
1 teaspoon lemon juice
1 egg
¼ cup shortening
½ cup sugar

1½ cups flour
½ teaspoon baking powder
½ teaspoon soda
½ cup seedless raisins
½ cup nuts

Combine bran, apple butter and lemon juice. Add egg to bran mixture. Let stand 5 minutes. Cream shortening and sugar. Add bran mixture, then add flour with salt, baking powder and soda. Stir until dry ingredients are moistened. Add raisins and nuts. Put in loaf pan lined with waxed paper. Bake at 325° for 1 hour. Yields 1 loaf.

PECAN-RAISIN LOAF
Can be frozen

1 cup coarsely chopped pecans
1 cup seedless raisins
6 tablespoons ground
   cinnamon
½ cup margarine, softened
½ cup sugar
1 tablespoon flour
3 packages dry yeast
2½-3 cups warm water

3 eggs
1 cup sugar
1 cup solid vegetable
   shortening
6 cups flour
1 cup additional flour
2 teaspoons salt
1 cup melted margarine

Mix pecans, raisins, cinnamon, softened margarine, sugar and flour well; set aside. Dissolve yeast in warm water, add eggs, sugar and shortening, flour, mixing well until smooth and spongy. Combine salt with additional flour and mix well into yeast dough. In a bowl grease top of dough with ¼ cup melted margarine, cover loosely with foil. Let rise in a warm, draft-free area until doubled in bulk, about 2 hours. Punch down and knead well on floured surface for 5 minutes. Separate into 4 parts; roll each out to 1 inch thickness and in rectangular shape. Spread each with filling (¼ portion for each), then roll, sealing edges with melted margarine. Allow dough to rise in greased loaf pans for 1 hour or until doubled in bulk. Bake in 350° oven 45 minutes. Turn out immediately onto cooling racks. Yields 4 loaves.

BREAD GLAZES FOR DIFFERENT CRUSTS

Soft, buttery crust: brush loaves with softened or melted butter or margarine after baking.

Crisp, shiny crust: brush loaves with a mixture of one egg and 1 tablespoon water just before baking. May be sprinkled with poppy or sesame seed.

Delicatessen bread crust: remove loaves from oven 5 minutes before done; brush with mixture of ½ teaspoon cornstarch and ¼ cup water that has been heated to boiling. Return loaves to oven to finish baking.

Cinnamon sugar crust: brush loaves with 2 tablespoons melted butter; sprinkle with mixture of 2 tablespoons sugar and ½ teaspoon cinnamon.

Slightly crisp, shiny, sweet crust: brush loaves with a mixture of 1 tablespoon each sugar and water after baking.

Mrs. Robert T. Thetford
(Elizabeth Goodwyn)

QUICK SALLY LUNN
Great with Brunswick Stew

2 eggs, separated
½ cup sugar
2 cups sifted flour
3 teaspoons baking powder

½ teaspoon salt
¾ cup milk
2 tablespoons butter, melted
¼ cup sugar

Preheat oven to 350°. Beat egg yolks with sugar. Mix flour, baking powder, and salt. Add dry ingredients to sugar mixture, alternately with milk. Add melted butter. Beat egg whites until stiff and fold in batter. Pour into greased loaf pan. Sprinkle ¼ cup sugar on top. Bake 40-45 minutes. Yields 1 loaf.

Mrs. Joseph S. Costanzo
(Frances Beazlie)

HINTS

A rib of celery in a bread bag keeps the bread fresh longer.

SOUPS
AND
SANDWICHES

BEEF STOCK

2 pounds beef shin, cut up
1 pound beef marrow bones
2 onions, quartered
1 carrot, diced
4 quarts water, divided

2 ribs celery, quartered
1½ teaspoons salt
pinch thyme
pinch marjoram
Bouquet garni

In a pan spread first 4 ingredients. Brown in oven at 450°. Transfer meat to roaster. Deglaze pan with 2 cups water at high temperature, stirring up brown bits. Add brown bits to roaster with 3½ quarts cold water. Add remaining ingredients. Boil, then reduce heat to simmer. (If necessary, add more boiling water to make 4 quarts to cover ingredients). Simmer 6-7 hours or until liquid is reduced to 2 quarts. Strain stock through a fine sieve and let cool. Chill and remove fat. Can be frozen. Yields 2 quarts.

VEGETABLE BEEF SOUP
Thick Soup

1 soup bone
2 pounds stew meat
2 (10½ ounce) cans chicken
  broth
1 (10½ ounce) can beef broth
4 soup cans water
1 chicken bouillon cube
1 beef bouillon cube
2 stalks celery, coarsely cut
1 large onion, chopped
2 (14½ ounce) cans tomatoes

1 (10 ounce) package frozen cut
  okra
2 (16 ounce) packages frozen
  mixed vegetables (succotash)
6 peppercorns
2 bay leaves
½ cup chopped parsley
few pieces spaghetti or rice
1 potato, diced (optional)
dash of soy sauce

In large covered 12 quart soup pot, brown soup bone and stew beef in a little oil. Drain off grease. Add broths, water and bouillon cubes, and bring to a boil. Cover and let boil gently for 30 minutes. Add vegetables, seasonings and spaghetti or rice. Cover and simmer 4 to 5 hours. Be sure to skim off foam during cooking. If soup gets too thick, add more water. You may also add any fresh or leftover vegetables and meat. Correct seasonings before serving. Serves 16-20.

Mrs. H. P. Persons, III
(Liz Cole)

HINTS
Add lettuce to pot of soup to absorb grease.

VEGETABLE SOUP CHINESE

4 cups chicken broth
1 cup cooked chicken, cut in
thin strips
½ (10 ounce) package frozen
peas
6 water chestnuts, sliced very
thin

1 teaspoon soy sauce
6 mushrooms, sliced very thin
¼ pound fresh spinach,
chopped
½ head iceberg lettuce,
shredded
salt and pepper to taste

Bring broth to a boil. Add chicken, peas, chestnuts, soy sauce, mushrooms and spinach. Bring to a boil again and add lettuce. Season to taste. Simmer about 3 minutes and serve. Serves 4.

OLD-FASHIONED MUSHROOM SOUP

1 pound fresh mushrooms
6 tablespoons butter or
margarine, divided
2 cups finely chopped carrots
2 cups finely chopped celery
1 clove garlic, finely minced
1 cup finely chopped onions
2 (10½ ounce) cans condensed
beef broth

2 (10½ ounce) cans water
3 tablespoons tomato paste
¼ teaspoon salt
1⁄16 teaspoon pepper
4 sprigs parsley
celery leaves
1 bay leaf
3 tablespoons dry sherry
sour cream (optional)

Rinse, pat dry, and finely chop ½ pound mushrooms. Slice remaining ½ pound. Set aside. In a large saucepan, melt 4 tablespoons of butter. Add the chopped mushrooms and sauté for 5 minutes. Add celery and carrots and sauté 5 more minutes. Stir in broth, water, tomato paste, salt and pepper. Tie together parsley, celery leaves and bay leaf and add to saucepan. Bring to boiling point. Cover, reduce heat and simmer 1 hour. Remove and discard parsley, celery leaves and bay leaf. Purée soup in blender. Return to saucepan. In a medium skillet, melt remaining 2 tablespoons butter. Add reserved sliced mushrooms, and sauté 5 minutes. Add to soup along with sherry. Reheat and serve. Garnish with a dollop of sour cream, if you wish. This soup can be frozen. When ready to use, add sherry and sour cream. Serves 10-12.

Mrs. Chris Sheridan, Jr.
(Beth Childress)

CREAM OF MUSHROOM SOUP
Rich and Good

2 cups fresh mushrooms
¼ cup butter
¾ cup chopped green onions,
  including tops

2 tablespoons flour
1 cup chicken stock or broth
1 cup half and half
¼ teaspoon pepper

Chop mushrooms in food processor or finely chop by hand. Put butter in large skillet and cook onions over low heat for 5 minutes or until tender. Add chopped mushrooms and cook mixture for 2 minutes. Add flour and stir for 3 more minutes. Remove pan from heat and add chicken stock and half and half slowly while you whisk mixture. Return to moderate heat and simmer for 5 minutes. Continue stirring. Add salt and pepper to taste. (Better if made ahead and reheated. Also can be frozen.) Serves 4.

Mrs. George Glock
(Mary Ruth Allensworth)

ONION SOUP

5 cups thinly sliced yellow
  onions
3 tablespoons butter
1 tablespoon oil
1 teaspoon garlic salt
¼ teaspoon sugar
3 tablespoons flour
5 cups canned beef broth
3 cups water
½ cup dry white wine

salt and lemon pepper to taste
12-16 slices French bread cut in
  ¾ inch slices
olive oil
garlic clove
2 ounces Swiss cheese,
  slivered
1 tablespoon grated onion
1½ cups grated Swiss cheese
1 tablespoon butter, melted

Cook onions in butter and oil in covered 4 quart saucepan 15 minutes. Uncover, increase heat, stir in garlic salt and sugar. Cook slowly 30-40 minutes. Onions should be tender. Sprinkle with flour and stir 3 minutes. In another saucepan, bring liquids to a boil. Stir into onion mixture. Simmer partially covered 30 minutes. Add salt and lemon pepper to taste. To make bread as topping: Place sliced bread in one layer in roasting pan. Bake at 325° for 30 minutes. After 15 minutes baking time, baste each side of bread with olive oil. After baking rub with garlic. Set aside. Bring soup to boil. Stir in 2 ounces Swiss cheese. Pour into serving dish. Float toast rounds on top. Sprinkle with 1½ cups grated Swiss cheese, and melted butter. Bake at 325° for 20 minutes. Serve immediately. Serves 8.

CHICKEN SOUP
Hearty and Delicious

baked hen
1 large onion, chopped
1 large bay leaf
3 stalks celery, chopped
7-8 tablespoons uncooked
  oatmeal
¼ cup uncooked rice

1 (10¾ ounce) can tomato
  soup, undiluted
1 pint milk
salt
pepper
cayenne
paprika

When most of the meat of a baked hen has been used, cover with water in a large pot, and add chopped onion, bay leaf, chopped celery, and 3 or 4 tablespoons uncooked oatmeal as a thickening agent. Cook at low heat until meat comes off the bones and add any leftover broth or gravy. Cool, remove bones and cut up the pieces of chicken. Chill mixture in refrigerator. Skim off fat. Put mixture back on stove, and when it begins to simmer add uncooked rice. Stir occasionally to prevent sticking. Add undiluted tomato soup and several tablespoons more oatmeal to attain desired thickness. When the tomato soup and oatmeal are absorbed, stir in milk, and season to taste with salt, pepper, and cayenne. Simmer on low heat before serving with a dash of paprika. Serves 6.

Mrs. Margaret H. Duncan
(Margaret Haley)

CHEDDAR CHEESE SOUP

1 onion, sliced
1 cup diced celery
¼ cup butter
¼ cup flour
½ teaspoon dry mustard
1 teaspoon Worcestershire
  sauce
½ teaspoon garlic salt
½ teaspoon lemon pepper

½ teaspoon monosodium
  glutamate
2 chicken bouillon cubes
2 cups water
1 carrot, diced
4 cups milk
8 ounces sharp Cheddar
  cheese, shredded
salt and pepper

Cook onion and celery in butter 5 minutes. Blend in next 6 ingredients. Add bouillon cubes, water, and carrot. Bring to boil and simmer covered 15 minutes. Add milk and heat almost to boiling. Add cheese. Stir until cheese is melted. Season to taste with salt and pepper. Yields 6 cups.

BLACK BEAN SOUP

2 quarts water
2 cups (1 pound) dried black
  beans
3 tablespoons butter
2 cups finely chopped onion
½ cup finely chopped carrots
½ cup finely chopped celery
1½ teaspoons finely chopped
  garlic
1-2 quarts fresh or canned
  chicken stock
1½ pounds smoked ham hocks
1 tablespoon distilled white
  vinegar
1 large bay leaf
1 teaspoon salt
1 tablespoon lemon juice
freshly chopped pepper
½ cup dry Madeira wine
1 lemon, cut in ⅛ inch slices
2 hard-cooked eggs, finely
  chopped
1 tablespoon parsley

Bring water to a boil. Drop in beans. Cook uncovered 2 minutes. Then turn off heat and set aside to soak uncovered for 1 hour. Meanwhile, melt butter in a 5 quart casserole. When foam begins to subside, add onion, carrots, celery, and garlic. Cook for 5 minutes while stirring over medium heat, or until vegetables are soft. Drain beans. Transfer to a casserole. Measure the soaking liquid. Add enough stock to make 1½ quarts and pour mixture in casserole. Stir in ham hocks, vinegar, bay leaf, and salt. Bring to a boil. Reduce heat to low. Cover casserole partially. Simmer 2 hours. Discard ham hocks and bay leaf. Purée soup through food processor. Add lemon juice and a few pepper grinds. Return to casserole and simmer. Stir in Madeira. Use the lemon, eggs, and parsley for garnish. Serves 8-10.

CREAM OF ARTICHOKE SOUP

¼ cup butter
2 tablespoons finely chopped
  onion
2 tablespoons flour
½ cup milk
1 (14 ounce) can diced
  artichoke hearts, reserving
  juice
1 (14 ounce) can chicken broth
3 egg yolks
½ cup cream
1 teaspoon lemon juice
¼ teaspoon nutmeg
salt
lemon slices
parsley

Sauté onion in butter until transparent; add flour. Using a mixer or wire whisk, blend milk, juice from artichokes and chicken broth into flour mixture. Bring to boil. In separate bowl, mix egg yolks and cream; continue using mixer, and add yolks and cream mixture to boiling soup. Lower heat; add lemon juice and nutmeg. Continue using mixer until blended. Add diced artichokes and salt. Serve warm garnished with lemon slices and parsley. Serves 4.

CREAM OF ZUCCHINI SOUP

1 pound young, green zucchini
  squash, sliced
2 tablespoons butter
2 tablespoons finely chopped
  spring onion
1 clove garlic, finely minced

1 teaspoon curry powder
½ teaspoon salt
½ cup half-and-half
1½ cups chicken broth,
  fresh or canned

Scrub unpeeled squash clean. Heat butter, add sliced squash, spring onion and garlic. Cover tightly. Simmer 10 minutes. Shake saucepan in order to avoid browning vegetables. Add curry powder and steam for 2 minutes. Spoon mix into blender, then add remaining ingredients. Serve hot with croutons or cold with chopped chives or parsley.
(You can make and freeze the soup *without* the cream. When ready to serve, melt soup in a boiler, then add cream). Serves 4.

Mrs. Hugh Moss Comer
(Virginia Bateman)

FRESH TOMATO SOUP

8 cups crushed, seeded, peeled
  tomatoes
½ cup minced onion
1 cup chicken stock or broth
1 cup dry white wine
2 teaspoons salt
1 teaspoon sugar

1 teaspoon minced fresh mint
  leaves or ⅓ teaspoon dried
  mint leaves, crumbled
1 teaspoon white pepper
sliced mushrooms
mint sprigs

Combine tomatoes and onion in large bowl; let stand covered at room temperature 1 hour. Press tomato mixture through sieve; discard pulp. Stir in stock, wine, salt, sugar, mint, and the pepper. Refrigerate covered until cold. Garnish with sliced mushrooms and mint sprigs. Serves 6-8.

HINTS

To clarify stock—for each quart of stock add 1 egg white beaten slightly with 2 teaspoons cold water and 1 crumbled egg shell. Stir and heat to boiling. Boil 2 minutes, remove from heat and let stand without stirring for 20 minutes. Pour stock through a strainer lined with cheesecloth.

CREAM OF CORN SOUP

5 ears sweet corn
2 small onions, chopped
1 medium bell pepper, seeded
 and chopped
3 tablespoons butter

salt and pepper to taste
2 cups milk
2 egg yolks
1 cup heavy cream
slivered almonds to garnish

Scrape corn from cobs. Sauté onions and bell pepper in butter and season with salt and pepper. Add corn and milk. Simmer 10 minutes. Put soup in blender and purée. Beat yolks; bring cream up to the boiling point slowly. Pour over egg yolks, then add to hot soup. Garnish with toasted slivered almonds. Serves 6.

COLLARD GREEN SOUP

½ pound hambone
2 Spanish sausages
¼ pound white bacon (salt
 pork)
1 (16 ounce) can turnip greens

1 (16 ounce) can white beans
1 small onion, minced
1 tablespoon bacon fat
4 potatoes, pared
salt and pepper to taste

In 1 quart of water, place the hambone, Spanish sausages, and white bacon. Let cook for ½ hour. Add turnip greens and white beans. Allow to cook slowly for ½ hour. Sauté onion in bacon fat until transparent. Add to greens. Cut the potatoes in medium-size pieces and add to greens. Season with salt and pepper and allow to cook another ½ hour or until potatoes are done. Serves 6.

Mrs. Herbert M. Ponder, Jr.
(Saynor Johnson)

SHERRIED CREAM OF CARROT SOUP

1 cup chicken broth
½ cup peeled sliced carrots
¼ cup diced onion
¼ cup diced celery
3 tablespoons cooked rice

salt and pepper to taste
dash cayenne
⅓ cup whipping cream
2 tablespoons sherry
watercress to garnish

Combine first 4 ingredients. Place in saucepan and boil. Reduce heat, cover and simmer 20 minutes. Transfer mixture to food processor or blender and add rice, salt and pepper, cayenne and whipping cream. Purée until mixture is smooth. Stir in sherry and serve hot or cold. Garnish with watercress. Serves 4.

LETTUCE SOUP
Different and Good

1 large onion, chopped
¼ cup margarine or butter
1 cup milk
3 tablespoons flour

1 pound Boston lettuce, in large
  pieces
½ teaspoon lemon pepper
½ teaspoon salt

Sauté onion in butter until transparent. Add milk and flour. Simmer until thickened. Drop lettuce leaves into boiling water. Cook until leaves are wilted (about 5 minutes). Drain leaves. Put into blender and purée leaves. Add purée to milk mixture. Salt and pepper to taste. Serve with garlic croutons. Serves 4-6.

Mrs. E. Max Crook
(Susan McNeill)

BEVERLY'S ASPARAGUS SOUP

½ pound fresh asparagus
¼ pound fresh mushrooms
1 small onion, chopped
5 or 6 tablespoons butter

3 cups chicken broth
3 cups skim milk, heated
salt and black pepper to taste
parsley

Cook asparagus, including stems, in water to cover, until tender. Save tips; blend stems in blender. Sauté mushrooms with onion in 3 tablespoons butter until tender. Add 2 or 3 remaining tablespoons butter in small pieces. Blend well in blender. Add chicken broth, heated skim milk, and blended asparagus stems. Add whole tips. Sprinkle lightly with fresh ground black pepper and salt to taste. Garnish with fresh parsley. Serves 6.

Mrs. Roger Mills
(Priscilla Bagby)

HINTS

To remove excess fat from soup stock, drop in an egg white while simmering then remove when cooked.

To simmering stock add 1 tablespoon of cold water to bring more film (residue) to the surface.

To garnish vegetable soup, top with grated cheese. To garnish consommé, garnish with lemon slices.

MISSY'S CAULIFLOWER SOUP

3 tablespoons butter
½ small onion, chopped
3 tablespoons whole wheat
  flour
3 cups milk

1 head cauliflower broken into
  flowerettes
salt and cayenne pepper to
  taste
sprigs of parsley to garnish

In a large pot melt butter and add onion. Cook a few minutes. Add flour and stir to make a paste. Slowly add milk, allowing mixture to thicken. Add cauliflower and simmer about 30 minutes. Add salt and cayenne pepper to taste. Garnish with parsley and serve. Serves 6.

Mrs. Donald W. Rhame
(Alacia Lee)

FISH STOCK

2 pounds skinned flounder, fish
  head, bones and trimmings
1 onion, sliced
6 parsley sprigs
1 teaspoon lemon juice

¼ bay leaf
pinch thyme
¼ teaspoon salt
1 cup dry white wine

Put ingredients in a pot with water to cover. Simmer uncovered 30-45 minutes. Strain. Boil before reusing. Yields 2 cups stock.

EASY CRAB MEAT SOUP

1 (10¾ ounce) can condensed
  green pea soup
1 (10¾ ounce) can condensed
  tomato soup
1 pound crab meat (canned,
  fresh or frozen)

¾ pint half-and-half
1 cup dry sherry wine
dash of onion salt

Place soups and crab meat in a double boiler and heat 20 minutes. Add half-and-half, sherry and onion salt. Heat thoroughly, but do not boil. Serves 4-6.

Mrs. Robert C. Dunlap, Jr.
(Mary Virginia Gates)

BOUILLABAISSE

1 cup olive oil
1 bay leaf, crushed
¼ teaspoon whole thyme
   leaves
1 clove garlic, minced
½ cup diced onion
½ cup diced green pepper
¼ cup diced celery
¼ cup sliced carrots
1 (48 ounce) can tomato juice

6 fresh crab bodies and claws
1 cup bite-size pieces fresh
   lobster
2-3 cups bite-size pieces
   filleted bass
1½ cups peeled and deveined
   shrimp
1 cup clams, cleaned
1 cup white wine
½ cup lemon juice

Heat oil slowly in Dutch oven. Add bay leaf, thyme leaves and garlic. Sauté 1-2 minutes. Stir vegetables into oil and sauté until onion is tender. Add tomato juice and crab. Bring mixture to a boil. Cover and simmer 2 hours. Pour tomato juice-crab mixture through a strainer, reserving liquid. Stir crab liquid into reserved tomato juice mixture. Discard crab and vegetables. Return tomato juice mixture to Dutch oven. Add remaining seafood. Cook over medium heat 10 minutes. Stir in wine and lemon juice. Cook 5 additional minutes. Serves 10-12.

OYSTER STEW

garlic salt or 1 clove garlic
1½ cups oysters and liquid
4 tablespoons butter
1½ tablespoons Worcestershire
   sauce

1 quart milk, scalded
1 pint half-and-half

Rub inside of kettle with crushed garlic clove or sprinkle bottom with garlic salt. Heat butter and Worcestershire in kettle. Add oysters with liquid and cook over medium heat until the edges curl and the oysters begin to swell (about 3 minutes). Add scalded milk and half-and-half and reheat. DO NOT BOIL. Serves 4-6.

Mrs. John D. Carey
(Sandra Ballentine)

HINTS

If soup is pale and colorless, add a beet while soup is cooking. Remove beet when soup is done and soup will be golden.

CRAB CHOWDER SUPREME

½ cup chopped celery
½ cup chopped onion
3 tablespoons margarine
3 cups milk
1 (10¾ ounce) can condensed
   potato soup
1 (7½ ounce) can crab meat
1 (8 ounce) can cream style
   corn

2 tablespoons chopped
   pimiento
¼ teaspoon salt
¼ teaspoon crushed thyme
1 bay leaf
¼ cup dry sherry
parsley

In large saucepan, cook onion and celery in margarine until tender. Add remaining ingredients, except sherry and parsley. Cook until heated thoroughly, stirring often, about 15 minutes. Stir in sherry, heat 2 minutes more. Remove bay leaf. Garnish with parsley. Serves 6.

Mrs. Thomas W. Talbot
(Betty Wilson)

SHRIMP GUMBO

3 tablespoons bacon grease
3 tablespoons flour
4 stalks celery, chopped
   (leaves Included)
½ bell pepper, chopped
1 medium onion, chopped
1½ gallons water
2 or 3 beef bouillon cubes
2 (16 ounce) cans chopped okra

1 (16 ounce) can tomatoes
3-4 pinches dried thyme
2 tablespoons Worcestershire
   sauce
6 or 7 drops Tabasco sauce
2 or 3 bay leaves
salt and pepper to taste
2 tablespoons dried parsley
2-3 pounds cleaned shrimp

Brown the flour in the bacon grease. Add the celery, bell pepper, and onion and sauté until limp. (You may need to add more grease.) Add the water and bouillon cubes. Bring to boil and let simmer. Add okra and tomatoes. Cook for 20-30 minutes. Add spices and simmer for 15 more minutes. Add shrimp while water is boiling. The shrimp will be done in about 5 minutes or when they turn pink. Serve over rice. Serves 10-12.

Mrs. John E. Oswald
(Melissa Ruth Johnston)

NEW ENGLAND CLAM CHOWDER

2 (7½ ounce) cans minced
  clams, reserving liquor
¼ pound salt pork, minced
1½ cups water
4 cups diced, peeled potatoes

½ cup chopped onion
2 cups milk
1 cup light cream
3 tablespoons flour
1½ teaspoons salt

Drain clams, reserving ½ cup liquor. Fry pork until crisp. Remove bits of pork from skillet and drain on absorbent towel. To pork drippings, add ½ cup clam liquor, water, potatoes and onion. Cook covered for 20 minutes or until potatoes are tender. Add clams, 1¾ cups milk and cream. Blend remaining ¼ cup milk and flour; stir into chowder. Heat to boiling, stirring occasionally. Add pork bits and salt. Serves 6.

Mrs. Edgar Y. Mallary, III
(Lloyd Washington)

SHRIMP SOUP
Excellent

¼ cup minced onion
¼ cup minced carrot
2 tablespoons butter
2 tablespoons flour
2 (10½ ounce) cans chicken
  broth
½ bay leaf

⅛ teaspoon thyme
2 (10½ ounce) cans Campbell's
  mushroom soup
2 cups ground, cooked shrimp
¼ cup fresh parsley
½ pint heavy cream
1 fresh lemon

Cook onion and carrot in butter until soft. Add flour, cooking 1 minute. Add hot chicken broth, bay leaf and thyme. Cook 15 minutes over low heat. Add canned soup and shrimp. Heat thoroughly. Add parsley, then cream. Serve in soup bowls. Garnish with sliced lemon. Serves 6-8.

SENEGALESE

3 (10¾ ounce) cans cream of
  chicken soup
1 tablespoon curry powder

1 (16 ounce) carton sour cream
1 cup heavy cream
1½-1¾ cups half-and-half

Blend soup, curry powder, and sour cream. Add heavy cream. Thin mixture by slowly adding half-and-half. Chill and serve. Serves 8.

GAZPACHO ANDULUZ
Easy

2 large tomatoes, peeled
1 large cucumber, pared and halved
1 medium onion, peeled and halved
1 medium green pepper, quartered and seeded
4 ounces pimiento, drained
12 ounces tomato juice, divided

⅓ cup red wine vinegar
¼ teaspoon Tabasco
⅓ cup olive oil
1½ teaspoons salt
⅛ teaspoon pepper
2 garlic cloves, peeled and split
½ cup croutons (optional)
¼ cup chives (optional)

In blender combine: 1 tomato, ½ cucumber, ½ onion, ¼ green pepper, the pimiento, ½ cup tomato juice. Blend 30 seconds on high speed to purée. Mix puréed vegetables with rest of tomato juice, ½ of the olive oil, vinegar, Tabasco, salt and pepper. Refrigerate. Sauté croutons with rest of the olive oil and 1 garlic clove, chopped. Chop separately the remaining vegetables and just before serving time, sprinkle the soup with the chopped vegetables, 1 crushed garlic clove and chives. Serve in chilled bowls and pass croutons. Can be made several days ahead. Serves 6-8.

Mrs. James C. Sikes
(Ginny Sowell)

COLD CUCUMBER AND SPINACH SOUP

1 bunch scallions, sliced
2 tablespoons butter
4 cups diced, peeled, and seeded cucumbers
3 cups chicken broth
1 cup chopped spinach

½ cup sliced, peeled potato
½ teaspoon salt
lemon juice, white pepper to taste
1 cup light cream

In a saucepan sauté the scallions in the butter until softened. Add remaining ingredients except cream and simmer the mixture until the potatoes are cooked. Transfer the mixture to a food processor or blender and purée it in batches. Freeze at this point if desired. Prior to serving, add 1 cup of light cream. Chill. Serve in chilled bowls and garnish each serving with a thin stick of cucumber or thin slices of radishes or scallions. Yields approximately 2-2¼ quarts.

Mrs. Alexander H. S. Weaver
(Adele Burgin)

BORSCHT

1 (20 ounce) can beets, drained, reserving juice
2 cucumbers, peeled and seeded
salt to taste
1 (16 ounce) carton sour cream
2 (10½ ounce) cans beef broth, undiluted

2 (10½ ounce) broth cans of buttermilk
½ cup beet juice
sour cream for topping
caviar to garnish

Purée beets and cucumber. (Reserve beet juice when draining beets before blending with cucumber). Drain puréed mixture. Add salt and sour cream and blend until mixture is smooth. Add beef broth, buttermilk and beet juice. Chill mixture. Top with sour cream and caviar before serving. Yields 2½-3 quarts.

COLD TOMATO SOUP

2 (10¾ ounce) cans tomato soup
1 (8 ounce) carton sour cream
1 tablespoon horseradish
¼ teaspoon curry powder

1½ soup cans water
1 jigger sherry or to taste
4 tablespoons sour cream
dash curry powder

Mix soup, sour cream, horseradish, and curry powder. Add water and sherry and mix well. Refrigerate to chill. Serve with 1 table-spoon sour cream on top of each serving and sprinkle top of soup with curry powder. Serves 4.

EASY VICHYSSOISE

1 (10¾ ounce) can potato soup
1 cucumber, peeled and seeded

1 pint half-and-half
pinch of salt

Place soup and cucumber in blender. Add half-and-half. Season to taste. Chill and serve. Serves 4.

Mrs. Bert Struby
(Jane Spearman)

URSULA'S STRAWBERRY WINE SOUP

1 cup sugar
½ cup cornstarch
1 cup red wine
1 cup water
2 teaspoons vanilla extract
2 (1 pint) baskets strawberries
¼ cup lemon juice

½ cup orange juice concentrate
½ cup red wine
16 ounces sour cream
1½ cups apple or orange juice
8-10 almond macaroons,
   crumbled

Mix sugar and cornstarch together. Then add red wine, water, and vanilla extract. Heat and stir constantly. When mixture comes to a boil, remove from heat and cool. Purée 1½ baskets strawberries with lemon juice and orange juice concentrate, and add to soup mixture. Reserve the remaining ½ basket of berries. Add ½ cup wine to cold soup and refrigerate. Add sour cream to soup. Then add apple or orange juice until you obtain desired consistency. Slice remaining ½ cup strawberries and add to soup. Just prior to serving soup, top soup with crumbled macaroons. Serves 10.

Ursula Knaeusel
Ursula's Cooking School
Atlanta, Georgia

CHILLED RASPBERRY SOUP

1½ envelopes unflavored
   gelatin
⅓ cup cold water
¾ cup hot water
3 (10 ounce) packages frozen
   raspberries, thawed

3½ cups sour cream
1⅓ cups pineapple juice
1⅓ cups half-and-half
1⅓ cups dry sherry
⅓ cup Grenadine
2 tablespoons lemon juice

Soak gelatin in cold water 5 minutes. Stir in hot water and dissolve over low heat. Force raspberries through sieve and then purée. Combine with remaining ingredients, cover, and refrigerate. Garnish with mint. Serves 12.

HINTS

Freeze leftover stock in ice trays. When frozen, remove from ice trays and freeze in plastic bags.

If soup is too salty, add a teaspoon each of cider vinegar and sugar or a raw potato.

STROGANOFF STEAK SANDWICH

⅔ cup beer
⅓ cup cooking oil
1 teaspoon salt
½ teaspoon garlic powder
¼ teaspoon pepper
2 pounds flank steak, about 1
 inch thick
2 tablespoons butter or
 margarine

½ teaspoon paprika
salt
12 slices French bread, toasted
4 cups sliced onion
1 cup sour cream, warmed
½ teaspoon prepared
 horseradish
paprika (optional)

In shallow dish, combine beer, oil, salt, garlic powder, and pepper. Place steak in marinade and cover. Marinate overnight in refrigerator or several hours at room temperature; drain. Broil steak 3 inches from heat for 5 to 7 minutes on each side for medium rare, or cook on grill. In saucepan, melt butter and blend in paprika and a dash of salt. Add onion; cook until tender, but not brown. Thinly slice meat on the diagonal across grain. For each serving, arrange meat slices over 2 slices bread. Top with onions. Combine sour cream and horseradish; spoon onto each sandwich. Sprinkle with paprika, if desired. Serves 6.

Mrs. John A. Draughon
(Sally Hines)

VEGETABLE SANDWICHES

1 (8 ounce) package cream
 cheese, softened
¼ cup chopped celery
¼ cup chopped green pepper
¾ cup grated carrots

1 medium onion, minced
¼ cup grated cucumber
1 tablespoon mayonnaise
1 teaspoon lemon juice
salt and pepper to taste

Drain juice from vegetables. Add vegetables to softened cream cheese and cut in mayonnaise. Season to taste. Spread on bread slices. Yields spread for 6 sandwiches.

Mrs. Paul A. Cable
(Susan Watt)

FROSTED SANDWICH LOAF

2 (8 ounce) packages cream
   cheese
milk
1 (2 ounce) jar pimientos
1 teaspoon finely minced onion

1 loaf unsliced sandwich bread
mayonnaise
2-3 peeled, sliced tomatoes,
   (drain on paper towel)
lettuce

Soften 1½ packages cream cheese with milk. Set aside. Make pimiento cheese spread with remaining cream cheese, pimientos and finely minced onion. Remove crust from bread. Cut loaf into 4 lengthwise slices. Spread bottom slice with mayonnaise. Cover with tomato slices. Spread next slice of bread with mayonnaise. Place on top of tomatoes. Spread top side with mayonnaise. Cover with lettuce. Spread third slice of bread with mayonnaise. Place on layer of lettuce. Spread top side with mayonnaise. Cover with pimiento cheese mixture. Top with last slice of bread lightly spread with mayonnaise. Frost top and sides of loaf with softened cream cheese. Refrigerate for several hours. Slice in 1-1½ inch servings.

Mrs. J. Wilbur Coggins, Jr.
(Sue Moss)

HAM AND CARROT SANDWICHES

1 cup ground cooked ham
½ cup grated carrot
½ cup salad dressing or
   mayonnaise
1½ teaspoons prepared
   horseradish

¼ teaspoon salt
⅛ teaspoon pepper
1 loaf bread, crusts removed
soft butter

Mix ham, carrot, salad dressing, horseradish, salt and pepper. Cut bread in desired shapes. Moisten bread with soft butter. Spread filling on bread and serve as a luncheon sandwich.

APPLE-CREAM CHEESE SPREAD

1 (3 ounce) package cream
   cheese, softened
1 tablespoon orange juice

2 teaspoons confectioners'
   sugar
½ cup peeled, grated apple

Combine cream cheese, orange juice, and confectioners' sugar; mix until smooth. Stir in apple. Chill. Use as a spread for banana bread or other fruit-nut bread. Yields about 1 cup.

INDIVIDUAL CHEESE PIZZAS

1 pound fresh pork sausage
1 pound ground beef
1 (15 ounce) can tomato sauce
1 (4 ounce) can sliced
   mushrooms, drained
2 teaspoons oregano
⅛ teaspoon garlic salt

5 English muffins, split and
   toasted
½ cup grated Parmesan
   cheese
10 slices Mozzarella cheese or
   2 cups shredded Mozzarella
   cheese

Preheat oven to 400°. In large skillet, slowly cook sausage for 10 minutes; add ground beef and continue cooking until browned; drain. In bowl, combine tomato sauce, mushrooms, oregano, garlic salt and meat. Place muffins on baking sheet. Spread with about ⅓ cup meat mixture. Sprinkle each muffin with about 2 teaspoons Parmesan cheese and top with a slice or about 2 tablespoons shredded Mozzarella. Bake 5-8 minutes or until sandwich is hot and cheese melts. Serves 10.

Mrs. E. Max Crook
(Susan McNeill)

PITA BURGERS

2 tablespoons lemon juice
1 teaspoon dry mustard
1 garlic clove, minced
¼ cup salad oil
¾ teaspoon salt
¼ teaspoon pepper
½ medium head romaine
   lettuce, in bite-size pieces
1 cup red cabbage, finely
   shredded

2 medium carrots, finely
   shredded
1½ cups fresh bean sprouts
6 pita bread pockets
1½ pounds lean ground meat
½ cup minced walnuts
¼ cup red wine
¼ teaspoon ginger
½ teaspoon salt
¼ teaspoon pepper

For dressing: mix first 6 ingredients, set aside. In large bowl, mix lettuce, cabbage, carrots and sprouts. Set aside. In medium bowl, mix ground meat, walnuts, wine, ginger, salt and pepper. Shape meat into patties. Cook patties. To serve, place a patty in a pita pocket and add some salad mixture that has been tossed in dressing. Serves 6.

HINTS

To clean breadboards, use a mixture of baking soda and water.

OPEN-FACED SHRIMP SANDWICHES

1 pound fresh shrimp, cleaned,
  cooked and diced
1 tablespoon minced onion
1 teaspon minced celery
1 teaspoon minced green
  pepper
2 teaspoons lemon juice

½ teaspoon grated lemon rind
¼ teaspoon salt
4-5 drops Tabasco
dash pepper
¾ cup mayonnaise
parsley to garnish

Cut shrimp into fine pieces. Mix together all ingredients with the shrimp and add more seasoning, if desired. Cut 36 rounds of bread about the size of a half dollar, ¼ inch thick. Put a heaping teaspoon of shrimp mixture on each round. Serve garnished with parsley.

Mrs. Leo B. Huckabee
(Jane Odom)

HIGH PROTEIN SANDWICH SPREAD

1 cup peanut butter
½ cup honey
½ cup crumbled bacon

½ cup wheat germ
1 cup crushed pineapple,
  drained

Mix all ingredients together and serve on whole wheat bread.

HOT BAKED CHICKEN SANDWICH
Great with Soup

1 loaf (24 slices white bread)
4 boneless chicken breasts,
  cooked and chopped
4 eggs, boiled and chopped
½ cup chopped olives
⅔ cup mayonnaise

2 (5 ounce) jars Old English
  cheese spread
1 raw egg
½ cup soft butter
salt and pepper

Make 3 layer sandwiches with spread made from chicken, eggs, olives and mayonnaise. Mix together Old English cheese spread, raw egg, butter, salt and pepper to taste. Frost top and sides of sandwiches with cheese mixture. Prepare at least 12 hours ahead of time and refrigerate. Bake at 350° for about 15 minutes before serving. Yields 8 whole sandwiches.

Ms. Susan S. Everett
(Susan Sprayberry)

SALADS
AND
SALAD
DRESSINGS

BING CHERRY MOLD

1 (3 ounce) package cherry
  gelatin
1 (16 ounce) can dark sweet
  pitted cherries, halved
1 (8 ounce) can crushed
  pineapple

1 cup cold Coca-Cola
½ cup chopped pecans

Drain cherries and pineapple and measure liquid. Add water, if necessary, to make 1 cup liquid. Heat liquid and add to gelatin in medium-size bowl. When gelatin is dissolved, add Coca-Cola. Chill until the consistency of egg whites. Add halved cherries, pineapple and pecans. Pour into 3½-cup mold. Chill. Unmold when congealed and serve with mayonnaise or cream cheese softened with a little milk. Serves 6.

Mrs. Charles J. Cartwright
(Stella Blum)

BLUEBERRY SALAD

2 (3 ounce) packages blueberry
  gelatin
2 cups boiling water
1 (15 ounce) can blueberries,
  drained, reserving juice

1 (8¼ ounce) can crushed
  pineapple, drained,
  reserving juice

DRESSING:
1 (8 ounce) package cream
  cheese, softened
½ cup sugar

½ pint sour cream
½ teaspoon vanilla extract
½ cup chopped pecans

Dissolve gelatin in boiling water. Combine juices from fruits and, if necessary, add enough water to equal 1 cup. Add this 1 cup mixture to gelatin. Stir in well-drained fruit. Pour into an oblong 2-quart casserole dish and refrigerate until firm.
Dressing: Combine all ingredients except nuts. Spread over congealed gelatin. Sprinkle with pecans. Serves 10.

Mrs. Charles F. Causey
(Alice Jackson)

RASPBERRY-BING CHERRY SALAD

1 (10 ounce) package frozen
  raspberries, thawed
½ cup currant jelly
2 cups water
2 (3 ounce) packages red
  raspberry flavored gelatin

½ cup sherry
¼ cup lemon juice
1 (16 ounce) can pitted dark
  sweet cherries, drained

Drain raspberries, reserving syrup. Combine jelly and ½ cup of water. Heat and stir until jelly melts. Add remaining 1½ cups of water and heat until gelatin dissolves. Remove from heat; add sherry, lemon juice and raspberry syrup. Chill until partially set. Fold raspberries and cherries into gelatin. Pour into a 6-cup mold. Chill until firm and serve. Serves 8-10.

APRICOT SALAD

1 (8 ounce) package cream
  cheese, softened
1 (6 ounce) package apricot
  gelatin
1 cup boiling water

1 (20 ounce) can crushed
  pineapple, reserving liquid
½ cup chopped nuts
1 (13 ounce) can evaporated
  milk, chilled

Place cream cheese, gelatin and water in double boiler. Mix well and add pineapple juice. Then add crushed pineapple and nuts. Cool. Whip chilled milk. Fold into cooled mixture. Yields 2 molds.

Mrs. Henry J. Lamar, IV
(Katherine Kilpatrick)

WATERGATE SALAD

1 (9 ounce) container Cool Whip
1 (20 ounce) can crushed
  pineapple
1 cup chopped pecans

1 (3¾ ounce) package pistachio
  instant pudding
1 cup miniature marshmallows
3 tablespoons lemon juice

Mix pudding and pineapple in large bowl. Add nuts, lemon juice and marshmallows. Fold in thawed Cool Whip. Chill in 8 x 12-inch dish for 24 hours. Cut in squares. Serves 10-12.

Mrs. V. J. Adams, Jr.
(Angela Gaultney)

STRAWBERRY PRETZEL SALAD
Strawberry Festival Winner

¾ cup margarine
3 tablespoons brown sugar
2½ cups crushed pretzels (not too fine)
1 (6 ounce) package strawberry gelatin
2 cups boiling water
3 cups chilled strawberries (measured after hulled) or 1 pound package frozen berries, slightly thawed

1 (8 ounce) package cream cheese
1 scant cup sugar
1 (8 ounce) carton whipped topping

Combine margarine, brown sugar and pretzels. Mix well and put into lightly buttered 9 x 13-inch baking pan. Bake at 350° for 10 minutes. Dissolve strawberry gelatin in boiling water. While hot add to chilled strawberries. Cool until mixture begins to set. Meanwhile cream sugar and cream cheese and fold into whipped topping. Spread cream cheese mixture over cooled crust. When gelatin begins to set, pour it over top of cheese mixture. Refrigerate until firm. Serves 8-10.

Mrs. Oliver C. Bateman
(Mary Jane Gosline)

RASPBERRY RING

1 (10 ounce) package frozen raspberries, thawed
2 (3 ounce) packages raspberry gelatin
2 cups boiling water

1 pint vanilla ice cream
1 (6 ounce) can frozen lemonade
¼ cup chopped pecans

Drain raspberries and reserve syrup. Dissolve gelatin in boiling water and add ice cream gradually until melted. Stir in lemonade and reserved raspberry syrup. Chill until partially set. Fold in raspberries and pecans. Pour into 6-cup mold. Serves 8-10.

Mrs. Rufus Dorsey Sams, III
(Sidney Tucker)

HINTS

To prevent discoloration of bananas, slice fruit with a silver knife.

FROZEN STRAWBERRY SALAD

2 (3 ounce) packages cream
  cheese
2 tablespoons pineapple juice
  (reserved from pineapple)
2 tablespoons mayonnaise
1 (20 ounce) can chunk
  pineapple, drained

2 sliced bananas
1 (10 ounce) carton frozen
  sliced strawberries
1 (8 ounce) carton whipping
  cream, whipped, divided
⅓ cup mayonnaise
1 cup chopped nuts (optional)

Cream together cream cheese. pineapple juice and mayonnaise.
Add drained pineapple, bananas, and strawberries. Reserving ⅔
cup whipped cream, fold remainder into above mixture. Freeze. Use
the reserved whipped cream and ⅓ cup mayonnaise for dressing
over salad. Sprinkle with nuts, if desired. Serves 10.

Mrs. Girard Jones
(Susan Smith)

SWISS WALDORF SALAD

3 tart apples, pared and diced
2 pears, pared and diced
2 tablespoons lemon juice
¾ cup diced Swiss cheese

½ cup sliced celery
½ cup broken walnuts
⅔ cup mayonnaise

Sprinkle lemon juice over fruit. Add other ingredients; toss lightly.
Chill. Serve on salad greens. Serves 4-6.

Mrs. George O. Haskell, III
(Katrin Kunze)

HOLIDAY AMBROSIA

1 cup pineapple chunks,
  drained
1½ cups mandarin oranges,
  drained
1 cup maraschino cherries,
  quartered
1 cup seedless grapes

2 apples, unpeeled and cubed
1 tablespoon sugar
½ cup flaked, toasted coconut
1 (8 ounce) carton sour cream
2 tablespoons mayonnaise
1 tablespoon light cream
lettuce

Combine fruits and sprinkle with sugar. Add coconut. Set aside.
Mix sour cream, mayonnaise and light cream. Fold into fruit
mixture. Serve on lettuce. Serves 6.

FROZEN FRUIT SALAD
Exceptionally tasty

1 (8-ounce) package cream
  cheese
1/4 cup maple syrup
1 large banana, mashed
1 tablespoon lemon juice
1/2 cup pecans, chopped

1/2 cup chopped dates
2 cups Dream Whip (prepared)
  or cool whip
1 (8-ounce) can crushed
  pineapple

Cream cheese and maple syrup together. Add mashed banana and pineapple; add remaining ingredients. Freeze in cupcake papers in muffin tins. Remove from freezer just prior to serving. Remove paper wrapper before serving. Serves 18.

Mrs. William W. Williams
(Ann Warlick)

APPLE CIDER SALAD

1 (6 ounce) package lemon-
  flavored gelatin
2 cups apple cider
2 cups chilled apple juice
2 tablespoons fresh lemon juice

2 tablespoons grated orange
  rind
2 cups diced, unpeeled apple
1 cup sliced dates
1 cup chopped pecans

Dissolve gelatin in cider, heated to boiling; stir in apple juice, lemon juice and orange rind. Chill until partially set. Fold in remaining ingredients. Pour into an oiled, 6-cup mold and chill until firm. Unmold salad and serve. Serves 8-10.

Mrs. William M. Gibson
(Bonny D. Denton)

SAUTERNE SALAD

1 (3 ounce) package lemon
  gelatin
1 cup pineapple juice
1/2 cup sauterne

1/4 cup lemon juice
sugar to taste
1 cup sliced seedless grapes
1 cup diced pineapple, drained

Dissolve gelatin in fruit juice which has been brought to a boil. Add sauterne, lemon juice and sugar. Chill until partially set. Add grapes and pineapple. Pour into 3 1/2-cup mold and congeal. Serves 6.

EGGNOG CRANBERRY SALAD
Colorful and delicious!

1 (3 or 3¼ ounce) package
  regular vanilla pudding mix
1 (3 ounce) package lemon
  flavored gelatin
2 cups cold water
2 tablespoons lemon juice
1 (3 ounce) package raspberry
  flavored gelatin

1 cup boiling water
1 (16 ounce) can whole
  cranberry sauce
½ cup finely chopped celery
¼ cup chopped pecans
1 envelope dessert topping mix
  (yields one cup)
½ teaspoon ground nutmeg

In saucepan, combine pudding mix, lemon gelatin, and 2 cups cold water; cook and stir until mixture boils. Stir in lemon juice; chill until partially set. Dissolve raspberry gelatin in 1 cup boiling water; cook and stir until dissolved. Beat in cranberry sauce. Fold in celery and pecans. Chill until partially set. Prepare dessert topping according to package directions, adding nutmeg; fold into pudding mixture. Pour half the pudding into an 8 x 8 x 2-inch pan. Carefully pour cranberry layer over pudding; top with remaining pudding. Chill 6 hours or overnight. Serves 9.

CHRISTMAS CRANBERRY SALAD
Great with Turkey Sandwiches

1 envelope unflavored gelatin
¼ cup cold water
1 (20 ounce) can crushed
  pineapple, reserving juice
1 (3 ounce) package orange
  gelatin
2 cups canned applesauce

1 (16 ounce) can cranberry
  sauce
¼ cup sugar
1 tablespoon grated orange rind
1 cup diced celery
1 cup chopped nuts

Soak gelatin in cold water. Heat juice of pineapple (1½ cups) and dissolve both unflavored gelatin and orange gelatin in hot liquid. When cooled, add other ingredients. Will fill two 5-cup ring molds. Serves 16-20.

Mrs. Guy B. Eberhardt
(Melanie Roberts)

HINTS

To select a ripe pineapple, pull a leaf from the pineapple crown. If it pulls out easily, the pineapple is ripe.

ORANGE RELISH—CRANBERRY SALAD

1 cup orange juice
1 (3 ounce) package cherry
  gelatin
1 envelope unflavored gelatin
1 (14 ounce) jar cranberry-
  orange relish

1 cup boiling water
1 (1 pound 4 ounce) can
  crushed pineapple, drained,
  reserving juice

Soak gelatin in ¼ cup orange juice. Add cherry gelatin and boiling water. Stir until gelatins are well dissolved. Add cranberry-orange relish, stirring well until smooth. Add remaining orange juice, pineapple juice and pineapple. Refrigerate. Stir several times while congealing as it has a tendency to separate. Serves 12.

Mrs. Milford Hatcher
(Marion Campbell)

FROZEN TOMATO SALAD

2½ cups tomato juice
1 teaspoon minced onion
1 teaspoon minced parsley
1 teaspoon horseradish
3 teaspoons wine vinegar
½ teaspoon celery seed

½ teaspoon allspice
juice of one lemon
½ teaspoon salt
Tabasco to taste
2 egg whites, stiffly beaten

Blend all ingredients except egg whites in blender; freeze. When partially frozen, stir in beaten whites and return to freezer. Scoop out on lettuce and serve with favorite dressing. Serves 4-6.

Mrs. H. M. Comer Train
(Anne Bush)

MARINATED TOMATOES

1 clove garlic, minced
1 teaspoon salt
½ teaspoon thyme
¼ cup chopped fresh parsley
¼ teaspoon pepper

¼ cup sliced green onion and
  tops
6 fresh peeled tomatoes, sliced
⅔ cup salad oil
¼ cup vinegar

Combine first 6 ingredients and sprinkle over tomatoes. Mix oil and vinegar. Pour over tomatoes. Chill 8 hours. Baste tomatoes occasionally. Drain to serve. Serves 6.

TOMATO-AVOCADO-CHEESE SALAD

AVOCADO LAYER:

1 envelope unflavored gelatin
½ cup water, divided
1 teaspoon salt
3 tablespoons lemon juice

5 drops Tabasco
1½ cups sieved avocado
few drops of green food
  coloring

CHEESE LAYER:

2 teaspoons unflavored gelatin
¼ cup cold water
4 (3 ounce) packages cream
  cheese, softened
½ cup milk
1 teaspoon salt

⅔ cup mayonnaise
¼ teaspoon Worcestershire
  sauce
½ teaspoon chopped green
  onion

TOMATO LAYER:

3 cups tomato juice
½ bay leaf
2 whole cloves
2 sprigs parsley
2 ribs celery
¾ teaspoon salt

dash cayenne pepper
1½ envelopes unflavored
  gelatin
⅓ cup cold water
1½ tablespoons vinegar
1½ teaspoons grated onion

Avocado Layer: Soften gelatin in ¼ cup cold water; add ¼ cup boiling water. To this mixture, add salt, lemon juice, and Tabasco. Cook until mixture thickens. Add avocado and green food coloring. Pour mixture into a 9 x 5-inch loaf pan. Chill until almost firm. *Cheese Layer:* Soften gelatin in cold water and dissolve over boiling water. Beat together the cheese and milk. Stir in remaining ingredients. Stir in gelatin. Pour over the Avocado Layer. Chill this mixture until it is almost firm. *Tomato Layer:* Bring tomato juice, bay leaf, cloves, parsley, celery, salt and pepper to a boil. Then simmer 10 minutes. Strain. Soften gelatin in cold water, then add to hot tomato juice; add vinegar and onion. Pour over Cheese Layer and chill until set. Serves 12-14.

Mrs. Rufus Dorsey Sams, III
(Sidney Tucker)

HINTS

When lemons become dry, place them in a warm oven for a few minutes. They become plump and juicy.

AVOCADO MOLD

2 ripe avocados
1 teaspoon curry powder
dash cayenne
2 envelopes unflavored gelatin
½ cup cold water
½ cup boiling water
2 tablespoons Ac'cent
2 cups mayonnaise
4 tablespoons lemon juice

salt to taste
4 drops Tabasco
2 tablespoons grated onion
½ cup chopped green pepper
½ cup chopped parsley
12 hard-boiled eggs put through sieve
green food coloring (optional)

Mash avocados with curry powder and cayenne. Soften gelatin in cold water then dissolve in boiling water. Add Ac'cent, mayonnaise, lemon juice, salt, Tabasco, onion, green pepper, and parsley. Add cooled gelatin that has been colored green. Oil bundt mold and line bottom with hard-boiled egg slices. Add avocado mixture and refrigerate until firm. Serves 10.

Mrs. Leo B. Huckabee
(Jane Odom)

CALICO SALAD

1 (16 ounce) can shredded sauerkraut, drained
1 medium onion, chopped
1 green pepper, chopped
1-2 pimientos, chopped
½ cup vinegar

½ cup sugar
¼ cup salad oil
1 teaspoon salt
½ teaspoon black pepper
½ teaspoon garlic salt
1 teaspoon celery seed

Drain and rinse sauerkraut. Add onion, green pepper, pimiento. Mix together vinegar, sugar, salad oil, salt, pepper, garlic salt, and celery seed. Pour over sauerkraut mixture, cover and store in refrigerator for 24 hours or more. Serves 4-6.

Mrs. C. Wesley Walker, Jr.
(Karen Kennedy)

HINTS

To ripen avocado, place avocado completely covered in a flour canister.

CUCUMBER MOUSSE WITH CELERY SEED DRESSING

6 large cucumbers
3 cups boiling water
6 tablespoons lemon juice
3 teaspoons Worcestershire
  sauce
2 teaspoons salt
1½ teaspoons pepper

1½ cups mayonnaise
3 envelopes unflavored gelatin
3 tablespoons cold water
3 tablespoons hot water
1 (8 ounce) carton sour cream
green food coloring

DRESSING:
½ cup sugar
1 teaspoon salt
1 teaspoon celery seed
1 teaspoon dry mustard

1 teaspoon grated onion
1 cup salad oil
¼ tarragon vinegar
paprika

Mousse: Cut cucumbers in half, lengthwise. Seed, peel and grate. Blanche in 3 cups boiling water to which lemon juice has been added. Drain well and cool. Add Worcestershire, salt, pepper and mayonnaise. Soften gelatin in 3 tablespoons cold water, then dissolve in 3 tablespoons hot water. Add to cucumber mixture with sour cream and blend well. Add food coloring as needed. Pour into an 8 x 8-inch pan. Chill well and cut into squares.
Dressing: Mix dry ingredients. Gradually add oil and vinegar alternately, mixing with a whisk. Color with paprika. Serves 6-8.

Mrs. Hubert C. Lovein, Jr.
(Ann Elliott)

CARROT SALAD

2 (3 ounce) packages lemon-
  flavored gelatin
2 cups boiling water
1 (20 ounce) can crushed
  pineapple, drained, reserving
  liquid

1 cup grated carrots
1 cup grated Cheddar cheese
¾ cup chopped pecans

Dissolve gelatin in boiling water. Drain pineapple; add enough water to liquid drained from pineapple to make 2 cups and stir into gelatin. Refrigerate until partially congealed; then stir in pineapple, carrots, cheese and pecans and chill until firm. Serves 15.

Mrs. Andrew W. Young
(Pamela Watkins)

FLORRIE'S COOL CARROTS
Excellent with Ham

2 bunches carrots, sliced
¾ cup vinegar
1 cup sugar
1 teaspoon dry mustard
1 finely chopped bell pepper

1 (10¾ ounce) can tomato soup
3 tablespoons chopped chives
  or spring onion including
  tops

Clean carrots and slice. Cook in salted water until just tender, but still slightly crisp. Drain. Mix remaining ingredients well and pour mixture over carrots. Refrigerate. Keeps well covered in refrigerator. Serves 6.

Mrs. Wilbur I. Tucker
(Elizabeth Conner)

LAYERED SALAD

your choice of salad greens
1 cup sliced celery
1 cup bell pepper rings
sliced purple or green onions
1 (10 ounce) package thawed
  frozen peas

bacon bits
1 (0.4 ounce) package Hidden
  Valley Ranch Style Dressing
½ cup mayonnaise
½ cup sour cream

Wash and dry salad greens. Tear into bite-size pieces. Fill a glass bowl with straight sides two-thirds full of greens. Top with layers of celery, bell pepper rings, onions, peas (dry well) and bacon in that order. Sprinkle dry ranch style dressing mix on top. Mix mayonnaise and sour cream and spread over top. Spread to edges to seal. Cover with plastic wrap and place in coldest part of refrigerator for 24 hours.

Also use avocado, egg, and mushrooms in this salad. It's great for a party because it has to be made the day before. When serving, use two spoons and go from the top to the bottom. Do not toss.

Mrs. Robert T. Thetford
(Elizabeth Goodwyn)

HINTS

Dip apples in boiling water briefly to remove skin.

ASPARAGUS VINAIGRETTE

2 (14½ ounce) cans green
    asparagus

2 hard-boiled eggs, grated

DRESSING:
½ teaspoon prepared mustard
2 tablespoons vinegar
6 tablespoons salad oil

½ teaspoon salt
dash pepper
1 teaspoon finely grated onion

Drain asparagus. Thoroughly blend together dressing ingredients. Arrange in serving dish and marinate asparagus in the dressing a few hours in refrigerator. Grate eggs on top just before serving. Serves 6-8.

Mrs. R. Douglas Cole
(Anne Sturman)

TACO SALAD

1½ pounds ground beef
1½ cups diced onion
1 cup diced celery
1 cup diced green pepper
3 cloves garlic, diced (optional)
1 pound Velveeta cheese
1 (8 ounce) can Ortega
    tomatoes and green chili
    peppers

1 head lettuce
2 large firm tomatoes
1 pound package Fritos
salt, chili powder, ground
    cumin to taste

Fry ground beef with small amount of oil until brown. Sauté onion, celery, green pepper in oil. Combine meat and vegetables and simmer 15 minutes. Season with salt, chili powder and ground cumin. In top of double boiler melt cheese and add can of tomatoes and chili peppers. You may only add ½ can if desired. Cut lettuce coarsely and cut tomatoes in chunks and mix together. Add Fritos and mix all ingredients, except melted cheese mixture. Top with hot cheese and mix again. Serve immediately. Serves 10-12.

Mrs. Rick W. Griffin
(Sally Roberts)

HINTS

Put a clove of garlic in a bottle of French dressing to improve its flavor.

ASPARAGUS SALAD
Tangy

⅔ cup sugar
½ teaspoon salt
1 cup water
½ cup vinegar
2 tablespoons lemon juice
2 envelopes unflavored gelatin
½ cup cold water
½ teaspoon grated onion

2 (10 ounce) cans asparagus, chopped
1 cup chopped celery
1 (10½ ounce) can water chestnuts, chopped
1 (2 ounce) jar pimientos, chopped

Bring sugar, salt, 1 cup water, vinegar and lemon juice to a boil. Add to gelatin that has been softened in ½ cup cold water. Cool. Add onion, asparagus, celery, water chestnuts, and pimientos. Pour slightly congealed mixture into a greased 1-quart ring mold. Congeal, unmold, and serve. Serves 4-6.

Mrs. Leo B. Huckabee
(Jane Odom)

ORIENTAL SPINACH SALAD

1 pound fresh spinach
⅓ cup bean sprouts, drained
1 can water chestnuts, sliced
    and drained

2 hard-boiled eggs, chopped
1 cup sliced fresh mushrooms
4 slices bacon, fried and crumbled

DRESSING:
1 cup oil
½ cup sugar
⅓ cup catsup
1½ teaspoons salt

⅓ cup vinegar
2 tablespoons Worcestershire sauce
1 small onion, chopped

Wash and dry spinach thoroughly; remove stems. Purée dressing ingredients in blender. Add other ingredients to spinach leaves. Use dressing to taste. Serves 6-8.

Ms. Bettie Lawrence
(Bettie Atkinson)

HINTS
Grease mold with mayonnaise before pouring in gelatin.

ARTICHOKE-RICE SALAD

1 (6 ounce) package Uncle
  Ben's Rice for Chicken
4 green onions, thinly sliced
½ bell pepper, chopped
12 pimiento stuffed olives,
  sliced

2 (6 ounce) jars marinated
  artichoke hearts, drained,
  sliced, reserving liquid
¾ teaspoon curry powder
⅓ cup mayonnaise

Cook rice as directed on package. Cool in large bowl. Add green onions, bell pepper and olives. Drain artichoke hearts, reserving marinade. Combine artichoke marinade, curry powder and mayonnaise, and whisk until smooth. Add artichoke hearts to rice salad. Toss with dressing. Chill. Serves 8.

Mrs. Wallace Miller, III
(Jane Oliver)

MARINATED RICE SALAD

1 cup uncooked rice
6 tablespoons olive oil
3 tablespoons vinegar
1 teaspoon salt
ground pepper to taste
1 teaspoon tarragon
⅓ cup chopped green pepper
¼ cup chopped parsley

¼ cup finely chopped onion
1 (2½ ounce) jar sliced
  mushrooms, drained
½ cup sliced black olives
½ cup sliced green olives,
  stuffed with pimiento
tomato slices or wedges for
  garnish, if desired

Cook rice according to directions. Combine oil, vinegar, salt, pepper, and tarragon. Pour over hot rice and mix well. Cool. Add green pepper, parsley, onion, mushrooms, and olives. Cover and refrigerate at least 4 hours before serving. Just before serving, add tomato slices to garnish, if desired. Serves 6.

Mrs. Edmund E. Olson
(Beverly Knight)

HINTS

To preserve canned pimientos, cover the remaining unused portion with vinegar and refrigerate.

TOMATO ASPIC
From one of Montgomery's finest cooks!

3 cups tomato juice (V-8 can be substituted)
1 bay leaf
2 teaspoons sugar
6-8 peppercorns
5½ envelopes unflavored gelatin
1½ cups cold tomato juice
¾ cup tomato juice
1 cup tomato sauce
½ cup tomato catsup
¼ cup fresh lemon juice
1 teaspoon Worcestershire sauce
dash Tabasco sauce
1 tablespoon grated onion
2 teaspoons salt
1 tablespoon cider vinegar
1 (3 ounce) jar stuffed olives, sliced
artichoke hearts (optional)
asparagus spears (optional)

Heat 3 cups tomato juice, bay leaf, sugar and peppercorns for 5 minutes. Soften gelatin in 1½ cups cold tomato juice. Add gelatin mixture to hot juice and dissolve thoroughly. Take out bay leaf and peppercorns. Then add ¾ cup tomato juice, tomato sauce, tomato catsup, lemon juice, Worcestershire sauce, Tabasco sauce, grated onion, salt, vinegar. Add chopped celery and sliced stuffed olives. Pour into two 8-inch square pyrex dishes. Refrigerate to congeal. Serves 16-18.

Mrs. Robert T. Thetford
(Elizabeth Goodwyn)

BROCCOLI SALAD

2 (10 ounce) packages frozen chopped broccoli
1 (10¾ ounce) can condensed consommé, divided
1 envelope unflavored gelatin
4 hard-boiled eggs, sliced, divided
¾ cup mayonnaise
juice of 2 lemons
dash of Tabasco
1 tablespoon Worcestershire sauce
salt and pepper
curry to taste (optional)

Cook and drain broccoli. Soften gelatin in one-fourth of consommé; heat remaining consommé and dissolve gelatin. Let cool and add seasonings. Place half of boiled, sliced eggs in bottom of a 10-inch tube mold. Add mayonniase and broccoli to gelatin. Pour half of mixture over boiled eggs. Add another layer of boiled eggs and remaining mixture. Congeal. Serves 8-10.

Mrs. Cubbedge Snow, Jr.
(Edyth McKibben)

MAINE CHANCE SALAD
Served at the Greenhouse

½ cup carrots, in thin strips
½ cup turnips, in thin strips
½ cup green beans, in thin
   strips

½ cup Le Sueur peas
½ cup cauliflower flowerets
¼ cup dressing

MAINE CHANCE DRESSING:
½ cup Wesson oil
½ cup salad oil
½ cup tarragon vinegar
1 teaspoon vegetable salt
1 teaspoon Ac'cent
6 shallots, chopped

1 teaspoon dry mustard
1 teaspoon horseradish
3 egg yolks
1 bunch watercress, chopped
1 bunch parsley, chopped

Cook first 5 vegetables in a small amount of water until tender (about 1 minute). Drain. For dressing, put all dressing ingredients in blender and blend until smooth. Add 1 tablespoon cold water if mixture is too thick, toss salad with dressing. Yields 1 pint. Serves 4-6 if accompaniment to meal, 2 for main dish.

CREAMY PIMIENTO RING

1 (3 ounce) package lemon
   gelatin
½ cup warm water
½ tablespoon vinegar
½ teaspoon salt
½ cup milk

¼ teaspoon paprika
1 teaspoon minced onion
½ cup mayonnaise
½ cup grated cheese
⅓ cup chopped pimiento

Dissolve gelatin in warm water. Add vinegar and salt. Chill. Add milk, paprika and onion to mayonnaise and beat. When gelatin is slightly thickened, beat in mayonnaise mixture and then fold in cheese and pimiento. Turn into ring mold and chill until mixture is set. Serves 6.

Mrs. William M. Matthews
(Fran Flournoy)

HINTS

Before adding salad dressing to salad, lightly toss salad with a teaspoon of oil. This coats the leaves and prevents sogginess.

ASHEVILLE SALAD

2 envelopes unflavored gelatin
½ cup cold water
1 (10¾ ounce) can tomato soup
1 cup mayonnaise
2 (3 ounce) packages cream
   cheese

Any two of the following:
1 cup chopped celery
2 bell peppers, chopped
½ cup chopped pecans
½ cup sliced green olives
1 cup cooked shrimp, chopped

Soak gelatin in ½ cup of cold water. Heat soup slowly and stir in cream cheese. Add gelatin and stir until dissolved. Cool. Add mayonnaise and remaining ingredients. Mold into 12 individual salad molds. Chill. Unmold and serve. Serves 12.

Mrs. Jackson R. Holliday
(Cordelia Dessau)

THREE BEAN SALAD

1 (16 ounce) can wax beans
1 (16 ounce) can cut green
   beans
1 (16 ounce) can red kidney
   beans

1 (2 ounce) jar chopped
   pimiento
3 medium onions, sliced in
   rings

DRESSING:
1 cup sugar
⅔ cup tarragon vinegar
⅓ cup Mazola corn oil

1 teaspoon salt
1 teaspoon pepper

Drain beans and pimiento. Slice onions into thin rings. Set aside. Mix dressing and toss together with beans, pimiento and onions. Chill at least 8 hours. Serves 10.

Mrs. Sidney E. Middlebrooks
(Susan Rau)

HINTS

Fresh tomatoes keep longer if stored stem down.

Tomatoes cut vertically instead of horizontally tend to bleed less.

MOLDED VEGETABLE RELISH
Tangy, good with ham

1 (3 ounce) package lemon
  or lime gelatin
¾ teaspoon salt
1 cup boiling water
¾ cup cold water
2 tablespoons vinegar
2 teaspoons grated onion

½ cup finely chopped cabbage
  (cut in slivers)
½ cup grated carrot
¼ cup finely chopped celery
3 tablespoons chopped green
  peppers (optional)

Dissolve gelatin and salt in boiling water. Add cold water, vinegar and grated onion. Chill until thickened. Fold in vegetables. Pour into a 3 or 4-cup mold or individual molds. Chill. Serves 5.

Mrs. Lee B. Murphey
(Judy Meier)

MARINATED VEGETABLE SALAD

MARINADE:
¾ cup salad oil
1 tablespoon cider vinegar
¼ teaspoon garlic salt
1 tablespoon Dijon mustard
1 tablespoon Parmesan cheese
¼ teaspoon dill weed
¼ teaspoon pepper
1 teaspoon salt

SLICE INTO MARINADE:
1 green pepper, sliced
1 small onion, sliced
½ pound fresh mushrooms,
  sliced
1 (14 ounce) can artichokes,
  drained and sliced
½ cup sliced celery
1 cucumber, sliced thin
1 cup cubed Mozzarella cheese
bacon, crumbled to garnish

Mix marinade ingredients together. Toss vegetables in marinade and refrigerate mixture several hours. Can be served with crumbled bacon and cheese to garnish. Serves 8.

Mrs. T. Baldwin Martin, Jr.
(Joyce McAfee)

HINTS

To crisp celery, wash and cut an Irish potato into pieces and drop in container with celery. Add ice and water and store in refrigerator until serving time.

YANKEE COLESLAW

1 cup red kidney beans, drained well
2 cups shredded cabbage
¾ cup finely chopped celery
⅓ cup finely chopped onions
½ cup chopped fresh parsley
3 strips bacon, fried crisp, crumbled

DRESSING:
1 teaspoon salt
½ teaspoon pepper
½ cup Kraft mayonnaise
2 tablespoons vinegar
1½ tablespoons sugar

Mix all salad ingredients together, reserving crumbled bacon for just before serving. Mix dressing ingredients together and toss or mix with salad ingredients. Sprinkle bacon on top before serving. Serves 8.

Mrs. William F. Ladson, Jr.
(Betty Sweet Simmons)

NANCY'S SLAW
Good with Barbecue

1 large head cabbage
1 large white onion, sliced
1 cup white vinegar
1 cup sugar
¾ cup Wesson oil
1 tablespoon salt
1 tablespoon celery seed

Slice cabbage and onion rings thin. Separate onion rings. Make alternate layers of cabbage and onions in large salad bowl. You will have more cabbage than onions so just cover layer of cabbage with onion rings. Take 2 tablespoons sugar from 1 cup and put in saucepan with vinegar, oil, salt, celery seed and bring to boil. Sprinkle remaining sugar over cabbage and onions. Pour marinade over slaw. Do not stir. Cover and chill 12 hours. Serves 10-12.

Mrs. C. Emory Johnson
(Wendy Bernhardt)

HINTS

If homemade mayonnaise separates, gradually beat in an egg yolk.

HORSERADISH MOLD
Great with Ham

1 (3 ounce) package lemon
  gelatin
¾ teaspoon salt
1 cup boiling water
1 tablespoon white vinegar

dash pepper
1 (8 ounce) carton sour cream
¼ cup prepared horseradish
1 teaspoon grated onion

Dissolve gelatin and salt in boiling water. Add vinegar and pepper. Chill until slightly thickened. Combine sour cream, horseradish and onion. Add gelatin, blending well. Pour into greased mold. Chill until firm. This mold can be served with crackers as an appetizer. Serves 4-6.

Mrs. Wilbur I. Tucker
(Elizabeth Conner)

MUSTARD RING
Good with Ham and Barbecue

¾ cup sugar
1½ tablespoons dry mustard
⅔ cup cider vinegar
⅓ cup water
4 eggs, well beaten

1 envelope unflavored gelatin
1 tablespoon cold water
½ pint whipping cream,
  whipped
salt to taste

Sift and mix dry ingredients. Add vinegar, water and well-beaten eggs. Put gelatin in double boiler with 1 tablespoon water and stir over hot water until gelatin dissolves. Add vinegar mixture slowly. When thoroughly mixed, add salt to taste, then remove from heat. Set in cold water to cool. When partially set, add whipped cream. Pour into mold and allow mixture to congeal. When unmolded, center may be filled with coleslaw. Serves 6-8.

EGG SALAD

6 hard-boiled eggs
3-4 spring onions, chopped
½ teaspoon French dressing

½ teaspoon dry mustard
4 tablespoons mayonnaise
salt and pepper to taste

Grate eggs and combine with remaining ingredients. Serve in a tomato or spread on a sandwich. Serves 4-6.

Mrs. L. Rodney Crutchfield
(Coleman Crandall)

GERMAN POTATO SALAD

2 pounds potatoes
½ pound bacon
2 tablespoons bacon drippings
3 tablespoons sugar
2 tablespoons minced onion
1 tablespoon flour

¼ teaspoon pepper
1½ teaspoons salt
1½ teaspoons celery seed
½ cup water
⅓ cup wine vinegar

Boil potatoes, peel and slice. Cook bacon, drain and break in small pieces. Reserve 2 tablespoons of drippings. To drippings, add sugar, onion, flour and seasonings. Gradually add water and wine vinegar. Heat to boiling, stirring constantly. Boil 1 minute. Add potatoes and bacon and mix gently. Serve hot. Serves 6-8.

SOUR CREAM POTATO SALAD

8 medium potatoes, boiled and
  sliced
1 (8 ounce) carton sour cream
3 green onions, thinly sliced
2 tablespoons dry parsley

½ teaspoon salt
2 teaspoons prepared
  horseradish
1½ cups mayonnaise

Make a sauce of sour cream, green onions, parsley, salt, horse-radish and mayonnaise. Alternate layers of potatoes and sauce in a flat dish and refrigerate. The flavors in this salad are penetrated if allowed to sit for at least 12 hours. Serves 8-10.

Mrs. William W. Baxley, Jr.
(Charlene Carpenter)

WATERCRESS-WALNUT SALAD

⅔ cup imported olive oil
⅓ cup red wine vinegar
1 teaspoon Dijon mustard
¼ teaspoon or more salt
¼ teaspoon or more pepper
2 bunches watercress, broken
  into small pieces

1 head Boston lettuce
1 avocado, peeled and sliced
2 green apples, sliced
¼ cup chopped walnuts

Mix olive oil, vinegar, mustard, salt and pepper in jar and shake to mix. Chill. In salad bowl, mix watercress, lettuce, avocado, apples and walnuts. Pour dressing over and toss. Serve at once. Serves 6.

CHEESE MOLD

2 envelopes unflavored gelatin
½ cup cold water
1 cup crumbled Roquefort
  cheese
1 cup grated New York State
  cheese
1 (8 ounce) package cream
  cheese, softened

1 teaspoon onion juice
¼ cup diced green pepper
½ cup diced celery
½ teaspoon salt
2 cups whipped cream, lightly
  whipped
½ cup chopped olives

Soak 2 tablespoons gelatin in ½ cup cold water for 5 minutes. Dissolve over hot water and cool. Mix cheeses, onion juice, green pepper, celery and salt. Add gelatin. Fold in lightly whipped cream. Add chopped olives. Pour into a mold to chill. Unmold and fill the center with shrimp or crab salad.

G'S CURRIED SHRIMP SALAD

4 pounds shrimp
1½ tablespoons curry powder
6 tablespoons sour cream
1 cup mayonnaise
1½ tablespoons grated onion
2 tablespoons lemon juice

1½ cups chopped celery
1½ teaspoons salt
1 honeydew melon
coconut, nuts, chutney to
  garnish (optional)

Cook and clean shrimp. Blend curry powder into sour cream. Add shrimp to the mixture and then add remaining ingredients. Chill several hours. In meantime, scoop out honeydew melon balls. Marinate in French dressing. When ready to serve, fill scooped out honeydew melon cut into 8 wedges, with shrimp salad to which melon balls have been added. Garnish with coconut, nuts, and/or chutney. Serves 8.

HOT SHRIMP SALAD

½ cup chopped onions
¼ cup chopped bell pepper
½ cup sliced fresh mushrooms
½ cup butter
1 tablespoon Worcestershire
  sauce
1 teaspoon curry powder
2 pounds small cooked shrimp

4 drops Tabasco
2 cups cooked long grain and
  wild rice
1 (10¾ ounce) can cream of
  mushroom soup
1 (13½ ounce) can chicken
  broth

Sauté onions, pepper and mushrooms in butter. Add seasonings, rice, soups, and shrimp. Bake at 325° for 30 minutes. Serves 6.

CHILLED SCALLOPS

1 pound scallops
2 tablespoons melted butter
½ cup vegetable oil
2 egg yolks, beaten
2 tablespoons instant minced
 onion
2 tablespoons chopped fresh
 parsley
1 tablespoon chopped chives
2 tablespoons lemon juice

2 tablespoons sour cream
1 teaspoon dill weed
1 teaspoon lemon pepper
1 teaspoon Dijon mustard
½ teaspoon tarragon
½ teaspoon salt
½ teaspoon anchovy paste
1 (2 ounce) jar pimientos
parsley and tomatoes to
 garnish

Sauté scallops in butter 2 minutes. Cool. Drain scallops and spoon into shallow dish. Combine remaining ingredients except garnish. Stir well and spoon over scallops. Chill overnight. Serve on bed of lettuce with garnishes of parsley and sliced tomato. Serves 6-8.

AVOCADO-SHRIMP SALAD

1½ envelopes unflavored gelatin
½ cup cold water
2 well-ripened avocados, peeled
 and mashed
1 (8 ounce) package cream
 cheese
1 cup finely chopped celery
2 cups finely chopped cooked
 shrimp (canned shrimp may
 be substituted)

1 cup mayonnaise
1 tablespoon lemon juice
2 teaspoons finely grated onion
salt, pepper and Tabasco to
 taste
greens, cherry tomatoes,
 parsley to garnish

Soak gelatin in cold water and dissolve over hot water. Peel and mash avocado into soft pulp, (blender may be used). Fold softened gelatin into cream cheese; blend. Add celery, mayonnaise, lemon juice, onion, shrimp and avocado pulp. Season with salt, pepper and Tabasco. Chill until firm. Garnish with greens, cherry tomatoes and parsley. Serves 12.

Mrs. V. J. Adams, Jr.
(Angela Gaultney)

HOT CHICKEN SALAD

2 cups cubed cooked chicken
2 cups chopped celery
½ cup toasted almonds
2 tablespoons grated onion
2 tablespoons lemon juice

½ cup mayonnaise
½ (10¾ ounce) can cream of
  chicken soup, undiluted
½ cup grated Cheddar cheese
1 cup crushed potato chips

Mix all ingredients except cheese and potato chips. Place in casserole. Sprinkle cheese and potato chips on top. Bake 25 minutes at 325°. Serves 4.

Mrs. William P. Brooks
(Veronica White)

CURRIED CHICKEN SALAD

2 cups boiling water
1 (4 ounce) envelope dry
  chicken noodle soup mix
1 cup instant rice
1 cup chopped celery
2 tablespoons chopped onion
2 cups chopped cooked
  chicken

1 teaspoon curry powder
1 teaspoon salt
½ teaspoon dry mustard
⅛ teaspoon pepper
¾ cup crushed pineapple
¾ cup mayonnaise

Add soup mixture and rice to boiling water. Cover and simmer until water is absorbed. Stir to fluff. Cover and set aside for 15-20 minutes. When rice mixture is cold, add remaining ingredients. Blend well. Cover and chill thoroughly. Serves 6-8 generously.

Mrs. Bayne Mallary
(Lester Hart)

SHRIMP AND POTATO SALAD

1 cup chopped boiled shrimp
2½-3 cups cubed cooked
  potatoes
1 cup diced celery
½ cup sweet pickle relish
2 hard-cooked eggs, chopped

½-1 teaspoon salt
½ cup sour cream
2 tablespoons mayonnaise
½ envelope Italian salad
  dressing mix

Mix potatoes, celery, relish, eggs and salt. Add mayonnaise and dry salad dressing mix to sour cream. Combine potato mixture with sour cream and chill. Add shrimp just before serving. Serves 8.

CHICKEN MOLD

2 envelopes unflavored gelatin
1½ cups cold water
1 cup Miracle Whip salad
   dressing
1 cup condensed beef broth
1 teaspoon salt

2 cups cubed, cooked chicken
1 cup chopped celery
2 tablespoons chopped onion
2 tablespoons chopped
   pimiento
1 cup slivered almonds (optional)

Sprinkle gelatin on water in small saucepan to soften. Place over moderate heat, stirring constantly, until gelatin is dissolved (about 3 minutes). Combine Miracle Whip with broth, gelatin, and salt. Chill, stirring occasionally until mixture mounds when dropped from spoon. Add chicken, celery, onion and pimiento. Add almonds if desired. Mix well, chill until firm in 1-quart mold. Garnish with green pepper strips and pimiento strips if desired. Serves 9.

Mrs. W. Cobb Matthews
(Marguerite Baxter)

CORNED BEEF SALAD

2 envelopes unflavored gelatin
¼ cup cold water
1½ cups tomato juice
juice of ½ lemon
½ teaspoon salt
1 (12 ounce) can corned beef,
   shredded

3 hard-boiled eggs, chopped
2 cups chopped celery
½ cup chopped cucumber
1 tablespoon chopped onion
1 cup mayonnaise

Soak together gelatin and cold water for a few minutes in a bowl. Bring tomato juice to boil, stir into gelatin until dissolved. Add lemon juice and salt. Let cool, but do not set. Fold in remaining ingredients and mold in lightly oiled mold or loaf pan. Chill until set. Unmold and serve. Serves 6-8.

Mrs. Thomas L. Bass
(Patricia Walker)

HINTS

Use yogurt instead of sour cream for salad dressings.

E. B.'s CONGEALED HAM SALAD

1 envelope plus 1 teaspoon
  unflavored gelatin
½ cup cold water
2 cups ground baked ham
2 tablespoons capers
¾ cup mayonnaise
¼ cup Durkee's dressing

1 tablespoon pickle relish
cayenne pepper
1 tablespoon lemon juice
½ cup chopped celery
2 hard-boiled eggs, chopped
1 pimiento, chopped

Dissolve gelatin in cold water. Place in double boiler and soften and melt over hot water. Combine remaining ingredients. Add gelatin and mix well. Use for sandwich filling or 6-8 individual molds.

Mrs. Wilbur I. Tucker
(Elizabeth Conner)

CURRIED TUNA SALAD

2 (6½ ounce) cans tuna in oil,
  drained
½ cup raisins
½ cup chopped bell pepper

½ cup dry roasted peanuts
¼ cup shredded coconut
2-3 tablespoons finely chopped
  chutney

DRESSING:
¼ cup plain yogurt
¼ cup Hellmann's mayonnaise
1 teaspoon lemon juice
1 teaspoon curry powder

2 tablespoons chopped green
  onion
¼ teaspoon salt

Mix tuna, raisins, bell pepper, peanuts, coconut and chutney. Mix together dressing ingredients. Toss tuna mixture with dressing. Serves 4.

MINCEMEAT SALAD

2 (3¾ ounces each) packages
  cherry gelatin
2½ cups water

1 (9 ounce) package mincemeat
juice and rind of a lemon
½ cup sherry wine
chopped pecans (optional)

Dissolve gelatin in water according to package instructions. Add mincemeat, lemon juice, rind, sherry and pecans. Mold and chill to congeal. Serves 8.

CREAMY ITALIAN DRESSING

1 egg yolk, whisked
1 sweet gherkin pickle
1 clove garlic
2 tablespoons chopped parsley
1 cup vinegar
1 teaspoon oregano

1 teaspoon Worcestershire
  sauce
1 teaspoon salt
½ cup oil
⅓ cup sour cream

Blend together first 8 ingredients by hand for creamier dressing. Add oil gradually. Whisk in sour cream. It will keep in refrigerator for several weeks.

Mrs. Kenneth D. Sams
(Harriet Newton)

AVOCADO SALAD DRESSING

1 large ripe avocado
1 cup mayonnaise
½ cup sour cream
¼ cup tarragon vinegar
1 tablespoon lemon juice
1 garlic clove, chopped

¼ cup white vinegar
5 tablespoons finely chopped
  anchovy fillets
2 tablespoons finely chopped
  onion

Peel avocado and remove seed. Mix all ingredients in the blender. Chill before serving on lettuce or other salad greens. Yields 2½ cups.

ROQUEFORT SALAD DRESSING

1 (8 ounce) carton sour cream
⅓ cup chopped green onion
2 cloves garlic, pressed
½ cup chopped parsley
2 cups mayonnaise

½ pound Roquefort or bleu
  cheese
lemon juice or vinegar (optional)
2 tablespoons anchovy paste
  (optional)

Mix ingredients well and refrigerate. If dressing is too thick, thin with more sour cream.

MARTINI GARLIC DRESSING
Delicious on Spinach Salad

½ cup olive oil or salad oil
1 tablespoon wine vinegar
1 tablespoon dry vermouth
1 tablespoon gin

1 clove garlic, pressed
¼ teaspoon dry mustard
½ teaspoon sugar
1 teaspoon salt

Combine all ingredients in a jar with tight cover. Shake well.

POPPY SEED DRESSING

1 egg
¼ cup sugar
¼ cup lemon juice
1 tablespoon poppy seed
1 teaspoon dry mustard

1 teaspoon grated onion
½ teaspoon paprika
½ teaspoon salt
1½ cups salad oil
¼ cup honey

Place egg, sugar, lemon juice, poppy seed, dry mustard, onion, paprika, and salt in a blender. Blend at high speed, adding oil gradually. Add honey; blend at medium speed until well mixed. Yields 2 cups.

Mrs. Albert S. Hatcher, III
(Deryl Howington)

SHERRY DRESSING FOR FRUIT

3 eggs, beaten slightly
1 cup sugar
1 tablespoon flour
pinch of salt
¼ cup pineapple juice

¼ cup sherry
¼ cup lemon juice
¼ cup orange juice
whipped cream

To slightly beaten eggs, add sugar, flour, salt and liquids. Mix well and cook in a double boiler until thickened. Add whipped cream to mixture until desired consistency is obtained.

STRAWBERRY SOUR CREAM DRESSING

1 (10 ounce) package frozen
  sliced sweetened strawberries
1½ cups sour cream

pinch of salt
confectioners' sugar, to taste

Thaw strawberries. Mix all ingredients together. Refrigerate 1 hour before serving. Serve on any fruit salad.

MARSHMALLOW DRESSING FOR FRUIT

¾ cup sugar
1 teaspoon salt
1 teaspoon dry mustard
¼ teaspoon white pepper
¼ cup vinegar

¼ cup milk
2 eggs, beaten
1 dozen large marshmallows
1 cup whipping cream,
  whipped

Mix together all ingredients, except marshmallows and whipped cream. Stir mixture over medium heat until it boils and thickens. Add marshmallows and stir until melted. Let stand until cool. Fold in whipped cream. Serve with fresh fruit. Serves 8.

MISS BERTIE'S COOKED DRESSING
Good on cabbage, potato salad, or raw vegetables

½ teaspoon dry mustard
½ teaspoon flour
2 tablespoons plus 1 teaspoon
  sugar
2 tablespoons butter

2 eggs
4 tablespoons vinegar
2 tablespoons water
½ tablespoon grated onion

Mix mustard, flour and sugar together. Melt butter and add dry ingredients. Beat eggs well and add to mixture. Add vinegar and water and cook over medium heat, stirring constantly until thickened. Add onion while hot. Yields 1 cup.

Mrs. Steve L. Wilson
(Gena Ware)

MAYONNAISE

1 egg
½ teaspoon salt
½ teaspoon dry mustard
¼ teaspoon paprika

1 tablespoon vinegar
1 tablespoon lemon juice
¾ cup oil
cayenne pepper to taste
(optional)

Put egg, seasonings, vinegar, lemon juice and ¼ cup oil in blender. After blended, pour remaining oil in slow, steady stream.

Fabia T. Rogers
(Fabia Trice)

GOURMET SALAD DRESSING
Can be made a day ahead

2 (3 ounce) packages cream
  cheese
1 teaspoon grated onion
¼ teaspoon garlic salt
½ teaspoon salt
⅛ teaspoon paprika
¼ cup California dry white
  wine (optional)

½ cup sour cream
2 tablespoons chili sauce
¼ cup finely chopped green
  onions
1 (7½ ounce) can minced
  clams, undrained

Beat cream cheese until soft. Blend in grated onion, garlic salt, salt, paprika, and wine. Add other ingredients, beat until well blended. Refrigerate and serve over lettuce. (Do not toss.)

Mrs. Warren C. Grice
(Mary Joe Vandiver)

GREEN SALAD DRESSING
A tangy dressing

1 (10¾ ounce) can Campbell's
  tomato soup, undiluted
¼ cup tarragon vinegar or
  cider vinegar
1 onion, grated (large or small
  to taste)
½ cup salad oil
3 tablespoons sugar

1 tablespoon Worcestershire
  sauce
1 tablespoon prepared mustard
½ teaspoon black pepper
½ teaspoon paprika
1 clove garlic, peeled
1 teaspoon salt

Combine ingredients in blender and mix well. Chill.

Mrs. Roger W. Wilson
(Ruth Dunwody)

CAESAR SALAD DRESSING

1 quart mayonnaise
6 eggs
½ teaspoon curry powder
1 (2 ounce) package dry onion
  soup mix

1¼ cups grated Parmesan
  cheese
2 teaspoons anchovy paste
½ teaspoon garlic powder

Mix all ingredients well and serve.

HERBED BUTTERMILK SALAD DRESSING

1 egg
1 egg yolk
1 tablespoon white vinegar
2 teaspoons Dijon-style
  mustard
1 teaspoon dried dill
¾ teaspoon salt
1 garlic clove

½ teaspoon dried thyme
½ teaspoon dried marjoram
½ teaspoon dried basil
½ teaspoon celery salt
½ cup vegetable oil
1 cup buttermilk
white pepper to taste

Combine all ingredients except oil and buttermilk in blender. Turn motor on and off. With motor running, add oil and buttermilk. Makes 1½ cups.

RED ROQUEFORT DRESSING

1 small onion, finely chopped
1 cup mayonnaise or salad
  dressing
½ cup salad oil
¼ cup catsup
2 tablespoons sugar
2 tablespoons vinegar

1 teaspoon prepared mustard
½ teaspoon salt
½ teaspoon paprika
½-1 teaspoon celery seed
dash pepper
1 (4 ounce) package bleu
  cheese, crumbled

Put all ingredients except bleu cheese in blender and blend well. Remove and add bleu cheese. Cover and chill.

Mrs. Roger W. Wilson
(Ruth Dunwody)

FRENCH DRESSING

2 teaspoons salt
1 teaspoon fresh black pepper
1 teaspoon paprika
1 clove garlic
½ teaspoon confectioners'
  sugar

½ teaspoon dry mustard
few grains of cayenne
¼ cup vinegar
1 cup oil

Mix ingredients in blender or food processor. This recipe doubles easily. Keeps well in refrigerator. Yields 1 cup plus.

Mrs. Gary C. Ertel
(Holly Akre)

CHEESE
AND
EGGS

HIGH HAT CHEESE SOUFFLÉ

¼ cup butter	½ pound New York Extra Sharp
¼ cup flour	Cheddar cheese, thinly
½ teaspoon salt	sliced
dash cayenne pepper	4 egg yolks, beaten
1 cup milk	4 egg whites, stiffly beaten

Melt butter; blend in the flour, salt, and cayenne. Add milk; cook quickly, stirring constantly, until mixture thickens and bubbles. Add cheese; stir until cheese melts. Remove mixture from heat. Beat egg yolks until thick and lemon-colored. Slowly add cheese mixture to egg yolks, stirring constantly. Cool mixture slightly, then pour slowly into beaten egg whites, folding together thoroughly. Pour mixture into ungreased 1½-quart soufflé dish or casserole. For a top hat (it puffs in the oven), trace a circle through mixture 1-inch from edge and 1-inch deep. Bake at 300° for 1 hour and 15 minutes or until knife comes out clean. Serves 6.

Mrs. Robert J. Adams
(Madge Webb)

SAUSAGE CHEESE GRITS CASSEROLE

1 pound hot bulk sausage	¼ pound garlic cheese, grated
1 cup hominy grits	½ cup milk
4 cups boiling water	3 eggs, slightly beaten
1 teaspoon salt	paprika
½ cup margarine	

Fry and drain sausage; set aside. Cook grits for 5 minutes in boiling, salted water. Add margarine and cheese. Stir until melted. Remove from heat. Add milk, eggs and sausage. Pour in a 9 x 13-inch pan and bake at 350° for 30-45 minutes. Sprinkle paprika on top of casserole. Serves 6-8.

Can be frozen.

Mrs. Thomas Kendrick-Holmes
(Joann Cotton)

VARIATION: Parmesan Grits: Add to 1 cup cooked grits, 1 cup Parmesan chese, ¼ cup milk, 4 well beaten eggs, and ½ teaspoon baking powder. Bake at 400° in greased 1½-quart casserole for 30 minutes.

CHEESE CASSEROLE
Good with Barbecue

2 (4 ounce) cans green chilies,
   drained
1 pound Monterey Jack cheese,
   coarsely grated
4 egg whites, beaten
4 egg yolks
1 pound Cheddar cheese,
   coarsely grated

⅔ cup canned evaporated milk
1 tablespoon flour
½ teaspoon salt
⅛ teaspoon pepper
2 medium tomatoes, sliced

Preheat oven to 325°. Remove seeds from chilies and dice. In a large bowl, combine the grated cheese and chilies. Turn into well-buttered shallow 2-quart casserole or 12 x 8 x 2-inch pan. In large bowl, with electric mixer, beat egg whites just until soft peaks form. In small bowl, combine egg yolks, milk, flour, salt and pepper. Mix well. Using rubber scraper, gently fold beaten egg whites into egg yolks. Pour egg mixture over cheese mixture in casserole. Pierce cheese gently with fork to let egg mixture seep through. Bake 30 minutes; remove from oven. Overlap tomato slices around sides of casserole. Bake 30 minutes longer or until a knife inserted comes out clean. Serves 6-8.

Mrs. R. Douglas Cole
(Anne Sturman)

CREOLE EGGS

1 medium onion, chopped
2 stalks celery, chopped
1 large bell pepper, chopped
1 (16 ounce) can tomatoes
4 hard-boiled eggs, sliced

2 (16 ounce) cans English peas
6 tablespoons butter
1 tablespoon chili powder
Worcestershire sauce to taste
buttered bread crumbs

To make Creole sauce, brown onion, celery and pepper in butter; add tomatoes, simmer for ½ hour. Place layer of eggs, peas, and creole sauce in baking dish. Cover with bread crumbs. Warm at 250° until heated throughout.

Mrs. Frank W. James
(Erskine Wall)

HINTS

Egg whites beat better at room temperature.

RICE AND CHEESE SOUFFLÉ

1½ cups long grain rice, uncooked (Makes about 6 cups when cooked)
¾ pound grated sharp Cheddar cheese
2 tablespoons melted butter
¾ cup milk
3 eggs, separated
1½ teaspoons salt
¼ teaspoon paprika
1 medium onion, grated
1 tablespoon Worcestershire sauce
6 tablespoons chopped parsley
1 pimiento, chopped

Cook rice, drain and steam about 5 minutes. Add all the above ingredients, except egg whites, and mix thoroughly. Beat the 3 egg whites until stiff, and fold into mixture. Bake in 350° oven about 45 minutes in a 3-quart baking dish. This dish can be fixed the day before, adding the egg whites before cooking. This is an old favorite, especially good served with fried chicken. Serves 12 (½-cup) servings.

Mrs. John D. Comer, Jr.
(Mary Anderson)

CHEESE STRATA

8 slices white bread, trimmed and cubed
3 tablespoons melted butter
½ pound grated sharp Cheddar cheese (2 cups)
4 eggs
2½ cups milk
2 teaspoons prepared mustard
1 tablespoon Worcestershire sauce
½ teaspoon salt
⅛ teaspoon paprika

Cut off bread crusts. Cut bread in large cubes and dip in melted butter. Put one-third of bread in bottom of casserole. Sprinkle with one-third of cheese. Repeat with remainder. Beat eggs with milk, mustard, Worcestershire sauce, salt and paprika. Pour over bread and cheese. Chill 2 hours in refrigerator. Bake uncovered at 350° for 1 hour. Let stand 10 minutes and cool.

This is good if prepared the night before serving.

Mrs. Rhett L. Moody, Jr.
(Suzanne Pilcher)

EGGS FLORENTINE

2 onion flavored buns, halved
softened butter
1 (10 ounce) package frozen
  leaf spinach, thawed and
  drained

2 tablespoons melted butter
4 slices ham
4 slices tomato
4 poached eggs

HOLLANDAISE SAUCE:
3 egg yolks
1 tablespoon lemon juice
¼ teaspoon tarragon leaves

¼ teaspoon salt
½ cup hot melted butter

Cut onion buns in half and spread with butter. Place under broiler until lightly browned. Sauté spinach 2 minutes in 2 tablespoons butter. Place a slice of ham and tomato on each bun half; top with a small amount of spinach and poached egg. Spoon Hollandaise sauce over each prepared bun. Serves 4.

To make sauce: combine all ingredients except butter in blender. Blend until thick and lemon-colored. Add butter in a slow, steady stream and continue to process until thickened.

Mrs. Derry Burns, Jr.
(Juliette Smith)

MACARONI AND CHEESE BAKE

½ cup mayonnaise
2 teaspoons prepared mustard
1 tablespoon parsley flakes
1 teaspoon salt
¼ teaspoon pepper
2 tablespoons finely chopped
  onion

1 cup milk
2 cups uncooked elbow
  macaroni
½ pound grated cheese
bread crumbs
2 tablespoons thinly sliced
  butter

Boil macaroni. Combine first 6 ingredients and blend in 1 cup milk. Add elbow macaroni and cheese. Place in buttered casserole dish. Cover with bread crumbs and dot with butter. Bake 20 minutes at 350°. Serves 6-8.

Mrs. Paul A. Cable
(Susan Watt)

SCOTCH PRINTER'S EGGS
A British Pub Favorite

6 hard-boiled eggs
1 pound mild sausage meat
2 beaten eggs
flour—enough to coat eggs

3-3½ cups finely crushed bread
   crumbs
cooking oil

Encase each shelled egg in sausage meat, shaping with your hands. Dip the sausage-coated eggs in flour, then in eggs and roll them in fine bread crumbs. Let the eggs stand for about 1 hour or until the coating has set. This is very important or the casings will separate from the eggs. Fry the eggs in hot deep fat (385°) until the coating is well browned and the sausage meat is cooked and firm. Drain the eggs on paper. Cut with a serrated knife. The eggs may be served hot or at room temperature.
Cut eggs lengthwise for service on a tray. You should be able to cut 6 slices from each egg. Makes 36 slices.

In England and Scotland, you see these eggs cooked in rounds. Be sure to have plenty as they go quickly.

Mrs. Giles O'Neal
(Beth Mason)

HINTS

To measure half of an egg, beat the whole egg lightly, then measure 2 tablespoons.

Don't beat egg whites too long or they will get dry. They are dry if they lose gloss. They will break down easily. By adding another egg white, the dull whites will pick up their gloss.

To refrigerate egg yolks, place in a dish and cover with cold water.

Cottage cheese will keep twice as long if carton is stored upside down.

A soufflé will remain light and fluffy if ¼ teaspoon cream of tartar is added to egg whites during mixing.

PEACHES

PEACHY HINTS

The best indicator that a peach is ripe is that the background color is yellow or cream. A blush or reddish color is not a sign of ripeness.

A ripe peach will have a "Peachy" aroma.

The fresh ripe peach is firm but not hard.

A ripe peach should be refrigerated immediately.

Store fully ripe peaches in the refrigerator, spread out in one layer to minimize bruising. Fully ripe peaches will keep 1 week.

To allow peaches to ripen at room temperature spread evenly on a counter, away from sunlight or in a loosely closed bag.

When peaches are cut or peeled, keep their color bright by treating them with ascorbic acid, commercial color keeper, or a citrus juice.

Clingstone peaches are best for drying.

To pit a peach, run a sharp knife all the way around the peach on the crease line; hold peach between fingers of both hands; twist and pull apart gently.

Try pureeing peaches sweetened to taste and freeze in small quantities to be used as toppings for ice cream, cobblers, or pancakes.

Peaches with a dark green ground color will not ripen satisfactorily because they were not mature when picked.

Firm peaches with a creamy or yellowish background will continue to ripen at room temperature.

Peaches without fuzz need not be peeled. The skin is full of vitamins and minerals.

Keep a bowl of sliced fresh peaches covered in orange juice in the refrigerator. The slices will stay brightly colored in the orange juice.

Cover sliced fresh peaches with a mixture of ⅓ cup light corn syrup, ⅛ teaspoon fruit-freeze powder, and ½ cup of water.

When freezing or canning peaches for a year's supply, plan on 15 pints for each person in the family.

Skins will slip off a peach if you pour boiling water over peaches and let them stand 1 minute. If peaches are room temperature only 30 seconds is required.

PEACHY FACTS

1 pound of fresh peaches will equal:
3 - 4 medium sized peaches
2 cups sliced peaches
1½ cups pulp or puree
4 servings

2 pounds of peaches makes 1 nine inch pie.

1 10-ounce package of frozen peaches equals:
3 (½ cup) servings

1 bushel makes 18 to 24 quarts of canned peaches.

Middle Georgia Peaches appear in the market from late May to late August.

Peaches are customarily classified in two general categories:
Freestone and Clingstone

One medium fresh peach has 38 calories.

4 ounces of fresh frozen peaches has 89 calories.

Peaches are one of the most widely grown fruits in the United States.

The Peach is rich in Vitamins A and C and Iron.

Peaches are sodium free.

Clingstone peaches are recommended for canning.

BRANDIED PEACH PUNCH

1 cup peach brandy
4 fresh sliced peaches
⅔ cup sugar
1 cup lemon juice

1 cup orange juice
1 bottle sauterne
1 bottle rosé wine
2 quarts ginger ale

Mix first 4 ingredients in blender and purée. Chill this mixture and remaining ingredients. Combine in punch bowl just before serving. This can be strained if desired. Serves 20-25.

PEACH DAIQUIRI

1 (6 ounce) can frozen pink
   lemonade or limeade
6 ounces vodka or rum

2 ripe peaches, sliced (or more,
   if desired)
cracked ice

Place first 3 ingredients in blender and mix slightly. Fill remainder of blender container with cracked ice and blend well. Garnish with cherry. Serves 4.

May substitute bananas or strawberries for peaches.

Mrs. Donald C. Eubanks
(Martha McKay)

PEACH ROSÉ

1 (29 ounce) can
   peach halves
3 tablespoons butter
2 tablespoons lemon juice
3-4 tablespoons firmly
   packed brown sugar

⅓ cup rosé
½ cup whipping cream
1 tablespoon cornstarch

Drain peaches, reserving 2 tablespoons liquid. In an 8-inch skillet melt butter over medium heat; add peaches and lemon juice. Coat peaches with butter and sprinkle with brown sugar; add wine. Cover and simmer 5 minutes. Stir in whipping cream and simmer several minutes more. Combine 2 tablespoons peach liquid with cornstarch and stir until smooth. Add cornstarch mixture to peach mixture and cook over low heat stirring constantly until thickened. Serve warm. Serves 4-6.

This delicious topping is great with ice cream and pound cake.

PEACH MUFFINS

1 cup chopped fresh peaches
2 tablespoons light brown
   sugar
½ cup sugar
3 tablespoons butter
1 egg, separated

2 cups flour
2 teaspoons baking powder
½ teaspoon ground cinnamon
½ teaspoon grated nutmeg
1 cup milk
additional cinnamon and
   nutmeg

Put chopped peaches in a bowl. Sprinkle with light brown sugar; put aside. Cream butter and sugar. Add beaten egg yolk; beat well. Sift dry ingredients together and add them alternately with milk. Beat egg whites until stiff. Spoon peaches from bowl with slotted spoon and dredge in 1-2 tablespoons flour. Fold peaches together with egg white into the batter. Pour into greased muffin tins and sprinkle tops with nutmeg and cinnamon mixture. Bake in preheated oven at 350° for about 30 minutes or until golden brown. Yields 18 regular muffins.

Mrs. George G. Felton
(Anne Corn)

PEACH BREAD

1½ cups sugar
½ cup shortening
2 eggs
2¼ cups fresh peach purée (6-8
   medium)
2 cups flour

1 teaspoon cinnamon
1 teaspoon soda
1 teaspoon baking powder
¼ teaspoon salt
1 teaspoon vanilla extract
1 cup finely chopped pecans

Cream sugar and shortening together. Add eggs and mix thoroughly. Add peach purée (made by blending peeled peaches fine in blender). Fold in dry ingredients. Mix thoroughly. Add vanilla extract and chopped pecans and stir until blended. Pour into two 5 x 9-inch loaf pans that have been greased and floured. Bake at 325° for 55 minutes to 1 hour. Let bread cool for 20 minutes before removing from pan.

HINTS

To keep 'ready to use' whipped cream on hand, whip 1 pint cream with 4 tablespoons sugar, drop on cookie sheet and freeze. Transfer to airtight container and store in freezer. Remove 15 minutes before serving.

PEACHES'N CHEESE

1 (5 ounce) jar Old
  English Cheese
1/2 cup butter
1 cup flour

2 tablespoons cold water
1 (4 ounce) jar peach
  preserves

Using food processor, cut cheese and butter into flour with steel knife blade. Add cold water, shape into a ball and refrigerate several hours or overnight. Remove from refrigerator. Preheat oven to 375°. Roll dough on a floured surface until thin. Cut dough into 2 inch circles with a glass or a biscuit cutter. Spoon 1/2 teaspoon preserves into center of circle. Fold dough over and crimp edges with a fork. Bake for 10 minutes on an ungreased cookie sheet until golden brown. Let cool 5 minutes before removing from pan. Pastries may be frozen before or after baking. Yield: 2 1/2 to 3 dozen.

Must prepare ahead.

PEACH FRITTERS WITH ORANGE SAUCE

1 cup sifted flour
1 teaspoon salt
1 teaspoon baking powder
2 eggs
1 cup milk

2 tablespoons melted butter
6 firm, ripe peaches
1/4 cup sugar
oil for frying

ORANGE SAUCE:
1/2 cup sugar
1 tablespoon cornstarch
1 cup sweet wine

1 cup orange juice
1 tablespoon grated orange
  rind

Sift flour, salt and baking powder. Set aside. Beat eggs well; add milk and melted butter. Stir in dry ingredients gradually and continue stirring until batter is smooth. Allow mixture to stand at room temperature for 1 hour. Plunge peaches into boiling water; remove and put them into cold water. Slip skin from peaches. Halve peaches and remove stones. Cut peaches into 4 wedges. Put peach wedges in a bowl and sprinkle with sugar. Set aside. Heat enough oil to measure 1 1/2 inches deep when heated. Dry peach wedges on a paper towel. Dip peaches into batter with fork. Fry peaches a few at a time in 375° heated oil for 3-5 minutes or until golden. Drain fritters on paper towels. Serve hot with orange sauce.
Orange Sauce: Combine sugar and cornstarch. Stir in 1/4 cup wine gradually until mixture is smooth. Stir in remaining wine and orange juice. Bring mixture to a boil over low heat. Cook 1 minute. Remove mixture from heat and stir in orange rind. Serve warm over fritters. Sauce yields 2 cups. Serves 8.

IRRESISTIBLE PEACH SWIRLS

1 (8 ounce) can refrigerated
  crescent rolls
2 tablespoons butter or
  margarine, melted
1 cup finely chopped peaches

1 teaspoon ascorbic acid
  powder
¼ teaspoon sugar

PEACH GLAZE

1 cup powdered sugar,
  sifted
1½ tablespoons puréed
  fresh peaches

chopped pecans (optional)

Remove rolls from can. Do not separate. Place on lightly floured board and work them into a rectangle about ¼ inch thick. Brush with melted butter. Mix chopped peaches with ascorbic acid powder and sugar. Sprinkle over surface of dough. Sprinkle with nutmeg. Roll up jellyroll fashion beginning with the long side of the dough. Cut into 9 equal slices. Place swirls in buttered dish, cut side down. Dot with butter, if desired. Bake at 450° for 20 minutes. Ice with peach glaze.
Glaze: Mix powdered sugar with fresh peach puree until smooth and drizzle over baked swirls. Top with chopped pecans. Yield 9 swirls.

PEACH-APRICOT SALAD

⅓ cup sugar
2 envelopes unflavored gelatin,
  divided
1 (12 ounce) can apricot nectar
½ cup water
¼ teaspoon almond extract
2 cups canned apricots, drained
  and diced
¼ cup sugar

½ cup water
2 beaten eggs
1 (6 ounce) can frozen
  lemonade concentrate,
  thawed
1 cup peach yogurt
1½ cups canned peaches,
  drained and diced

In saucepan, combine ⅓ cup sugar and 1 envelope gelatin. Add apricot nectar, stir over low heat until gelatin is dissolved. Stir in ½ cup water and almond extract. Chill until partially set, then fold in apricots. Meanwhile in saucepan, combine ¼ cup sugar and remaining 1 envelope gelatin. Add remaining water, the eggs and lemonade concentrate. Cook and stir until thickened. Beat in yogurt. Chill until partially set and fold in peaches. Into 6½-cup mold, layer ½ of apricot and peach mixtures. Swirl to marble, repeat layers, swirling layer mixtures. Chill 8 hours. Serves 10-12.

PEACH PICKLE SALAD

2 (3 ounce) packages lemon
  gelatin
2 cups spiced pickled peach
  juice
1 cup cold water
1½ (29 ounce each) jars peach
  pickle, diced

1 (16 ounce) can Royal Anne
  white cherries, seeded and
  halved
1 cup chopped pecans

Bring spiced peach juice to a boil and add to gelatin. Add cold water and stir until gelatin dissolves. Chill until partially set. Fold in diced peach pickle, white cherries, and pecans. Refrigerate until completely congealed.

I always add 2 packages of plain gelatin to be sure it is firmly congealed.

Mrs. Donald Beaty
(Ann Chandler)

PEACH FROST SALAD

1 (3 ounce) package cream
  cheese
½ cup whipping cream,
  whipped
¼ cup Hellmann's mayonnaise
1-2 tablespoons lemon juice

few grains salt
1 (30 ounce) can sliced
  peaches, drained, or 3 cups
  fresh sliced peaches
½ cup coarsely chopped
  pecans

Have cheese at room temperature. Beat cheese and cream together until mixture is light and fluffy. Stir in mayonnaise, lemon juice and salt. Lightly fold in peach slices and nuts. Pour into square pyrex dish. Freeze several hours. Remove from freezer 15 minutes before serving. Serves 8.

Mrs. Oliver C. Bateman
(Mary Jane Gosline)

HINTS

Meringue will not shrink if spread on pie over to each side of pie shell.

FROZEN FRESH PEACH SALAD

3 cups peeled, crushed fresh
  peaches
2 cups miniature marshmallows
½ cup drained crushed
  pineapple
½ cup (3 ounces) slivered
  almonds

¼ cup (or 4 ounce jar)
  quartered maraschino
  cherries
½ teaspoon almond extract
⅛ teaspoon salt
2 cups sour cream

Mix all ingredients in a 2-quart bowl. Pour into 8-inch square pan or 12 muffin cups lined with paper baking cups. Cover with foil and freeze. Fifteen minutes prior to serving, cut salad into squares or peel off paper cups. Serves 12.

AMARETTO PEACHES

6 large ripe peaches
½ cup raspberry preserves
12 macaroons, coarsely
  crumbled

4 tablespoons unsalted butter,
  cut into bits
½ cup Amaretto liqueur

Preheat oven to 350°. Cut peaches in half, discarding stones. Scoop out a small amount of pulp from center of each half. Chop up pulp and reserve. Arrange halves in baking dish. Place a spoonful of preserves into each peach cavity. Put a small amount of pulp on top. Spoon some macaroons on top of pulp and dot with butter. Sprinkle a little Amaretto on each half. Pour water in pan ⅛-inch deep. Bake 20 minutes at 350° and baste with more Amaretto, if desired. Serve warm. Serves 12.

PEACH FANTASY

1 (12 or 16 ounce) package
  frozen peaches
⅓ cup grenadine

1 (16 ounce) carton sour cream
1 quart vanilla ice cream

Soften peaches enough to blend in blender with grenadine. Add sour cream and ice cream. Put in individual bowls to serve and refreeze until ready to serve. The taste is better than homemade ice cream and is quick and easy. Serves 6.

Mrs. Oscar S. Spivey
(Rosa Schofield)

PEACH SOUFFLÉ

1 (12 ounce) package frozen
   sliced peaches, thawed
1 envelope unflavored gelatin
½ cup peach syrup
4 eggs, separated
¼ cup water

1 tablespoon lemon juice
⅛ teaspoon salt
¼ teaspoon almond extract
½ cup sugar
1 cup heavy cream, whipped

Drain syrup from peaches into double boiler and set slices aside. Sprinkle gelatin on syrup to soften. Beat egg yolks and water together. Add to gelatin. Cook over boiling water 5 minutes stirring constantly until gelatin is dissolved. Remove from heat, stir in lemon juice, salt and almond extract. Chill slightly. Purée peaches in blender or food processor. Mix into gelatin mixture. Beat egg whites until stiff. Beat in sugar. Fold in gelatin mixture. Fold in whipped cream. Turn into 1½-quart soufflé dish and chill until firm. To add a collar to the soufflé dish, use a strip of aluminum foil or brown paper 4 inches deep and long enough to go around the dish. Fasten with tape so the collar is 2 inches above dish. Serves 6-8.

Mrs. Oliver C. Bateman
(Mary Jane Gosline)

LATTICE PEACH COBBLER

1 quart sliced peaches
¾-1 cup sugar

½ cup butter

PASTRY:
1½ cups flour
¾ teaspoon salt

½ scant cup shortening
5-6 tablespoons ice cold water

Combine peaches, sugar and butter in 1½-quart saucepan. Cook slowly, stirring until peaches are tender and syrup begins to thicken. To make pastry, sift flour and salt together and cut in shortening until it is a coarse crumb mixture. Work quickly. Add ice water, a tablespoon at a time until you have a soft pastry. Roll on floured pastry cloth with floured pastry sleeve until ⅛-inch thick. Cut into strips. Place half of strips in bottom of a lightly buttered deep cobbler dish in lattice weave design. Pour peach mixture on top of lattice and top filling with woven pastry strips. Sprinkle lightly with sugar. Bake at 350° until golden brown and bubbly. Top with vanilla ice cream. Serves 6.

Mrs. Joseph A. Wall
(Patricia Hammock)

EASY PEACH COBBLER
So Simple!

½ cup butter
1 cup self-rising flour
1½ cups sugar, divided

1 cup milk
4 cups sliced fresh peaches

Melt butter in 2-quart Pyrex baking dish or casserole. Stir together flour and 1 cup sugar; add milk and mix well. Pour into butter; stir gently. Add peaches that have been tossed with remaining ½ cup sugar; do not stir. Bake at 375° for 40 minutes. Serve warm with whipped cream or vanilla ice cream. Serves 6.

PEACH CRISP

4 cups peeled and sliced
   peaches
2-3 tablespoons lemon juice
1 cup flour

1 cup sugar
1 egg, slightly beaten
dash of salt

Slice firm, ripe peaches and fill a 9-inch baking dish and add lemon juice. Mix together the flour, sugar, egg and salt. Spread mixture over top of peaches. Dot with butter and bake in oven at 400° until golden brown on top. Good served with ice cream or whipped cream. Serves 6.

Simple but so good!

FRIED PEACH PIES

PASTRY:
2 cups flour
1 teaspoon salt

½ cup butter
⅓ cup cold water

FILLING:
4 quarts cut-up peaches
   (canned or frozen)

3-4 cups sugar
1 cup vinegar

Pastry: Sift flour and salt together, cut in the butter and mix with hands. Add water. Roll about ⅛-inch thick between waxed paper. Cut with large cookie cutter about 4 inches in diameter. In each round, place 1½ tablespoons peach pie filling. Moisten edges with water, fold to make a semi-circle and press edges together with a fork. Fry in deep fat.

Filling: Mix peaches, sugar, and vinegar and cook until very thick or consistency of peach preserves. Put in hot pint jars while mixture is boiling hot and seal, or use a peach pie pastry.

FRESH PEACH PIE

FILLING:
4 cups fresh sliced peaches
1¼ cups sugar
3 tablespoons flour

¼ teaspoon salt
2 tablespoons melted butter
1 tablespoon lemon juice

CRUST:
2 cups sifted flour
1 teaspoon salt
2 tablespoons confectioners'
  sugar

⅔ cup vegetable shortening
½ cup heavy cream
1 tablespoon melted butter

Precook peaches to shrink with 1 cup water. Drain a small amount of liquid and set aside to cool. Sift dry ingredients together and mix with peaches. Add melted butter and lemon juice. Allow filling to set a few minutes before filling pie shell. Sift flour, salt and sugar into a mixing bowl. Cut in shortening with pasty blender until mixture resembles fine bread crumbs. Add cream gradually by sprinkling 1 tablespoonful at a time over the mixture and tossing it lightly with a fork after each addition. Shape dough into a smooth ball. Cut it into 2 pieces, one slightly larger for bottom crust. Roll out dough and place in pie pan. Brush bottom crust with melted butter. Roll top and cut into lattice strips about ⅓ inch wide. Weave onto waxed paper. Pour filling into bottom crust. Turn latticed top onto pie and flute edge. Cover edge with collar of aluminum foil or pie tape. Bake at 375° for one hour. Serves 6-8.

Mrs. Steve L. Wilson
(Gena Ware)

FRESH PEACH SOUR CREAM PIE

1 unbaked 9-inch pastry shell
5-6 medium-size peaches,
  sliced
½ cup sugar

1 (8 ounce) carton sour cream
4 tablespoons flour
½ cup packed brown sugar

Preheat oven to 450°. Line pie shell with peaches. Blend sugars, flour, sour cream. Pour cream mixture over peaches. Bake 10 minutes, reduce heat to 325°. Bake 25-30 minutes longer. Serves 6.

Mrs. William W. Williams
(Ann Warlick)

FAMILY'S FAVORITE PEACH PIE

1¼ cups sugar
¼ teaspoon salt
juice of one lemon
3 tablespoons corn starch
1½ cups water
1 (3-ounce) package cream
  cheese

2 tablespoons milk
2 cups sliced, ripe
  peaches
½ pint whipping cream
¼ cup sugar
1 9-inch pie crust

To make a sauce, mix the first 5 ingredients. Cook until sauce is clear and thick, stirring constantly. Remove from heat and chill. (yellow or red food coloring may be added to make peach color more pronounced). One hour before serving, line pie shell with 3 ounces of cream cheese, softened with 2 tablespoons milk. Mix chilled sauce and peaches. Spread over cream cheese. Whip cream with ¼ cup sugar. Spread on top of pie and garnish with peach slices. Serves 6-8.

Mrs. Oliver C. Bateman
(Mary Jane Gosline)

PEACH CHANTILLY

4 cups puréed fresh peaches
2 tablespoons lemon juice
2 envelopes unflavored
  gelatin
½ cup reserved juices
2 tablespoons orange liqueur

4 tablespoons sugar
2 cups whipping cream
7 or 8 fresh peach halves to
  garnish
2 baked 9-inch pastry shells

Mix peach purée with lemon juice. Place mixture in fine sieve and allow juices to drain in bowl for 20 minutes. Reserve juices. Stir gelatin and juices over low heat until gelatin has completely dissolved. Mix purée with liqueur, sugar and cooled gelatin mixture. Whip cream and fold into purée. Spoon mixture into shell. Refrigerate for 4-6 hours. Garnish with fresh peaches and blueberries, grapes or raspberries. Serves 10.

Mrs. Oliver C. Bateman
(Mary Jane Gosline)

HINTS

Whipped cream that is whipped ahead will not separate if unflavored gelatin is added (¼ teaspoon per cup of cream).

PEACH CHIFFON PIE

¾ cup sugar
1½-2 cups mashed fresh
  peaches
1 envelope unflavored gelatin
¼ cup cold water
½ cup hot water

1 tablespoon lemon juice
dash salt
1 teaspoon vanilla extract
yellow food coloring (optional)
1 cup whipping cream
1 baked 10-inch pie shell

Add sugar to peaches and let stand 30 minutes. Soften gelatin in cold water. Dissolve in hot water. Cool. Add peach mixture, lemon juice, salt and vanilla extract. Chill until partially set. Fold in whipped cream. Pour into a baked 10-inch pie shell and chill thoroughly. Serves 8.

Mrs. Joseph N. Neel, III
(Marie Butler)

BEBE'S PIE

Crust:
¾ cup vanilla wafers,
  crushed
2 tablespoons sugar

½ stick melted butter
½ cup chopped pecans

Sauce:
2 tablespoons lemon juice
3 tablespoons butter

½ cup sugar
1 egg, beaten

Crust: Combine ingredients and press into greased pie pan. Cool. Soften 1 quart vanilla ice cream and put in crust.
Sauce: Cook lemon juice, sugar and butter until butter melts. Remove from heat and blend in egg. Cook until thickened. Stir constantly. Spoon sauce on top of ice cream. Freeze. When ready to serve, garnish with peaches and whipped cream.

HINTS

To prevent soggy pie crusts, coat the pastry shell with egg white before baking.

SOUTHERN COMFORT PEACH PIE

10-12 fresh peaches, peeled
  and diced
1/2 cup Southern Comfort
2/3 cup sugar

1/3 cup ground almonds
3 tablespoons butter
2 tablespoons flour
dash of salt

CRUST:
1 cup sifted flour
1/2 teaspoon salt
1/2 cup butter
2 1/2 tablespoons ice water

2 tablespoons whipping cream
whipped cream or sour cream
  for garnish

Fill a deep 10 inch pie pan with peaches. Pour Southern Comfort over fruit. Combine sugar, almonds, butter, flour, and salt in a bowl and mix well. (Cut butter into mixture with a fork). Sprinkle evenly over peaches. Prepare crust to cover peaches by mixing flour and salt in a bowl. Work butter into flour. Sprinkle mixture with water. Form mixture into a ball and refrigerate for approximately 10 minutes. Preheat oven to 450°. Roll out pastry and arrange on top of pie dish. Form designs in pastry, if desired. Brush pastry with whipping cream. Bake pie at 450° for 10 minutes. Reduce heat to 350° and continue baking 15-25 minutes or until pastry is golden. Serve warm with whipped cream or sour cream.

AMBROSIA PEACH PIE

CRUST:
2 cups shredded coconut
1/3 cup melted butter

Filling:
3 large fresh peaches,
  sliced
1 (3 ounce) package instant
  coconut pudding

1 cup milk
1/2 cup heavy cream, whipped
sugar

Crust: Combine coconut and melted butter and press into a 9-inch pie pan to form a pie shell. Refrigerate for one hour.
Filling: Fill crust with peach slices. Make coconut pudding with 1 cup milk and fold in whipped cream that has been sweetened with sugar. Cover peaches and chill pie. Serves 6-8.

UPSIDE-DOWN PEACH CAKE

¼ cup butter
½ cup packed light brown sugar
2 tablespoons light corn syrup
2 fresh peaches
¼ cup maraschino cherries
¼ cup chopped pecans
½ cup plus 2 tablespoons
  butter

1¼ cups sugar
1 teaspoon vanilla extract
2 eggs
1½ cups sifted flour
¼ cup cocoa
½ teaspoon baking soda
½ teaspoon salt
½ cup buttermilk

Melt and mix ¼ cup butter, ½ cup light brown sugar and 2 table-spoons corn syrup. Spread over bottom of 9-inch square pan. Slice, cook slightly, and drain peaches. Arrange slices in sunburst design over the pan mixture. Between the peach sections, arrange cherries and pecans. In large mixing bowl, cream ½ cup plus 2 tablespoons butter, 1¼ cups sugar, and vanilla extract. Add eggs, one at a time, beating well after each addition. Sift together remaining flour, cocoa, soda, salt and add alternately with buttermilk. Beat well and pour over fruit and nuts in pan. Bake 45-55 minutes at 350° and im-mediately invert to serving dish. Top with whipped cream, if desired. Serves 8.

OLD FASHIONED PEACH SHORTCAKE

2 cups flour
5 teaspoons baking powder
2 tablespoons butter

1 cup milk (scant)
½ teaspoon salt
sliced peaches, fresh or
  canned

Mix dry ingredients. Sift. Work butter in with tips of fingers. Add milk gradually, cutting in with knife to make soft dough. Use only enough milk to hold dough together. Roll out dough and fold over on itself in 4 layers. Roll and cut, using a large cutter for shortcake. Bake 12 minutes in hot oven (450°). Split and butter. While warm place peach slices between layers and cover tops. Add generous amount of whipped cream. Drizzle the juice of the peaches over the shortcake. Serve immediately.

PEACHY CAKE ROLL

1 cup minus 2 tablespoons
  all-purpose flour
1 teaspoon baking powder
1/4 teaspoon salt
3 eggs

1 cup sugar
1/3 cup water
1 teaspoon vanilla
powdered sugar

FILLING:
8 ounces cream cheese
1/2 cup powdered sugar

1/8 teaspoon almond flavoring
1 cup diced peaches

*Cake:*Mix together flour, baking powder and salt. In another bowl, beat eggs about 5 minutes or until thick and lemon-colored. Gradually beat in sugar. On low speed, gradually blend in water and vanilla. Gradually add dry ingredients beating just until batter is smooth. Line a 15 x 10 x 1 inch jelly roll pan with waxed paper, then lightly grease the paper. Pour batter into pan and spread evenly. Bake at 375° for 12-15 minutes or until toothpick inserted in center comes out clean. Remove cake from oven and loosen edges. Invert pan onto a clean towel that has been dusted heavily with powdered sugar. Remove waxed paper. While cake is still hot, roll the cake and towel together from the narrow end. Cool on wire rack. When cool unroll cake and spread with Peach Filling. Carefully roll cake again and sprinkle outside with powdered sugar. Cover and chill thoroughly before serving.
Filling: Beat softened cream cheese until smooth and fluffy. Add powdered sugar and almond flavoring and beat until smooth. Mix in 1 cup finely diced peaches. Serves 8-10.

GINGER PEACHES

1/2 cup almond macaroons,
  crumbled
1 (29 ounce) can peach
  halves

1/2 teaspoon ginger

Drain peaches and reserve syrup. Place peaches in greased baking dish. Mix macaroons and ginger with enough syrup to moisten and fill centers with this mixture. Bake at 350° for 15 minutes. Serve hot.

This is ideal with chicken or can be served with whipped cream as a dessert.

PEACH TORTE

CRUST:

1¾ cups graham crackers crumbs	⅓ cup butter
	¼ cup sugar

TORTE:

1 (8 ounce) package cream cheese, at room temperature	3 eggs
1 cup cottage cheese, small curd	1 (4 ounce) package vanilla pudding, not instant
1 cup sugar	½ cup milk
	½ teaspoon vanilla

TOPPING:

1 pint whipping cream	fresh, frozen, or canned peaches, chopped
½ cup sugar	

Crust: Mix the ingredients and place in an 8-inch springform pan. Press firmly against the bottom and 2 inches up the sides of the pan. Chill.
Torte: Mix together cream cheese and cottage cheese. Add remaining ingredients. Pour into crust and bake for 45 minutes to an hour at 350° until golden brown. Cool and refrigerate overnight. Top Torte with chopped peaches, then the whipped cream, whipped with the sugar. Garnish with peach slices. Serves. 8.

PEACH KUCHEN

2 cups sifted flour	1 teaspoon cinnamon
¼ teaspoon baking powder	2 egg yolks
½ teaspoon salt	1 cup heavy cream or sour cream
¾-1 cup sugar	
1 cup butter	
12 fresh peach halves or 2 packages frozen slices, drained	

Preheat oven to 400°. Sift baking powder, flour, salt and 2 tablespoons sugar. Cut in butter until mixture looks like coarse meal. Press half of this mixture on bottom and sides of a 8 x 8-inch baking pan. Bake crust until brown. Peel fresh peaches and arrange slices on pastry. Sprinkle with mixture of cinnamon and remaining sugar. Bake 15 minutes at 350°. Pour over this a mixture of lightly beaten egg yolks and cream. Bake 30 minutes longer. Serve warm. Serves 6.

PEACH-STUFFED CORNISH GAME HENS

½ cup chopped onion
¼ cup butter
1 cup rice
1¼ cups chicken broth
1 pound peaches, peeled
  and chopped
½ pound walnuts, chopped

¼ cup lemon juice
2 teaspoons sage
1 teaspoon grated orange rind
½ teaspoon cinnamon
salt and pepper to taste
6 (1 pound) cornish game hens
3 tablespoons melted butter

SAUCE:
1 cup chopped onion
½ cup chopped carrot
¼ cup butter
1 cup dry white wine
2 cups chicken broth
½ pound peaches, peeled
  and sliced
1 tablespoon lemon juice

1 teaspoon thyme
1 bay leaf
½ cup vinegar
3 tablespoons sugar
2 tablespoons arrowroot
¼ cup cold water
2 tablespoons butter
salt and pepper to taste

In saucepan, cook onion in butter over moderate heat 2-3 minutes. Add rice and cook until rice is translucent. Stir in chicken broth and simmer covered 10-15 minutes or until liquid is absorbed. In a bowl combine the remaining ingredients and the rice mixture and toss. Pack body cavities loosely with stuffing and truss the hens. Brush the hens with melted butter and roast in 400° oven for 20 minutes. Reduce heat to 350° and roast hens, basting twice, for 25 minutes more or until juices run clear when thigh is pricked. Split hens in half, pour sauce over hens and garnish with parsley.

Sauce: In saucepan, cook onion, carrot, and giblets in butter over moderate heat for 5 minutes, or until vegetables are lightly browned. Deglaze with wine and reduce liquid by half. Add chicken broth, peaches, thyme, bay leaf and cook for 30 minutes. Transfer peaches with slotted spoon to blender and purée them. Strain cooking liquid into bowl and reserve. In saucepan combine vinegar and sugar and cook over moderate heat until sugar is caramelized. Add strained cooking liquid, bring to boil and stir in arrowroot dissolved in cold water. Add peach purée, butter, lemon juice, salt and pepper. Cook until thick enough to coat spoon. Serves 6.

Mrs. Rufus Dorsey Sams, III
(Sidney Tucker)

HINTS

To tenderize chicken, rub inside and out with lemon juice.

SPICED CHICKEN WITH PEACHES

1½ cups sliced fresh peaches
1 cup orange juice
2 tablespoons brown sugar
2 tablespoons vinegar
1 teaspoon nutmeg
1 teaspoon sweet basil
1 clove garlic, minced

1 fryer, cut up
½ cup flour
1 teaspoon salt
¼ teaspoon freshly ground
   black pepper
vegetable oil

Put ½ inch oil in skillet; set on medium high heat. Combine peaches and orange juice with the brown sugar, vinegar, nutmeg, basil and garlic in saucepan; cook slowly 10 minutes. Dredge chicken in flour, salt and pepper; brown in skillet. Remove oil, replace chicken in skillet and cover with sauce. Simmer for 20 minutes. Serves 4.

CHICKEN GRAND MARNIER WITH PEACHES

4 large chicken breasts,
   split
salt and flour
peanut oil for frying
6 tablespoons brown sugar

2 tablespoons butter
2 large oranges, sectioned
4 fresh peaches, halved
½ cup Grand Marnier*
¾ cup toasted almonds

Lightly salt and flour chicken. Fry in peanut oil. Remove chicken from pan and set aside. Pour off all oil and drippings in pan, then add brown sugar and butter. Simmer, stirring until smooth. Add chicken and orange sections. Place a halved peach on each piece of chicken. Add Grand Marnier and simmer for 5 minutes. Baste. Arrange chicken and fruit on a serving platter. Sprinkle prepared dish with toasted almonds. Serves 6-8.

*Optional--use ¼ cup orange juice and ¼ cup Grand Marnier.

HINTS

Whip ½ pint whipping cream with 1 tablespoon vanilla ice cream and powdered sugar to taste. The cream will take longer to whip but will not turn to butter.

DUCK WITH PEACHES

6 fresh peaches, peeled
and halved
1/2 cup peach brandy
2 tablespoons brown sugar
PEACH BRANDY SAUCE:
peel of 1 orange, cut in
slivers
peel of 1 lemon, cut in
slivers
1/4 cup sweet butter
3 tablespoons flour
2 cups brown stock (4 beef
and 4 chicken bouillon cubes
dissolved in 2 cups water

2 (4-41/2) domestic ducklings
1 tablespoon salt
1 teaspoon pepper

juice of 1 orange
juice of 1/2 lemon
1/2 teaspoon salt
1/2-3/4 cup of peach brandy
juice from 6 drained peaches
(optional)
3/4 cup white port
pepper to taste

Place peach halves, cut side up, in a shallow baking dish and sprinkle 1/2 cup brandy and the brown sugar over them. Cover and let stand 4-6 hours. Drain peaches and set aside, reserving any juices for the Peach Brandy Sauce. Rub cavities of ducks with 1 tablespoon salt and 1 teaspoon pepper. Place ducks on a rack in a shallow roasting pan and roast in a preheated 400° oven for 45 minutes. Pour off the fat from time to time. Cool ducks at room temperature for 3-4 hours. About an hour before serving, cut the ducklings in half, and using a very sharp knife, remove the backbone, breastbone, and ribs. Cut into quarters. Place the ducks on a rack in the broiler pan, prick skin all over with a fork, and broil 10-15 minutes per side or until the skin is crispy and the fat has cooked out. Turn the ducks once or twice, again pricking thoroughly with a fork to release as much fat as possible from under the skin. Have the broiler heat moderate or place the ducks 7-8 inches below the flame so that the skin becomes crispy but not burned. Meanwhile, heat the peaches a few minutes in a 350° oven until just warm. Reheat Peach Brandy Sauce. Arrange the duck on a large platter. Slice the peaches and arrange them over and around the ducklings. Pour about 1/3-1/2 of the Peach Brandy Sauce over the ducklings and pass the rest separately. To prepare sauce, cook the orange and lemon peel for 5 minutes in 1 cup boiling water in a small saucepan. Drain, discarding the water, and set the peels aside. Melt the butter in the top of a double boiler over boiling water, skimming off foam as it forms. Slowly stir in flour and cook, stirring, until the roux is lightly browned, 5-7 minutes. Remove from the heat and cool slightly. Add brown stock and cook, stirring, over a low heat until smooth. Add the peels, the juices of the orange and 1/2 lemon, 1/2 teaspoon salt, 1/2-3/4 cup brandy, juice from peaches, and port. Cook over a moderate heat until it is reduced by 1/3. Strain sauce and season to taste with pepper. Set aside until ready to reheat just before serving.

This elegant entree is delicious with wild rice.

HAM AND PEACH CURRY

1 (16 ounce) can peach halves	1 teaspoon curry powder
1 tablespoon butter or margarine	2 tablespoons brown sugar
4 slices cooked ham	1 tablespoon butter or margarine

Drain peach halves, reserving syrup. Set aside. Melt 1 tablespoon butter in a large skillet. Brown ham in butter; remove and set aside. Add peach syrup and curry powder to pan drippings. Place peach halves, cut side down, in syrup mixture; cook over medium heat 2 minutes. Turn peaches; fill cavities with brown sugar, and dot with remaining butter. Return ham to skillet; cover and cook 3 minutes. Serves 4.

PEACH ICE CREAM

1 pint fresh peaches	1 pint fresh cream
dash lemon juice	1 quart milk
sugar to sweeten	

Put fresh peaches in a blender and blend well, adding a dash of lemon juice to retain freshness of peaches. Sweeten peaches to taste with sugar. Add fresh cream. Check sweetness and add more sugar if desired. Pour peach mixture into your electric churn. Add 1 quart of milk to churn and freeze. (The mixture should be very sweet prior to freezing if a 'sweet' ice cream is desired).

Mrs. Miles A. Brewer
(Patricia Coffee)

PEACH SAUCE FOR ICE CREAM

1 tablespoon tapioca	¾ cup peach syrup (from drained peaches)
¼ cup sugar	1 tablespoon lemon juice
dash of salt	
1 (10 or 12 ounce) package frozen peaches, thawed and drained	

Mix first 5 ingredients and heat to boiling; add lemon juice. Serve cooled on vanilla ice cream.

FRESH PEACH ICE CREAM

1½ quarts mashed ripe
  peaches
2 tablespoons vanilla extract
1 teaspoon salt
2 (14 ounce) cans sweetened
  condensed milk

1 (13 ounce) can evaporated
  milk
½ cup sugar
½ gallon of milk

In a 6-quart churn mix the peaches, vanilla extract, salt, condensed milk, evaporated milk, and sugar. Fill the churn to mixture line with milk. Freeze according to your churn's instructions.

A delicious, homemade recipe and very appealing.

Mrs. Robert L. Dickey, III
(Cynde Martin)

PEACH ICE CREAM

4 cups soft ripe peaches
2½ cups sugar
2 large cans Pet Milk
  (undiluted)

4 eggs
2 tablespoons vanilla
2% milk to make gallon of
  ice cream

Peel and cut up peaches. Put ½ cup sugar over the peaches and let stand while mixing other ingredients. Pour into 1 gallon freezer and fill with enough 2% milk to make the container full. Freeze according to your churn's instructions. Yield 1 gallon.

LUSCIOUS CUSTARD SAUCE

1 (3 ounce) package Jello
  Americana Pudding
6 ounces Cool Whip

Grand Marnier
Sliced peaches

Mix pudding according to directions except reduce milk amount to 1½ cups. Bring to a rolling boil. Remove from heat. When pudding is ½ way congealed whisk in Cool Whip until this is smooth. Add Grand Marnier to taste; usually ½ to 1 tablespoon. Use as a dip for sliced peaches.

This dip is also good with pound cake and other fruits such as strawberries, pears, apples, and pineapples.

PEACH BAVARIAN WITH RASPBERRY SAUCE

2 eggs, separated
1 (3 ounce) package peach
  jello
1/8 teaspoon salt
1 cup boiling water
1/4 teaspoon vanilla extract

1/4 teaspoon almond extract
2 tablespoons sugar
1 cup fresh peaches,
  drained and diced
1 cup heavy cream, whipped

Raspberry Sauce:
1 (16 ounce) package frozen
  red raspberries
1 teaspoon cornstarch
1 tablespoon water

1/4 cup sugar
1/2 cup red currant jelly
1/4 cup cherry cointreau
1 tablespoon flour

Beat egg yolks and add jello and salt. Add boiling water and stir until jello is dissolved. Add extracts and set aside. Beat egg whites and gradually add sugar. Fold gelatin into egg white mixture. Fold in peaches and whipped cream. Pour combined mixture into a 6-cup mold and chill until set. Serve with raspberry sauce.
Sauce: Thaw frozen berries. Heat and strain through a sieve. Mix cornstarch and water together and fold into strained berries. Cook this berry-cornstarch mixture in a saucepan, stirring for 5 minutes. Add sugar and jelly and heat until dissolved. Add flour and cointreau. Serve over peach bavarian. Serves 6-8.

PEACHES FLAMBÉ

1/4 cup butter
1 (16 ounce) can sliced
  peaches
1/2 cup orange juice
1 teaspoon grated orange
  peel

1 tablespoon sugar
1/4 cup brandy, heated
8 warm cooked crepes,
  folded into quarters
1/4 cup chopped pecans
  (optional)

Melt butter in skillet or chafing dish. Drain peaches and reserve juice. Combine peach juice (about 3/4 cup) with orange juice; pour in pan with butter. Simmer about 5 minutes or until slightly thickened. Stir in peaches. Sprinkle with orange peel and sugar. Add warm brandy and ignite with long match. When flame dies, spoon peaches and sauce over warm crepes on individual dessert plates. Sprinkle with pecans if desired. Yield: 8 crepes.

PEACHES AND CREAM DESSERT

1½ cups all-purpose flour
2 teaspoons baking powder
1 teaspoon salt
2 (3⅛ ounce) packages vanilla
   pudding mix, not instant
6 tablespoons melted butter

2 eggs
1 cup milk
1 (29 ounce) can sliced
   peaches, drained except for
   5 tablespoons of syrup

TOPPING:
12 ounces softened cream
   cheese
¾ cup sugar

5 tablespoons reserved peach
   syrup

Beat first 7 ingredients for 2 minutes. Pour into a greased 9 x 13-inch pan. Arrange peaches on top. Cover with topping.
Topping: Mix topping ingredients together and beat for 2 minutes. Spoon evenly over batter. Sprinkle with cinnamon and sugar. Bake at 350° for 30 to 35 minutes. Serve hot or cold. Serves 8.

FANNIE KATE'S PEACH CONSERVE

4 pounds peaches, peeled,
   pitted, and quartered
5 pounds sugar
20 ounces or 2½ cups crushed
   undrained pineapple, or 2
   fresh pineapples cut in
   small pieces

4 oranges, peeled and sliced
1 pint chopped pecans
5 cooking apples, peeled and
   chopped
juice of 4 lemons
¾ pound diced citron (optional)

Combine peaches and sugar; let stand until juice forms. Combine other ingredients and cook slowly until thickened at least 40 minutes. Seal in hot, sterilized jars. Yields 8 pints.

Serve over ice cream, pound cake or on hot biscuits.

PEACH MERINGUE

1 pint jar Dixieland
   (or other freestone)
   peach halves
2 egg whites, beaten
   until stiff

powdered sugar to taste
½ cup chopped almonds

Fill peach halves with beaten egg whites and almonds, covering all the peach. Heat in 375° oven until a delicate brown.

SPECIAL PEACH JAM

4 cups crushed peaches
5 cups sugar
½ teaspoon ground cloves
½ teaspoon ground cinnamon

½ teaspoon ground allspice
1 box pectin, powdered
red food coloring (optional)

Crush peaches. Measure sugar and set aside. Add spices and pectin to peaches and bring mixture to a boil. Stir in sugar and continue boiling. Boil only 1 minute, stirring constantly. Remove peach mixture from heat. Skim foam away and add food coloring. Place in 6 half-pint sterilized jars. Seal.

BRANDIED PEACHES

9 pounds yellow cling stone
  peaches
9 pounds sugar
1 quart water

2 sticks cinnamon
2 tablespoons whole cloves
3 pints brandy

Peel and weigh fruit. Boil sugar and water with spices tied in a cheese cloth bag. Boil until mixture is clear. Drop in peaches a few at a time and cook until tender. *The peaches must remain whole.* Place fruit on platter to drain. When syrup has cooled, add brandy and stir well. Place peaches in sterilized jars and cover with syrup. Seal. Yields 4 quarts.

MRS. E'S PEACH CHUTNEY

4 pounds peaches, chopped or
  sliced
½ cup chopped onion
1 cup chopped crystallized
  ginger
½ pound seedless raisins

1½ pounds brown sugar
3 cups cider vinegar
2 tablespoons white mustard
  seed
1 tablespoon salt
2 tablespoons chili powder

Mix ingredients well. Simmer together in an 8-quart kettle for 2 hours, or until fruit is glazed and syrup reduced and thickened. Pour into sterilized jars. Seal. Yields approximately 10 jars.

Pears or apples may be substituted.

Mrs. George G. Felton
(Anne Corn)

SEAFOOD

FILLETS OF SOLE

4 tablespoons butter
1 medium onion, finely
   chopped
½ pound mushrooms,
   finely chopped
2 tablespoons finely chopped
   parsley
salt and pepper
1 cup dry white wine

1 cup fish stock or clam juice
2 tablespoons shallots
6 fillets of sole, lemon sole, or
   flounder
2 tablespoons butter
2 tablespoons flour
2 egg yolks
1 tablespoon butter

In a saucepan, melt 4 tablespoons butter. Add onion and cook until transparent. Add mushrooms and cook until all moisture has evaporated. Stir in parsley and season onion-mushroom mixture with salt and pepper. Set aside. Lightly grease a sauté pan and pour in the wine and stock. Bring to a boil, then simmer for 10-15 minutes with shallots. Meanwhile, wash and pat dry fillets. Season with salt and pepper and line one side with mushroom onion mixture. Roll up fillet and fasten with a toothpick. Place fillets in liquid and simmer 6 minutes. While fish is poaching make a roux by melting 2 tablespoons butter and gradually adding 2 tablespoons flour. Remove fillets and keep warm. Strain two-thirds of cooking liquid into roux and make a sauce of desired consistency. Mix egg yolks with remaining 1 tablespoon butter. Pour in a small amount of the hot sauce and mix by whisking. Pour the warm mixture back into the saucepan and continue cooking to thicken. Pour sauce over fillets. Serves 4-6.

Mrs. Thomas H. Lowe
(Maribeth Wills)

FLOUNDER FLORENTINE

1 (10 ounce) package frozen
   chopped spinach, cooked
   and well drained
2 tablespoons chopped onion
1 teaspoon salt
¼ teaspoon pepper

½ teaspoon seasoned salt
2 tablespoons salad oil
4 fresh flounder fillets
½ cup medium white sauce
2 tablespoons Vermouth
½ cup grated sharp cheese

Place cooked spinach in a greased casserole. Add onion and seasonings that have been sautéed in oil. Lay fish over mixture. Make a white sauce and add Vermouth. Pour over spinach. Sprinkle with cheese and bake at 350° 40-50 minutes. Serves 2-4.

HERBED SHAD ROE

¼ cup butter
2 medium shad roe
salt and pepper
1 tablespoon chopped parsley

2 teaspoons lemon juice
2 teaspoons chopped chives
1 teaspoon tarragon
1 teaspoon chervil

Heat butter. Add shad roe and sprinkle with salt and pepper. Cook on both sides for a total of 12 minutes. When lightly browned, convert to a serving platter. Mix remaining ingredients and pour over the shad roe. Serves 4.

FISH CARDINAL

1 pound filleted fish
1 cup sherry wine
8 tablespoons butter
2 tablespoons lemon juice

¼ pound cooked shrimp
¼ pound cooked lobster
¼ pound crab meat

SAUCE:
4 tablespoons butter
2 tablespoons flour
1 pint half and half
dash Worcestershire sauce
salt and pepper to taste
¼ pound fresh mushrooms,
   stemmed or 4 ounces
   canned sliced mushrooms

¼ pound grated Parmesan or
   Gruyère cheese
1 tablespoon catsup

Poach fish in sherry wine with 8 tablespoons butter and lemon juice. Remove fish to a boiler. In the meantime, dip shrimp, lobster, and crab meat in wine mixture; then remove to boiler with fish. Strain fish-wine juices and reserve. (yields about 1 cup) To make sauce, melt 4 tablespoons butter and add 2 tablespoons flour gradually to thicken. Remove from heat and add half and half all at once. Mix well. Add fish-wine juices and continue cooking until mixture thickens. Add catsup, Worcestershire sauce, salt and pepper. If sauce is too thick, thin to desired consistency with additional half and half or mushroom juice from canned mushrooms, if used. Add mushrooms and cheese to fish, then fold in sauce. Heat well and serve in crepes or over rice. Serves 8.

Mrs. Edgar Y. Mallary, III
(Lloyd Washington)

TROUT AMANDINE

½ cup butter
1 clove garlic
½ teaspoon salt
1 teaspoon Worcestershire
  sauce
2 teaspoons lemon juice
4-6 tablespoons chopped
  almonds

2 eggs, beaten
salt and pepper to taste
fresh trout fillets
flour
Wesson oil
1 tablespoon chopped parsley
1 tablespoon dry sherry
lemon slices (optional)

One hour before serving, melt butter; add garlic, ½ teaspoon salt, Worcestershire sauce, and lemon juice. Keep sauce warm over the stove. Toast chopped almonds. Set aside. Beat eggs and add salt and pepper to taste. Dip fresh trout fillets in seasoned eggs, then roll in flour. Fry in Wesson oil until a golden brown. Arrange fish in warm serving dish. Sprinkle toasted almonds on fish. Just before serving, add parsley and sherry to sauce. Pour sauce over fish. Serve with slices of lemon.

Mrs. John B. Harris, Jr.
(Marie Doss)

SNOW-PATTERSON ISLAND
CRAB-STUFFED MUSHROOMS

20 medium mushroom caps
3 tablespoons melted butter
1 (6 ounce) package crab meat,
  thawed and drained
½ cup bread crumbs
1 heaping teaspoon Bama
  mayonnaise

1 heaping teaspoon Bama
  salad dressing
1 teaspon lemon juice
½ teaspoon curry powder
pimiento strips

Coat mushrooms with butter; place upside down, in shallow pan. Spoon ¼ teaspoon butter in each cap. Combine crab meat, bread crumbs, salad dressing, mayonnaise, lemon juice, and curry and spoon into mushroom caps and drizzle with butter. Place pimiento strip on each mushroom and broil 5 minutes.

Mrs. William A. Snow, Jr.
(Jean Lamar)

HINTS

Thaw frozen fish in milk for a more freshly caught flavor.

BAKED FISH

½ cup butter or margarine
½ cup chopped green pepper
1 clove garlic, finely chopped
½ cup chopped celery
½ cup chopped onion
2 tablespoons chopped parsley
2 tablespoons flour
1 (16 ounce) can tomatoes (or 3 large tomatoes, chopped)
sprig of thyme
1 teaspoon chili powder
1 teaspoon basil
1 bay leaf
1 tablespoon lemon juice
1 tablespoon Worcestershire sauce
1 teaspoon salt
4-6 pounds flounder, bass, red snapper, catfish, salmon perch or trout
oil
1 teaspoon paprika

Put butter or margarine in skillet or saucepan. Heat to frying point. Add green pepper, garlic and celery. Cook until soft. Add onion and parsley. Cook until soft. Add flour and stir well. Pour in tomatoes. Cook 5 minutes. Add all other ingredients except paprika. Simmer for 10 minutes. Rub fish with oil. Salt and pepper well. Place in a greased baking pan. Pour half of sauce over fish. If fish is thick, make about 3 slits across the fish to absorb juices. Cook 15 minutes at 400°, then add remaining sauce. Bake 15 more minutes. Sprinkle with paprika. Garnish with lemon and parsley sprigs. This recipe makes about 3 cups sauce, enough for a 4-6 pound fish. Serves 4-6, depending on size of fish.

Ms. Betty Moseley Ramsbottom
(Betty Moseley)

CRAB SOUFFLÉ

1 small onion, finely chopped
5 tablespoons butter
3 tablespoons flour
3 tablespooons tomato paste
½ cup cream
1 teaspoon salt
½ teaspoon ground pepper
dash Tabasco
1 teaspoon tarragon
2 tablespoons cognac
4 egg yolks
6 egg whites
1 pound crab meat

Sauté onion in butter. Add flour and stir; then add tomato paste and cream. Stir again until smooth. Add seasonings, including cognac, and cool slightly. Add yolks. Beat well. Beat whites until firm, not dry. Fold into mixture. Butter a 1½-quart soufflé dish. Place a layer of crab meat on the bottom. Add one-third soufflé mixture, then another layer of crab meat and the remaining soufflé mixture. Bake at 375° for 30 minutes. Serves 4.

CRAB-STUFFED FLOUNDER

1 (5 pound) flounder
½ cup chopped green onion
¼ cup butter
2 tablespoons chopped parsley
⅓ cup bread crumbs
2 hard-boiled eggs, chopped
½ pound crab meat

½ teaspoon pepper
1 teaspoon salt
dash Tabasco
paprika
seasoned salt
lemon slices

Clean flounder. Make a slit for stuffing. Brown onion in butter. Add parsley, crumbs, eggs, crab meat and seasoning. Mix and stuff in pocket of fish. Brush flounder with melted butter. Sprinkle with paprika and seasoned salt. Bake at 375° for 30 minutes. Garnish with lemon slices. Serves 6.

CAPE COD DEVILED CRAB

1 cup cold milk
¼ cup cream
1 tablespoon Worcestershire
  sauce
1 teaspoon chopped parsley
1 teaspoon dry mustard
¼ teaspoon salt
cayenne to taste

½ cup chopped onion
½ or 1 clove garlic, crushed
2 tablespoons flour
2 egg yolks
4 tablespoons cracker crumbs
1 pound crab meat, flaked and
  picked

CRAB BUTTER:
2 tablespoons butter
½ teaspoon dry mustard
1 teaspoon tarragon vinegar
1 teaspoon Worcestershire
  sauce

¼ teaspoon salt
cayenne
1 egg yolk
1 teaspoon minced tarragon

Mix milk, cream, Worcestershire sauce, parsley, mustard, salt and cayenne. Boil mixture 5 minutes. Brown onion and garlic. Pour in above mixture. Add flour, egg yolks, and cracker crumbs. Cook until thickened. Add crab meat and spoon in 6 crab shells. Top with crab butter. Mix crab butter ingredients together and pour over prepared crab meat. Bake at 400° for 10 minutes.

Mrs. Alfred Sams
(Betty Dunwody)

CRAB-CHEESE CASSEROLE

⅓ cup butter
¼ cup chopped onion
¼ cup diced green pepper
½ cup flour
1 teaspoon salt
⅛ teaspoon pepper
dash cayenne
1 teaspoon dry mustard
1½ cups milk

1 teaspoon lemon juice
1 teaspoon Worcestershire
  sauce
2 (6 ounce) cans crab meat,
  flaked
⅔ cup shredded American
  cheese, divided
½ cup bread crumbs

Melt butter in saucepan over low heat. Add onions and green pepper and cook slowly until tender. Blend in flour, salt, pepper, cayenne, and mustard. Add milk, stirring constantly. Cook until sauce is smooth and thickened. Fold in lemon juice, Worcestershire sauce, crab meat, and ½ cup cheese. Spoon mixture into individual casserole dishes, or 1 large casserole dish, or shells. Blend remaining cheese with crumbs and put around edge of dishes. Heat in a slow oven at 325° for 15-20 minutes. Serves 6.

Mrs. Randall H. Sanders
(Anne Bryant)

CRAB-RICE SQUARES

CRAB SQUARES:
1 cup minced onion
1 cup minced parsley
1 (2 ounce) bottle pimiento,
  drained and chopped
1 cup grated American cheese
3 cups cooked rice
1 teaspoon salt

½ teaspoon Ac'cent
1 tablespoon Worcestershire
  sauce
1 (6 ounce) can flaked crab
  meat
3 eggs, slightly beaten
2 cups milk

SAUCE:
2 (10¾ ounce) cans cream of
  shrimp soup

1 (8 ounce) carton sour cream
1 teaspoon lemon juice

Mix all crab square ingredients together and place in long greased 3-quart baking dish. Bake at 325° for 45 minutes. Cut into squares. To make sauce, heat together soup, sour cream, and lemon juice until heated throughout. Top warmed crab squares with warmed sauce. Serves 10.

Mrs. Jack Busbee
(Bruce Horton)

CRAB QUICHE

½ cup mayonnaise
1½ tablespoons flour
2 eggs, well beaten
½ cup milk
1 (6½ ounce) can flaked crab
  meat, drained and cleaned

5 slices Swiss cheese, diced
½ cup sliced green or spring
  onions
1 unbaked pie shell

Mix first 2 ingredients, then slowly add the remaining ingredients. Pour into a pie shell and bake at 350° for 40-45 minutes. Serves 6 for main dish, 8-10 for hors d'oeuvres.

Mrs. Wilber D. Owens, Jr.
(Betty Glenn)

SALMON QUICHE

CRUST:
1 cup whole wheat flour
⅔ cup grated sharp Cheddar
  cheese
¼ cup chopped almonds

½ teaspoon salt
¼ teaspoon paprika
6 tablespoons corn oil

FILLING:
1 (15½ ounce) can salmon,
  cleaned and flaked
3 beaten eggs
1 (8 ounce) carton sour cream
  or plain yogurt
¼ cup mayonnaise

½ cup grated sharp Cheddar
  cheese (or low-fat
  Mozzarella)
1 tablespoon grated onion
¼ teaspon dried dill weed
3 drops bottled hot pepper
  sauce

Crust: Combine whole wheat flour, grated cheese, almonds, salt and paprika in a bowl. Stir in oil. Set aside ½ cup of the crust mixture. Press remainder of mixture into the bottom and up the sides of a 9-inch pie plate. Bake crust in 400° oven for 10 minutes. Remove from oven. Reduce oven temperature to 325°. *Filling:* Drain salmon, reserving liquid. Add water to reserved liquid to make ½ cup. Flake salmon, removing bones and skin; set aside. In a bowl, blend eggs, sour cream, mayonnaise and salmon liquid. Stir in salmon, the ½ cup cheese, onion, dillweed and hot pepper sauce. Spoon filling into crust. Sprinkle with reserved crust mixtue. Bake in 325° oven for 45 minutes or until firm. Serves 6.

Mrs. Waldo E. Floyd, Jr.
(Joanne Peterson)

SHRIMP CREOLE PUGET SOUND

2 cups sliced green pepper
5 cups sliced onion
2 cups diced celery
1 cup celery leaves
1 cup salad oil
1 cup chili sauce
1 cup seedless raisins
1 cup chopped blanched
    almonds

2 (16 ounce) cans tomatoes
1 teaspoon thyme
1 teaspoon black pepper
3 large bay leaves
½ cup chopped parsley
1 teaspoon curry powder
5 pounds cleaned raw shrimp

Sauté green pepper, onion, celery and leaves in hot oil. Cook until onion is tender. Add remaining ingredients except shrimp. Simmer gently for 1 hour. Add shrimp and simmer until tender for about 5 to 7 minutes. Serves 16-20.

Mrs. James Elliott, Jr.
(Patricia Jarrard)

GINGER WOODARD'S
SHRIMP AND ARTICHOKE CASSEROLE

6½ tablespoons butter
4½ tablespoons flour
¾ cup milk
¾ cup half and half
salt and pepper
¼ cup dry sherry
1 tablespoon Worcestershire
    sauce

1 (13 ounce) can artichokes,
    drained
1 pound cooked shrimp
1 cup freshly grated Parmesan
    cheese
1 (4 ounce) can mushrooms

Preheat oven to 375°. To make a sauce, melt butter, stir in flour. When mixture is well blended, gradually add milk and half and half, stirring constantly. When smooth and thick, add salt and pepper, Worcestershire sauce, and sherry. Set aside. Arrange artichokes on bottom of baking dish and top with shrimp. Add Parmesan cheese, then mushrooms, and top with sauce. Top with paprika and additional Parmesan cheese. Bake covered 20-30 minutes or until mixture is bubbly. Serve over rice. Serves 6.

Mrs. Andrew W. Young
(Pamela Watkins)

SHRIMP BAKED IN AVOCADO

2 avocados
2 (10 ounce) packages frozen
   shrimp
2 tablespoons lemon juice
celery leaves
8 tablespoons butter
4 tablespoons flour

1 cup heavy cream
1 (8 ounce) jar sliced
   mushrooms
4 tablespoons sweet wine
1 cup Pepperidge Farm stuffing
   mix

Peel, split and lightly salt avocado. Boil shrimp 1 minute in salted water with lemon juice and celery leaves. Drain. Melt butter and add flour and cream to make a white sauce. Cook until thickened. Remove from heat. Add mushrooms, wine and shrimp to the sauce. Pour over each avocado half and top with stuffing mix. Heat thoroughly 15 minutes in 300° oven. Serves 4.

SHRIMP ROCKEFELLER

4 tablespoons butter or
   margarine
1 teaspoon celery seed
1 teaspoon Worcestershire
   sauce
½ teaspoon salt
1 cup chopped lettuce
¼ cup chopped green onion
1 small clove garlic, minced
2 (10 ounce) packages frozen
   chopped spinach, thawed
   and drained

1 cup light cream
1 beaten egg
8 ounces cleaned, cooked
   shrimp
2 tablespoons butter or
   margarine
¼ cup fine dry bread crumbs
¼ cup grated Parmesan
   cheese

In medium saucepan, combine the butter or margarine, celery seed, Worcestershire, and salt. Stir in the lettuce, green onion, and garlic; simmer, covered 2-3 minutes. Add the spinach, cream, and beaten egg. Cook and stir until mixture begins to simmer. Divide half the shrimp among 4 individual casseroles or baking shells. Add hot spinach mixture; top with remaining shrimp. Combine 2 tablespoons melted butter, bread crumbs, and cheese. Sprinkle evenly over the casseroles. Bake in a 375° oven for 15 minutes or until casserole is heated. Serves 4.

Mrs. Bayne Mallary
(Lester Hart)

SHRIMP OR LOBSTER NEWBERG

3 pounds shrimp or 2 cups
  boiled diced lobster meat
1 cup butter
2 teaspoons salt
cayenne pepper

1 cup cream
4 egg yolks
4 teaspoons lemon juice
4 tablespoons sherry

Cook shrimp or lobster in butter for 3 minutes. Add seasoning; cook 1 minute longer. Add cream and egg yolks. Cook untl mixture thickens. Add lemon juice and sherry. Serves 4.

Mrs. Henry B. Matthews
(Evelyn McArver)

SHRIMP BATTER
Good for Onion Rings, too!

1 cup flour
¾ cup water
2 tablespoons lemon juice
2 tablespoons cooking oil

1 teaspoon salt
½ teaspoon pepper
2 egg whites, stiffly beaten

Mix all ingredients except egg whites. Fold them in just before frying. If batter seems too thick, add water to obtain desired consistency. Fry shrimp after dipping in batter, being careful to keep them separate as you are frying. (This prevents batter from adhering to one another.)

Mrs. James E. Carpenter, Jr.
(Patricia Reynolds)

JANIE'S SHRIMP VERMOUTH
Simply wonderful!

5 pounds shrimp, deheaded
  only
2½ cups butter
1½-2 cups vermouth

1-1½ ounces coarsely ground
  black pepper
garlic salt to taste

In a large saucepan, add just enough water to cover bottom of pan. Add butter, vermouth, pepper, and garlic salt. Bring to a boil; add shrimp. Remove saucepan from heat, cover shrimp mixture, and allow to sit 15 to 20 minutes or until shrimp are desired doneness. Drain shrimp and serve. Pass the butter vermouth sauce as a dip for French bread. Serves 8.

BARBECUED SHRIMP

1-2 cloves garlic, crushed
½ cup cooking oil
1 teaspoon salt
1 teaspoon ground pepper
3 tablespoons chili sauce
1 tablespoon Worcestershire
  sauce

3 tablespoons vinegar
¼ cup chopped parsley
dash of hot pepper sauce
3 pounds shrimp, shelled,
  deveined, uncooked

Using a blender, blend the garlic with cooking oil, salt, pepper, chili sauce, Worcestershire, vinegar, parsley and hot pepper sauce. Rinse shrimp; drain and arrange on 8 skewers. Brush with sauce, cover with Saran wrap, and refrigerate 4 to 6 hours or overnight. Broil 10 minutes, turning and brushing with sauce. Shrimp can be cooked on the grill. Serves 4-6.

Mrs. Henry J. Lamar, IV
(Katherine Kilpatrick)

GOLDEN SHRIMP CASSEROLE

5 slices buttered bread, cut in
  ½-inch cubes
2 cups cooked shrimp, cut in
  pieces
2 cups grated American cheese

3 eggs
2 cups milk
½ teaspoon dry mustard
½ teaspoon salt

Put a layer of bread cubes on bottom of 1½-quart casserole. Alternate layers of shrimp, cheese, and bread. Beat eggs with milk and seasonings. Pour over mixture in casserole. Bake in a pan filled with 1 inch hot water in slow 325° oven 1 hour and 25 minutes. Serves 6.

Mrs. Calder W. Payne
(Eugenia Coleman)

HINTS

To minimize shrimp odor, drop fresh celery leaves in the cooking container or 1 tablespoon caraway seed.

The freshest shrimp have a grey cast and are referred to as green shrimp; pink shrimp are those that are half cooked and are likely to be less fresh.

SEAFOOD DIVAN

2 (10 ounce) packages frozen
  chopped broccoli
5 ounces canned or frozen
  lobster
1 cup canned or fresh shrimp
1 tablespoon butter

2 tablespoons flour
1½ cups skim milk
¼ teaspoon salt
2 ounces shredded processed
  Swiss cheese (½ cup)
paprika

Cook the broccoli, drain and arrange in a greased 11¾ x 7½ x 1¾-inch baking dish. Flake the lobster; toss with the shrimp and spoon over broccoli.
Make a sauce of the butter, flour, milk and seasoning. Cook until thick and bubbly and add the Swiss cheese. Pour over seafood to cover. Sprinkle with paprika. Bake at 400° for 20-25 minutes. Serves 6-8.

Low caloried at only 115 calories per serving.

Mrs. B. L. Register
(Mary Richardson)

SHRIMP CURRY

½ cup butter
½ cup chopped onion
¼-½ cup chopped green
  pepper
2 cloves garlic, pressed
1 (16 ounce) carton sour cream
2 teaspoons lemon juice
2 teaspoons curry powder
¾ teaspoon salt

½ teaspoon ginger
dash chili powder
dash of pepper
3 cups cleaned cooked shrimp,
  (about 2 pounds in shell)
condiments: chopped peanuts,
  chutney, coconut, bacon
  bits, grated egg, to garnish

Melt butter; add onion, green pepper, and garlic. Cook until tender but not brown. Stir in sour cream, lemon juice, and seasonings; add shrimp. Cook over low heat stirring constantly, just until hot throughout. The sauce will be thin. Serve over rice. Offer condiments. Serves 6.

Note: Adjust curry according to taste

Mrs. Charles F. Causey
(Alice Jackson)

COQUILLES GRATINÉES

2 cups sliced fresh mushrooms
3 tablespoons butter
¼ teaspoon salt
2 tablespoons flour
2 tablespoons butter
1¼-1½ pounds scallops,
   poached, reserving liquid

½ cup shredded medium
   Cheddar cheese
1½ cups dry white wine
   (or ¾ cup wine,
   ¾ cup water)

To poach scallops, wash and drain 1¼ to 1½ pounds scallops. Place them in a pan with 1½ cups dry white wine (or ¾ cups wine, ¾ cup water). Bring liquid to a boil, cover, reduce heat, and simmer 8 to 10 minutes. Remove scallops and reserve liquid. Set liquid aside. Sauté sliced mushrooms in 3 tablespoons butter. Drain. Make a roux of salt, flour and butter. Slowly pour in 1 cup poaching liquid stirring until smooth and thick. Add cheese and continue to cook. Add mushrooms and scallops to the sauce and spoon into scallop shells. Bake at 375° for approximately 8 minutes. Serves 4-5.

Mrs. Donald W. Rhame
(Alacia Lee)

GRILLED SCALLOPS AND PINEAPPLE

1½ pounds scallops
2 cups pineapple chunks
2 cups mushroom caps
1 green pepper, cut in cubes
¼ cup soy sauce

¼ cup lemon juice
¼ cup finely chopped parsley
½ teaspoon salt
pepper to taste

Combine all ingredients in a bowl and marinate 30 minutes. Drain and reserve marinade. Heat in saucepan. Put scallops, pineapple, mushrooms and green peppers on 8 skewers. Broil on grill 5 minutes on each side, brushing with marinade. Serves 4.

HINTS

The redder the salmon, the higher the price.

Canned shrimp loses its canned taste by soaking in 2 tablespoons vinegar and 1 teaspoon sherry for 15 minutes.

SHERRIED OYSTERS

1 quart oysters, drained
salt and pepper to taste
½ cup butter
½ cup sherry (or more)

2 tablespoons flour mixed with
½ cup cold water
dash cayenne pepper

Lay oysters dotted with butter in shallow pyrex dish. Salt and pepper. Broil until edges curl, stirring often so liquid will brown and turn into brownish gravy. After about 15 minutes add sherry and thicken with flour-water mixture. Add cayenne and brown before serving on crispy toast. Serves 4.

Great for an easy Sunday night party.

Mrs. Oscar S. Spivey
(Rosa Schofield)

LOW-COUNTRY OYSTERS

1 pound fresh mushrooms,
  sliced
1 (2 ounce) jar pimientos
8 tablespoons butter

8 tablespoons flour
4 cups cream
salt and white pepper to taste
1½ quarts oysters

Sauté mushrooms and pimientos in butter. After mushrooms have cooked a few minutes, sift flour over mixture and when it begins to thicken, add cream, salt and pepper. Let oysters simmer in own liquid in another pan until edges curl. Add oysters to mushroom sauce and add more cream if mixture is too dry. Serve from chafing dish with toast triangles.

Mrs. Crawford B. Edwards
(Mildred Taylor)

HINTS

Lemon juice combined with plain yogurt and dillweed makes a refreshing sauce for poached fish.

To preserve the freshness of fish, sprinkle fish with lemon juice and cover with lemon slices.

OYSTERS IN PATTY SHELLS

2 quarts oysters, drained
(reserving liquid)
1 cup butter
1 cup flour
2 garlic cloves, finely chopped
1 tablespoon grated onion
1 tablespoon chopped parsley
1 tablespoon paprika
1 tablespoon monosodium
glutamate
3 tablespoons A-1 sauce
1 tablespoon basil
½ cup sherry
1 tablespoon Scotch
3 tablespoons catsup
3 tablespoons Worcestershire
sauce
3 tablespoons lemon juice
¼ teaspoon Tabasco
1 tablespoon dill weed

Drain oysters well. Simmer. Drain again and reserve some of the liquid. Brown butter and add flour to make a sauce. Thin slightly with oyster liquid. Add remaining ingredients and oysters. Serve in patty shells.

MEUNIÈRE SAUCE

½ cup butter
1 tablespoon chopped parsley
1 tablespoon chopped green
onion
2 tablespoons lemon juice
½ teaspoon salt
½ teaspoon pepper
dash hot sauce
dash Worcestershire sauce

Mix all ingredients and heat. Serve warmed sauce over baked fish. Serves 4.

MUSHROOM SAUCE FOR FISH

1 (10¾ ounce) can mushroom
soup
1½ teaspoons Worcestershire
sauce
1 tablespoon lemon juice
¼ teaspoon dry mustard
2 tablespoons milk
dash black pepper
2 onions, chopped
3-4 drops hot sauce
1 teaspoon chopped parsley
2 tablespoons white wine
1 pound fresh shrimp

Mix all ingredients and pour over a pound of fresh shrimp. Bake at 375° for 30 minutes. Serves 2-4.

GAME
AND
POULTRY

DUCK WITH WILD RICE

2 ducks
1 onion, chopped
2 ribs celery, chopped
1 (5 ounce) package Uncle
  Ben's wild and long grain rice
½ cup butter
½ cup chopped onion
¼ cup flour
1½ cups half-and-half

1 tablespoon chopped fresh
  parsley
1½ teaspoons salt
¼ teaspoon pepper
1 (8 ounce) can mushrooms
  and liquid
1 (4 ounce) package slivered
  almonds, toasted

Boil duck, onion and celery until tender. Remove meat from bones. Set aside. Cook rice. Set aside. Melt butter and sauté onion. Stir in flour; add half-and-half to make cream sauce. Add parsley and seasonings. Add cooked duck, rice, mushrooms and almonds to cream sauce. Bake mixture in a casserole at 350° for 30-45 minutes. Serves 6-8.

Mrs. Charles S. Simmons
(Kathy Tucker)

BESSE'S BIRDS

12 birds (dove or quail)
1 cup uncooked rice
¼ cup chopped bell pepper
¼ cup chopped onion

1 cup beef consommé
1 (10¾ ounce) can onion soup
½ cup flour
salt and pepper

Sauté salted and floured birds in small amount of butter or bacon drippings to brown well. Put rice in bottom of a buttered oblong casserole. Place birds on top of rice. Sprinkle peppers and onion on top. Pour consommé and onion soup over casserole. Cover casserole with aluminum foil and bake at 350° for 45 minutes. Serves 6.

12 pieces chicken may be substituted for the birds.

Mrs. Hugh Moss Comer
(Virginia Bateman)

HINTS

Salt game birds and refrigerate 2 days before freezing.

ROAST WILD DUCK IN ORANGE SAUCE

6 wild ducks (preferably wood
  duck)
3 oranges
flour

thyme
sage
salt and pepper
vegetable oil

ORANGE SAUCE:
¾ cup orange marmalade
1 teaspoon grated orange rind
½ cup orange juice
¼ cup tarragon vinegar

1 tablespoon prepared mustard
2 teaspoons cornstarch
¼ teaspoon salt
¼ teaspoon rosemary

Preheat oven to 325°. Pat ducks dry and salt inside. Insert half an orange in cavity, cut side up. Rub outside with vegetable oil. Season with thyme, sage, salt and pepper. Dust with flour and place in roaster, breast side up. Moisten with small amount of boiling water and place uncovered in oven. Watch carefully adding small amounts of water, turning as ducks brown (1 hour). When brown, cover roaster and cook until tender (depending on size). Remove ducks and make gravy from pan drippings, skimming off fat if necessary.
Orange Sauce: Mix together ingredients in small saucepan. Cook until thickened. Pour over ducks. Serves 6.

Mrs. Joseph N. Neel, III
(Marie Butler)

SMOTHERED DOVE
Serve with Wild Rice and Tart Salad

12 doves
½ cup butter
1 bell pepper, sliced
1 large onion, chopped
seasoned salt
garlic powder

salt and lemon pepper
2 (4 ounce) cans mushrooms
Worcestershire sauce
½ cup white wine
lemon juice

Flour, salt and lemon pepper birds. In an aluminum pot, on top of stove, add seasoned birds and remaining ingredients except wine. Cover birds partially with water and simmer covered 30 minutes. Add ½ cup white wine. Simmer 30 more minutes or until tender. Serves 8.

Mrs. A. S. Durkee, Jr.
(Harriett Murphey)

WILD DUCK IN MADEIRA

4 wild ducks, cleaned and
  halved
½ cup flour
2 teaspoons salt, divided
1½ teaspoons pepper, divided
¼ cup olive oil
1 large onion, chopped

2 cups Madeira
½ cup sherry
4 tablespoons chopped parsley
1 (4 ounce) can ripe olives,
  chopped
1 orange, thinly sliced
parsley

Dust duck with seasoned flour (1 teaspoon salt and 1 teaspoon pepper). Brown in olive oil. Remove duck to a 3-quart baking dish. Simmer the onion in the same olive oil. To make a sauce, add Madeira, sherry, parsley, olives, 1 teaspoon salt and ½ teaspoon pepper. Cook 1 minute and pour over duck. Bake 40 minutes at 350°. Baste with sauce. Garnish with orange slices and parsley. Serves 4.

WALTHALL'S BEST BIRDS

8 dove or quail
McCormick's Season-All
  seasoning
McCormick's Lemon Pepper
  seasoning

½ cup butter, melted
2 lemons, juice and zest
⅓ slice bacon per bird
add water to ½ inch in frying
  pan

Season birds well inside and out and with Season-All and Lemon Pepper seasoning. Dip birds in melted butter coating well. Brown well in frying pan on all sides, ending with doves turned breast side up. Turn heat to low. Pour lemon juice over birds dousing breasts well. Place ⅓ strip bacon on each breast. Add enough water to bring up ½ inch in bottom of pan. Bruise lemon peelings and place over birds and in juice of pan. Cover. Cook slowly for several hours. Baste birds about every 30 minutes adding hot water as needed to maintain level of liquid. Cook until they are fork tender (as in cooking a chicken). They are better after sitting in the liquid for several hours. Serves 4.

Mrs. Frank W. Walthall, Jr.
(Janet Fortson)

HINTS

To reduce the gamey taste of venison, soak it overnight in milk.

BRANDIED PHEASANT

8 green onions, thinly sliced
¼ cup butter
3 pheasants, cleaned
½ cup brandy
2 cups chicken broth

1 teaspoon salt
pepper
6 slices bacon
2 cups heavy cream
¼ cup horseradish

Sauté onions in butter. Add pheasants and cook until birds are browned. Pour brandy over birds and ignite. When flame subsides, add chicken broth, salt, and pepper. Lay bacon over birds and cook 45 minutes at 375°. Stir in cream and horseradish and roast 10-15 more minutes. Serves 6.

ROAST WILD GOOSE

1 (6-8 pound) young wild goose
juice of one lemon
salt and pepper to taste
¼ cup butter
¼ cup chopped onion
1 cup chopped tart apple

1 cup chopped dried apricots
3 cups finely crushed bread
 crumbs
4-6 slices of bacon
melted bacon fat

Preheat oven to 325°. Season the goose inside and out with lemon juice, salt, and pepper. In a saucepan, heat the butter and add the onion. Cook until onion is transparent. Stir in the apple, apricots, bread crumbs, ½ teaspoon salt and ⅛ teaspoon pepper. Spoon the stuffing into the goose cavity. Tie up the cavity. Cover the breast with bacon slices and cheesecloth that has been soaked in bacon fat. Put the prepared goose, breast up, on a rack in a roasting pan. Roast 2-3 hours, basting frequently. Serves 8.

TOMMY'S VENISON CHILI

1 pound ground venison
½ pound sausage
1 large garlic clove, crushed
1 large onion, chopped
2-3 tablespoons chili powder
1 (32 ounce) can tomato sauce
½ teaspoon thyme

1 teaspoon oregano
1 bay leaf
1 (32 ounce) can red kidney
 beans, drained
12 ounces beer
salt and pepper to taste

Brown venison and sausage. Drain meat, add onions and garlic to grease and sauté. Mix meat, onion, garlic, chili powder, tomato sauce, thyme, oregano, bay leaf, kidney beans, and beer. Simmer mixture covered for 1 hour minimum. Season to taste.

VENISON BURGERS

2½ pounds ground venison
½ cup minced onion
1 clove garlic, minced
4 tablespoons chopped parsley

⅔ cup dry red wine
2 tablespoons soy sauce
salt and pepper

Mix all ingredients and form meat into patties. Cook on coals or broil 10 minutes on each side. Serves 8.

WILD GAME SAUCE

1 ounce black pepper
10 ounces Worcestershire
    sauce
1 ounce soy sauce
2 tablespoons salt

2 tablespoons sugar
5 ounces Louisiana hot sauce
1 pint cider vinegar
juice of 3 lemons

Combine all ingredients and refrigerate. Yields 1 quart.

DEER MARINADE

½ cup dry red wine
½ teaspoon cardamon
⅛ teaspoon garlic powder

⅓ cup vegetable oil
3 tablespoons soy sauce
2-4 deer steaks

Combine first 5 ingredients and pour over meat. Allow meat to marinate 3 hours, turning occasionally. Cook as desired. Serves 2-4.

PEPPER JELLY SAUCE

½ cup pepper jelly
¼ cup Port wine
¼ cup catsup

2 tablespoons butter
½ tablespoon Worcestershire
    sauce

Heat all ingredients over low heat and serve with your favorite wild game. Yields 1 cup.

HINTS

Game birds weighing 3½ to 4 pounds should serve 4.

AUNT MYRTLE'S CHICKEN BREASTS WITH OYSTERS
Can be prepared in advance

8 chicken breasts, boned
32 smoked oysters (4 per
 breast)
16 slices bacon (2 slices per
 breast)
1 (10¾ ounce) can cream of
 celery soup

1 (10¾ ounce) can cream of
 mushroom soup
1 cup sherry
salt and pepper to taste

Salt and pepper breasts. Stuff boned chicken with smoked oysters. Wrap each with bacon and seal with toothpicks. Place breasts in buttered pan and pour over the celery soup, mushroom soup and part of sherry. Sprinkle with salt and pepper. Bake at 350° for 1 hour. Baste chicken with remaining sherry from time to time. Serve chicken over rice with the gravy. Serves 6.

Mrs. V. J. Adams, Jr.
(Angela Gaultney)

OVEN-BARBECUED CHICKEN
Sauce can be made ahead of time

15 chicken breasts halved or
 equal amount chicken parts

oil for browning

SAUCE:
½ cup margarine, melted
¾ cup finely chopped onion
½ teaspoon salt
1¼ teaspoon dry mustard
½ cup brown sugar
¼ teaspoon chili powder

1¼ cups catsup
1¼ cups water
¼ cup vinegar
1 tablespoon Worcestershire
 sauce

Wash, dry and flour chicken parts. Brown lightly in oil. Place in large baking dish and cover with warmed sauce made from remaining ingredients. Bake 2 hours at 300°. Serves 12-15.

Mrs. Joseph A. Wall
(Patricia Hammock)

CHICKEN BOURSIN

6 boneless chicken breats,
  skinned
seasoned flour
7 ounces herbed Boursin
  cheese
6 slices Proscuitto ham
1 tablespoon oil

3 tablespoons butter
½ pound mushrooms, sliced
4 onions, chopped
2 tablespoons brandy
½ cup white wine
1 cup chicken stock
¼ cup chopped parsley

Skin breasts. Coat with flour, seasoned with salt and pepper. Spread ½ tablespoon cheese on each breast, then cover with slice of ham. Roll and secure with toothpicks. Brown in oil and butter. Add mushrooms and onions and sauté. Add brandy and ignite. Add wine, chicken stock and parsley. Cover and simmer 30-40 minutes. Remove toothpicks and serve with wild rice. Serves 6.

Mrs. Rufus Dorsey Sams, III
(Sidney Tucker)

CHICKEN DIVAN
Really delicious!

3 whole chicken breasts, boiled
  and chopped
2 (10 ounce) packages frozen
  chopped broccoli, cooked
2 (10¾ ounce) cans cream of
  chicken soup
1 cup mayonnaise
1 (8 ounce) carton sour cream

1 cup grated sharp cheese
1 tablespoon lemon juice
1 teaspoon curry
salt and pepper to taste
grated Parmesan cheese
paprika
butter

Boil chicken and chop. Cook and drain broccoli. Mix soup, mayonnaise, sour cream, grated cheese, lemon juice, curry, salt and pepper. In a greased casserole, put broccoli in bottom and top with chicken. Sprinkle with Parmesan cheese. Pour soup mixture over all. Sprinkle with more Parmesan and paprika. Dot with butter. Bake at 350° for 30 to 40 minutes. Serves 6.

Mrs. Larry E. Landers
(Valery Wrenn)

CRAB-STUFFED CHICKEN

4 large breasts, boned and
  halved
¼ cup butter, divided
¼ cup flour
¾ cup milk
¾ cup chicken broth
⅓ cup dry white wine
¼ cup chopped onion
1 (7½ ounce) can crab meat,
  drained, flaked
1 (4 ounce) can chopped
  mushrooms, drained
½ cup coarsely crumbled
  saltine crackers
2 tablespoons parsley
½ teaspoon salt
pepper to taste
1 cup grated Swiss cheese
paprika

To make sauce, melt 3 tablespoons butter, blending in flour. Add milk, broth and wine all at once. Cook and stir until bubbly. Set aside. In skillet, cook onion in remaining butter until tender, stirring in crab, mushrooms, crumbs, parsley, salt, and dash of pepper. Stir in 2 tablespoons sauce. Top each chicken piece with ¼ cup crab meat mixture. Roll up. Pour sauce over chicken. Bake at 350°, uncovered for 1 hour. Top with cheese and dash paprika, and bake 2 more minutes. Serves 8.

CHICKEN WITH WILD RICE

2 (6 ounce) boxes wild rice mix
  (Uncle Ben's)
1 large onion, diced
1 cup butter
½ cup flour
2 (2½ ounce) jars whole
  mushrooms, reserve liquid
1 diced large hen, saving broth
  (approximately 4 cups)
3 cups light cream
1 cup slivered almonds
1 (2 ounce) jar pimientos
1 teaspoon parsley
3 teaspoons salt
½ teaspoon pepper

Prepare rice according to package directions. Sauté onion in butter until tender; remove from heat. Stir in ½ cup flour. Drain mushrooms, saving liquid. Combine mushroom liquid with enough skimmed chicken broth to make 4 cups. Stir slowly with flour mixture. Add cream. Cook and stir until thickened. Add cooked rice, mushrooms, chopped chicken, almonds, pimientos, and seasonings. Bake at 350° in a 2½-quart casserole dish until bubbly, about 35 minutes. Serves 8-10.

Best to use a fork when adding rice.

Mrs. Mack B. Minton
(Bonnie Tuttle)

CHICKEN, ARTICHOKE, AND MUSHROOM CASSEROLE
Make ahead of time and freeze

1 (5-pound) stewing hen or
  equivalent in mixed fryer
  pieces
1 cup butter
¾ cup flour
2 cups milk
2 cups chicken stock
1 teaspoon salt
1 teaspoon seasoned salt
¼ teaspoon cayenne pepper
  (or to taste)

2 cloves garlic, pressed
¼ cup tomato sauce
3 ounces Gruyere or Swiss
  cheese
2 ounces extra sharp Cheddar
  cheese
3 (14-ounce) cans artichokes
3 (4½-ounce cans button
  mushrooms
grated cheese
paprika

Simmer chicken in water seasoned with 1 rib celery, 1 onion, 1 bay leaf, and 1 teaspoon salt. Remove chicken from bones and cut into large pieces. Make cream sauce of butter, flour, milk, stock and seasonings. When thickened stir in tomato sauce and cheeses, cooking until cheese melts. Add artichokes and mushrooms. Mix all ingredients well. Pour in 3-quart shallow casserole. Top with additional grated cheese and paprika. Bake at 350° for 35 minutes. Serves 12-15.

Mrs. John Marbut, Jr.
(Katie Dickey)

CHICKEN SPECTACULAR

2 cups diced cooked chicken
1 (18 ounce) can tiny English
  peas
2 cups cooked rice
½ cup mayonnaise
1 (10¾ ounce) can cream of
  celery soup, undiluted
¼ teaspoon salt

1 (8 ounce) can sliced water
  chestnuts
2 tablespoons chopped
  pimiento
2 tablespoons chopped onion
pepper to taste
buttered bread crumbs
paprika

Mix all ingredients except paprika and bread crumbs; place in 2-quart casserole. Cover with paprika and buttered bread crumbs. Bake 25 minutes at 350°. More chicken can be added if desired.

Mrs. J. Lon King, Jr.
(Jean Trammell)

CHICKEN COUNTRY CAPTAIN

12 breasts and thighs
½ cup bacon fat
seasoned flour
2-3 onions, finely chopped
2 green peppers, finely chopped
½ cup butter
2 teaspoons curry powder
⅔ teaspoon thyme
⅔ teaspoon cayenne pepper

2 (16 ounce) cans tomatoes
1-3 tablespoons currants
1-3 tablespoons blanched
   almonds
1 tablespoon chopped parsley
1 clove garlic, chopped
currants, parsley, almonds, and
   chutney to garnish

Dredge chicken in flour and brown in fat. Brown onions and peppers in butter. Add remaining ingredients and simmer. Place chicken in Dutch oven. Pour sauce over chicken. Cover tightly. Bake at 300° for 2-3 hours. Serve chicken over rice and cover with sauce. Garnish with additional currants and parsley. Garnish with almonds and chutney. Serves 8.

CHICKEN SPINACH NOODLE

6-8 chicken breasts
1 (16 ounce) package spinach
   noodles
½ cup margarine, melted
1 cup green pepper, chopped
1 cup celery, chopped
1 cup onion, chopped

1 pound Velveeta cheese
1 (10¾ ounce) can mushroom
   soup
1 (3 ounce) jar stuffed olives,
   sliced
1 (4 ounce) can mushrooms
crushed cheese crackers

Boil chicken breasts in salted water until tender. Remove chicken and set aside until cool. In chicken stock (after removing ½ cup of stock and reserving), boil the noodles until done. Drain noodles. In a skillet, sauté margarine, green pepper, celery, and onion. Add Velveeta cheese and stir until smooth and soft. Add mushroom soup, sliced stuffed olives, and mushrooms. Cut chicken into small pieces after removing all bones and add cut-up chicken and cooked noodles to other mixture. You may add extra ½ cup stock if it seems dry. Pour into casserole and top with crushed cheese crackers. Bake 25 minutes at 375°. Serves 10-12.

This may be doubled and will make 3 casseroles. Freezes well.

Mrs. Benjamin Allen Rives, IV
(Jeanne Lindley)

CHICKEN KIEV
Easy

¼ cup minced onion
½ cup plus 2 tablespoons
   butter
3 tablespoons minced fresh
   parsley
8 flattened chicken breasts,
   (four whole ones, boned, split
   and pounded, ask butcher to
   do this)

salt and pepper
flour
2 eggs, slightly beaten
24 butter crackers, finely
   crushed
shortening

Sauté onion in the 2 tablespoons butter in large skillet just until tender, but not browned; combine with parsley. Sprinkle chicken lightly with salt and pepper. Place equal portions of onion mixture on each piece of chicken and 1 tablespoon butter over onion mixture; roll up chicken, tucking in sides, making a package. Secure with wooden picks. Roll in flour, dip in egg, then roll in crumbs. Refrigerate at least 1 hour or overnight. Fry in ½ inch vegetable shortening until golden brown; drain on absorbent paper; remove wooden picks before serving. Serves 8.

Chicken may be frozen after frying. Wrap individually to freeze. To serve, unwrap frozen chicken; let stand at room temperature for 1 hour, then bake on rack in shallow pan at 425° about 20-25 minutes or until heated through and crisp.

Mrs. Andrew W. Young
(Pamela Watkins)

PAM'S CHICKEN
Quick and Easy

2 whole chickens, cut in pieces
1 (8 ounce) bottle Russian
   dressing

1 (2 ounce) envelope onion
   soup mix
1 (17 ounce) can apricots

Place chicken in pan. Mix last 3 ingredients. Pour over chicken. Bake in preheated 350° oven for 1 hour.

Mrs. W. Lee Wood, Jr.
(Frances Bush)

CHICKEN TORTILLA BAKE

1 (10¾ ounce) can cream of mushroom soup
2 (10¾ ounce) cans cream of chicken soup
1½ cups milk
1 chopped onion
1 (8 ounce) can mild taco sauce
1 dozen corn tortillas
2 whole chickens, cooked, boned, and chopped
½ pound grated Cheddar cheese

Combine sauce ingredients (mushroom soup, chicken soup, milk, onion, taco sauce). In buttered casserole, layer tortillas, chicken and sauce. Repeat layers. Top with cheese. Refrigerate 24 hours. Bake at 300° for 1½ hours. Serves 8.

For serving four, use 1 chicken, 1 (10¾ ounce) can chicken soup, 1 cup milk, and same amount of other ingredients.

Mrs. William L. Tift
(Sherry Follette)

CHICKEN TETRAZZINI
Family Dish

6 chicken breasts, boiled and diced
salt, celery salt, pepper
½ pound spaghetti
3 tablespoons butter
½ pound sliced mushrooms
1 tablespoon lemon juice
½ cup butter
2 tablespoons flour
½ cup sherry
1 cup heavy cream

Cover chicken with water seasoned with salt, celery salt, and pepper. Boil until tender. Remove chicken from bone. From kettle reserve 2½ cups stock. Add 6 cups of water to remaining stock. When liquid boils, add spaghetti and cook 6 minutes. Drain and place in baking dish on top of chicken. In skillet heat 3 tablespoons of butter, add mushrooms and sprinkle with lemon juice. Sauté and pour over chicken and spaghetti. In double boiler melt butter; add 2 tablespoons flour; stir until smooth; add stock slowly; pour in sherry; last pour in 1 cup heavy cream. Stir until thickened. Pour over chicken and spaghetti. Bake 25 minutes at 400° in a greased casserole. Serves 6-8.

OPTIONAL: Add 3 stalks celery and ½ cup green pepper. Chop fine and sauté in three tablespoons of butter. Add to mushrooms.

Mrs. W. Elliott Dunwody, III
(Martha Brumback)

OPULENT CHICKEN
Low Cholesterol Cooking

4 whole chicken breasts (may be boned, if desired) with skin removed—season with paprika, salt and pepper
½ cup Mazola margarine
1 (15 ounce) can artichoke hearts, halved

½ pound fresh mushrooms, sliced
pinch of tarragon or rosemary
3 tablespoons flour
1½ cups chicken bouillon
⅓ cup sherry

Mix paprika, salt and pepper on platter or in paper bag and coat chicken as for frying. Shake excess coating from chicken pieces, then sauté in margarine until brown. Place chicken pieces in large casserole and add artichokes among the breasts of chicken. Sauté fresh mushrooms in same skillet, and add margarine if needed; sprinkle crushed herbs over them and sauté 3-5 minutes longer; then pour over chicken. Shake flour and bouillon together in jar with tight lid until well blended. Next stir in sherry. Pour in saucepan and stir over medium heat until thickened to consistency of medium cream sauce. Pour over chicken, cover casserole with lid or foil and bake 45 minutes to 1 hour at 350°. Serves 4 whole breasts or 8 half-breast servings.

Mrs. Waddell Barnes
(Martha Davis)

OVERNIGHT TURKEY
Very moist

turkey
1 large onion
2 stalks celery

salt
pepper
butter or margarine

Wash turkey and place onion and celery in the cavity; butter outside generously (even if butter basted) and season with salt and pepper. Place in roaster with tight fitting cover adding 1 cup cold water. Heat oven to 500°, cook turkey at 500° for 1 hour, turn off oven and leave turkey overnight without opening oven door.

Mrs. Henry H. Tift
(Christine Lee)

PARMESAN CHICKEN
Easy and Good

4 chicken breasts, skinned
  and boned
1 cup finely grated bread
  crumbs
⅓ cup grated Parmesan
  cheese

1 teaspoon salt
½ teaspoon pepper
½ teaspoon garlic powder or
  more to taste
softened butter
milk

Mix all dry ingredients together in a bowl. Dip chicken in milk, then in bread crumb mixture to coat. Sauté in butter over medium heat until done. Crumbs will be browned and crisp.

Mrs. John E. Oswald
(Melissa Ruth Johnston)

CHICKEN CRÊPES
Prepare ahead

CHICKEN CRÊPES
2 tablespoons butter
¼ cup chopped celery
1½ cups chopped cooked
  chicken
¼ cup walnuts

½ teaspoon salt
½ cup mayonnaise, divided
½ cup sour cream
2 tablespoons sherry
almonds

BASIC CRÊPE BATTER
2 eggs, beaten
1 cup milk
1 cup flour

1 tablespoon butter
pinch of salt

Chicken: Melt butter and sauté celery; combine celery with chopped chicken, nuts and salt; toss with ¼ cup mayonnaise; spoon mixture onto crêpes and place in a buttered casserole. Mix sour cream, ¼ cup mayonnaise and sherry and top crêpes with sherry sauce. Bake at 375° for 20 minutes. Sprinkle with almonds. *Crêpe Batter:* In mixing bowl, add milk to beaten eggs, and gradually stir in flour, stirring with a wire whisk. Add butter and salt. Mix until smooth (batter should be like fresh cream). Pour small amount into greased crêpe pan and crêpe is ready when bubbles form on the outer edge. Serves 8.

Mrs. Charles P. Deaton, Jr.
(Lynn Davis)

SAUSAGE-STUFFED CORNISH GAME HENS

1 pound pork sausage, cooked
and drained
1 medium onion, chopped
2 garlic cloves, minced
¼ cup butter

½ cup bread crumbs
1 teaspoon sage
salt and pepper to taste
4 Rock cornish game hens
4 tablespoons butter

Cook sausage until crumbled and brown. Transfer to a bowl. In the skillet, toss onion and garlic in butter over moderate heat for 1 minute and transfer to bowl. Add bread crumbs, sage, salt and pepper to sausage mixture. Combine well and let cool. Pack the cavities of game hens loosely and truss. Arrange on rack of roasting pan and spread each with 1 tablespoon softened butter. Roast at 400° for 20 minutes. Reduce heat to 350°, roast 25 minutes. Baste twice. Test fleshy part of thigh for doneness. When juices run clear, transfer to cutting board, remove strings and split hens in half, keeping stuffing in each half. Serves 8.

CHINESE CHICKEN

1 pound chicken breasts,
skinned, boned, diced
2 tablespoons margarine
1 beef bouillon cube
½ cup water
1 (10¾ ounce) can golden
mushroom soup
1 tablespoon soy sauce
1 teaspoon Worcestershire
sauce
½ teaspoon curry powder
½ teaspoon poppy seeds

1 (8 ounce) can bamboo shoots,
drained
½ cup sliced onion
½ cup sliced celery
1 (4 ounce) can sliced
mushrooms, drained
1 small green pepper, cut in
strips
3 tablespoons dry white wine
1 (3 ounce) can chow-mein
noodles

Cut chicken into small pieces. This is easier if chicken is partially frozen. In medium skillet brown chicken in margarine. Dissolve bouillon in water. Add the bouillon, soup, soy sauce, Worcestershire sauce, curry, and poppy seed to chicken. Mix well. You may prepare to this point before guests arrive. Simmer 15 minutes, stirring constantly. Add the bamboo shoots, onion, celery and mushrooms. Cover and simmer 10 minutes or until tender-crisp. Stir in the green pepper and wine and simmer 3 more minutes. Don't overcook. Serve over chow mein noodles. This recipe doubles easily. Serves 4-6.

Mrs. William W. Baxley, Jr.
(Charlene Carpenter)

PARTY CHICKEN CASSEROLE

18 boned chicken breasts, boiled
and diced, reserving broth
2 cups white wine
4 to 6 cups water (with salt
added)
2 (6 ounce) packages Uncle
Ben's white and wild rice with
herbs
3 ribs celery, chopped

1 medium onion, chopped
1 (4 ounce) can mushrooms,
sliced
4 tablespoons butter
1 (10¾ ounce) can cream of
mushroom soup
1 (8 ounce) carton sour cream
1 cup half and half
½ pint whipping cream

Simmer chicken in wine, salt and water to cover until done. Remove chicken, debone, and cut into bite-size serving pieces. Cook rice in 5 cups of broth for 25 minutes or until almost dry. Sauté celery, onions, and mushrooms in butter until tender. Add mushroom soup, sour cream, half and half, whipping cream and cut up chicken. Combine with cooked rice and mix gently. Bake in large buttered casserole at 350° for 30 to 40 minutes. The entire casserole may be made the day before needed and refrigerated until baking time. Serves 15.

Mrs. Frank W. Walthall, Jr.
(Janet Fortson)

CHICKEN AND BUTTER BEANS
Can be frozen

12 pieces chicken (breasts
and thighs)
salt
ginger
paprika

butter, enough to brown
chicken
2 (8 ounce) cartons sour cream
2 (10 ounce) packages frozen
butter beans

Salt chicken pieces, rub with ginger, and sprinkle with paprika to brown. Brown chicken in melted butter and place in casserole, no more than 2 layers. Spread generously with sour cream and some more salt. Spread the butter beans over the top of chicken. Cover and put in moderate oven 350° for at least 1 hour. This may be cooked ahead for about ½ hour and then cooked an additional ½ hour when serving, which enhances the taste. Serves 4-6.

Mrs. F. Daly Smith
(Berthenia Crocker)

YELLOW RICE AND CHICKEN

1 frying chicken (3 to 3½ pounds), cut in serving pieces
1 medium onion, diced
2 cloves garlic, peeled and cut
¼ cup olive oil
¾ cup tomatoes
1½ quarts chicken broth or water
1 bay leaf
2 cups raw white rice
½ teaspoon saffron
2 tablespoons salt
1 green pepper, diced
1 (16 ounce) can tiny green peas, drained
2 pimientos, sliced

Quarter chicken and fry with onions and garlic in olive oil for 45 minutes. Add tomatoes and broth. Boil for 5 minutes. Add bay leaf, rice, saffron, salt and green pepper. Blend. Place in baking dish in 375° oven for 20 minutes or until rice is just tender and has absorbed moisture. Garnish with peas and sliced pimientos. Serve hot. Serves 4-5.

Mrs. Marion H. Liles, Jr.
(Catharine Burns)

POULET VÉRONIQUE
Delicious over Rice

3 large chicken breasts, boned and halved
½ teaspoon salt
½ teaspoon white pepper
1 teaspoon season all seasoning
½ teaspoon paprika
10 tablespoons butter, divided
20 medium mushroom caps
1 cup diced ham
3 tablespoons sifted flour
1½ cups coffee cream
¾ cup wine
1 teaspoon lemon juice
1½ cups seedless green grapes

Split and bone chicken breasts. Season with salt, pepper, season all seasoning and paprika. Melt 6 tablespoons butter in large heavy skillet and brown chicken over medium heat. Wash skillet and melt 4 tablespoons butter in skillet. Sauté sliced mushroom caps over medium heat for 4 minutes. Place chicken, ham and mushroom caps in greased casserole. Stir flour in skillet for 1 minute. Add cream and wine slowly and stir until smooth. Add lemon juice. Pour sauce over chicken. Bake covered in 350° oven for 35 minutes. Uncover and spread grapes over chicken. Bake 10 more minutes. Serve over rice. Serves 6.

Mrs. William J. Buzzell
(Claude Burns)

MEAT

SIRLOIN STEAK WITH BORDELAISE SAUCE

BORDELAISE SAUCE:

2 tablespoons butter
½ cup finely chopped shallots
1½ cups dry red wine
1 bay leaf
10 whole black peppercorns
2 cloves garlic, unpeeled
2 level teaspoons meat essence

2 tablespoons hot water
2 cups water
¼ cup beef marrow
½ cup plus 2 tablespoons butter
1 tablespoon lemon juice
2 tablespoons finely chopped
  parsley

STEAK:

3 tablespoons rendered beef fat
3½ pounds sirloin steak,
  1-inch thick

salt

In a small saucepan, melt 2 tablespoons butter over low heat. Stir in
½ cup shallots and cook 3 minutes. Add wine, bay leaf, peppercorns, garlic cloves. Bring to a boil, reduce heat and simmer uncovered until reduced to half its original volume. Strain sauce
through fine sieve, return to saucepan and stir in 2 teaspoons meat
essence which has been dissolved in 2 tablespoons hot water. Set
aside until ready to cook steak. Bring 2 cups water to boil. Drop in
marrow, cut in quarter-inch rounds. Bring to full boil, remove pan
from heat. Allow marrow to heat through about 4 minutes, then
remove with slotted spoon to small dish. Cream butter until soft.
Beat in 1 tablespoon lemon juice and parsley. Start wine simmering. Then in heavy frying pan, heat beef fat until it begins to smoke.
Sear each side 1 minute. Reduce heat and cook 5 minutes each side
for medium rare. Remove to heated platter. Remove simmering
wine from heat and beat in creamed butter, 1 tablespoon at a time.
Stir in poached marrow. Spoon small amount of sauce over steak
and pass the rest in hot sauceboat. Serve steak sliced. You may
substitute 2 teaspoons granulated beef bouillon in ½ cup of hot
water for meat essence.

BEEF RIB ROAST

7 or 8 rib roast
ice cream salt

water

Heat oven to 350°. In heavy roasting pan put ice cream salt 2 inches
thick on bottom of pan. Sprinkle with water. Put roast on salt and
pour salt around roast and sprinkle with water. Cover roast with 2
inches salt and sprinkle with water. Bake uncovered 13 minutes per
pound. Serves 8.

STRIB'S STROGANOFF

2 cups lean top sirloin of beef
¼ cup vegetable fat
½ pound fresh mushrooms
¼ cup minced onion
1 clove garlic, minced
½ teaspoon dried chervil
3 tablespoons flour

4 cups stock, divided
2 tablespoons caraway seeds
2 tablespoons minced parsley
2 tablespoons tomato paste
1 cup sour cream
salt, pepper

The beef for this stew should be cut into 1-inch squares, ¼-inch thick. Melt the fat. Add the beef. Sauté slowly, stirring frequently until the meat turns brown. Detach the mushroom caps from the stems, wash well. Cut the caps and stems into slices ¼-inch thick. Add mushrooms, onions, garlic and chervil to pot. Sauté 5 more minutes. Stir in the flour, mixing well. Add 3 cups stock. Stir well. Pound caraway seeds in mortar until full aroma is released. In a separate, small saucepan, combine 1 cup stock and the caraway seeds. Simmer 15 minutes. Strain the caraway broth and add to the stew. Discard seeds. Add parsley and simmer slowly until meat is very tender, about 2-2½ hours. Skim fat from surface. Stir in tomato paste. Turn off the flame and slowly stir in the sour cream. When ready to serve, reheat, bringing the gravy up to the boiling point but do not boil. Add salt and pepper to taste. Serves 4.

Mrs. Robert W. Stribling
(Ginger Meadows)

STUFFED BEEF ROAST BOURGUIGNONNE

1 (6 ounce) package long grain
  wild rice mix
1 (13¾ ounce) can beef broth
¼ cup burgundy
1 (4 ounce) can sliced
  mushrooms, drained

1 (3 pound) beef ribeye roast
beef broth
4 teaspoons cornstarch
⅓ cup burgundy
salt and pepper to taste

In saucepan, prepare wild rice according to package instructions, using the can of beef broth, ½ cup water and ¼ cup burgundy. Fluff rice with fork and fold in mushrooms. Meanwhile, cut 6 pockets crosswise in roast. Season with salt and pepper. Fill pockets with rice stuffing. Place on rack in shallow pan. Cover with foil. Bake at 350° 1½ hours, for a well done roast. Remove roast to warm platter. Meanwhile, to make a sauce, measure pan juices, adding additional broth to pan juices to equal ¾ cup. Combine cornstarch and remaining ⅓ cup burgundy. Add to pan juices. Cook and stir until mixture thickens. Season to taste with salt and pepper. Pass the sauce. Serves 6.

STEAK TACOS

1 pound sirloin tip, cut in small
  pieces
1 (4 ounce) can mushrooms or
  fresh mushrooms
1 medium onion, chopped
1 teaspon garlic salt
½ to 1 (10½ ounce) can beef
  bouillon
1 teaspoon soy sauce
dash Tabasco

1 teaspoon Worcestershire
  sauce
1 (3¼ ounce) can chopped ripe
  olives
2 tomatoes, chopped
shredded lettuce
1 cup grated Cheddar cheese
8 ounces taco sauce
1 (4½ ounce) package taco
  shells

Brown first 4 ingredients in frying pan. Add remaining ingredients
except olives and simmer for 15-20 minutes. Add olives and spoon
mixture into taco shells. Top with tomatoes, lettuce, cheese and
taco sauce. Serves 4-6.

Mrs. L. Rodney Crutchfield
(Coleman Crandall)

COLD MARINATED STEAK

1 sirloin, 1½ inch thick
  (3¼ pounds)
½ cup soy sauce
½ cup dry red wine
⅓ cup vegetable oil
⅓ cup sliced green onion
½ teaspoon salt
½ teaspoon dry mustard
½ teaspoon leaf basil

½ teaspoon thyme
¼ teaspoon pepper
Optional:
1 pint cherry tomatoes, halved
½ pound mushrooms,
  quartered
1 (10 ounce) package frozen
  artichokes, cooked and
  drained

Combine the ingredients. Pierce steak with fork and put in a non-
metal dish. Pour half the marinade mixture over the steak. Cover
and let marinate in refrigerator at least 2 hours. Turn 2 times, or
more if you leave for a longer time. Put vegetables in a separate
container and pour the remaining marinade over them. Next, drain
the steak, reserving the marinade. Pat with paper towel. Broil on
each side 8 to 12 minutes for this size steak to be rare. Brush cooled
steak with remaining marinade, slice thin and put in refrigerator. To
serve, place on platter and garnish with vegetables. Serves 8.

Mrs. Stuart C. Davis III
(Kay Lamar)

BAKED STUFFED FLANK STEAK

¼ cup butter
½ cup chopped onion
1 clove garlic, crushed
1½ cups cooked rice
½ cup chopped parsley
½ cup grated Parmesan cheese
½ teaspoon salt
¼ teaspoon pepper
2 pounds flank steak
1 clove garlic, whole

1 tablespoon soy sauce
¼ teaspoon pepper
2 tablespoons butter
½ cup condensed beef broth
½ cup water
½ tablespoon chopped ginger
  or
¾ teaspoon confectioners'
  sugar

Sauté onion and crushed garlic in ¼ cup butter until golden brown. Remove from heat. Stir in cooked rice, parsley, Parmesan cheese, salt and pepper. Heat oven to 350°. Wipe the flank steak with a damp paper towel and score with a knife. Rub the steak with the garlic clove. Brush with soy sauce that has been mixed with the pepper. Spread with 1 tablespoon butter. Place the rice stuffing over the steak leaving 1½ inches around the edge. Roll up, jelly roll fashion. Fasten the edges with skewers and tie in 2 or 3 places with twine. Spread the remaining tablespoon of butter over the surface of the steak. Place in a roasting pan. Dilute beef broth in water. Pour over the steak roll. Sprinkle ginger on top. Bake at 350° for 45-60 minutes, basting occasionally. Serves 4.

Mrs. Thomas H. Woodcock
(Lash Lawton)

STEAK AU POIVRE

peppercorns
2 steaks—filet, rib eye or strip
3 tablespoons butter
¼ cup plus 1 teaspoon cognac

½ cup cream
½ teaspoon Dijon mustard
salt

Crush peppercorns and with heel of hand, press them into room temperature steaks. Brown steaks in butter 3-4 minutes per side for medium rare steaks. Pour ¼ cup cognac over meat and flame. Remove steaks and keep warm. Add cream to pan. Stir with wooden spoon. Add 1 teaspoon cognac, Dijon mustard and salt to taste. Pour over steaks and serve at once. Serves 2.

Mrs. Thomas H. Lowe
(Maribeth Wills)

FILETS MIGNONS IN WINE SAUCE

4 filets mignons, 1-inch thick
1 tablespoon butter
1 pound fresh mushrooms,
  thinly sliced

1 tablespoon minced green
  onions and tops
½ cup red wine

SAUCE:
1 teaspoon melted butter
1 teaspoon flour

2 tablespoons red wine
1 tablespoon butter

Grill filets 4 minutes on each side. Set aside and keep warm. In the meantime, sauté mushrooms and onions in 1 tablespoon butter for 3 to 5 minutes. Stir in ½ cup red wine and cook until wine is reduced to half. Lower heat to simmer and keep warm. To make a sauce, combine the 1 teaspoon melted butter with 1 teaspoon flour. Add sauce to mushroom mixture, and stir constantly until sauce thickens. Add 2 tablespoons red wine and 1 tablespoon butter and stir until butter melts. Spoon sauce over filets. Serves 4.

Mrs. James A. Berg, Jr.
(Martha Williams)

DEE'S SPECIAL STUFFED FILETS MIGNONS
Fabulous

4 tablespoons butter, divided
4 (8 ounce) filets mignons
½ pound fresh lump crab meat
3 shallots, sliced
1 tablespoon chopped chives

2 cups beef stock
8 medium-sized mushrooms,
  sliced
1 cup Madeira wine

In 2 tablespoons butter, sauté shallots, add crab meat and chives. Set aside. Butterfly filets, flattening slightly. To one side, add crab meat filling and secure. Sauté filets in remaining 2 tablespoons butter until brown on both sides. Place in 450° preheated oven and cook to desired doneness. To skillet, add beef stock, sautéed mushrooms, and wine. Salt and pepper to taste. Allow liquid to reduce by one-half. Place filets on plate and top with mushroom sauce. Serves 4.

Mrs. Rufus Dorsey Sams, III
(Sidney Tucker)

BEEF WELLINGTON

¼ cup butter
4 (4 ounces each) beef
 tenderloin fillets
salt and pepper
1 clove garlic, crushed
½ cup chopped fresh
 mushrooms
1 small onion, minced
6 fresh mushrooms, sliced
3 tablespoons flour

½ cup red wine
1 (10½ ounce) can condensed
 beef broth
1 bay leaf
salt and pepper to taste
1 (4 ounce) can liver pâté
1 (11 ounce) package pastry for
 double crust pie
¼ cup butter
1 beaten egg

Melt butter. Season fillets with salt and pepper and rub with garlic. Sauté fillets in butter. Remove fillets and chill. Add chopped mushroom to skillet and sauté. Remove and chill. Add onion and sliced mushrooms to skillet. Stir in flour gradually. Add wine and broth. Add bay leaf and cook until sauce bubbles. Season to taste. Remove bay leaf. Set sauce aside. Mix chilled chopped mushrooms with liver pâté and spread over fillets and refrigerate. Prepare pastry, cutting extra ¼ cup butter into pastry. Mix with cold water, roll out and cut into four 6-inch squares. Brush dough with beaten egg and place fillets (pâté side down) on pastry squares. Fold over and seal edges with egg. Place fillets on greased baking sheet, seam edge down. Brush tops with beaten egg. Bake at 425° for 20 minutes or until crust is brown. Serves 4.

SUKIYAKI

1 pound lean round steak,
 sliced
2 tablespoons fat
1 (4 ounce) can mushrooms,
 stems and pieces
1 bunch green onions, sliced
3 stalks celery, sliced

2 large onions, sliced
1 (8 ounce) can bamboo shoots
3 tablespoons sugar
½ cup soy sauce
1 chicken bouillon cube
½ cup hot water
3 cups hot cooked rice

Have butcher cut round steak diagonally in very thin slices. Brown meat well in fat. Add mushrooms, green onions, celery, sliced onions, bamboo shoots, sugar, bouillon cube, water and soy sauce. Stir to mix well. Cover and cook 1 hour over low heat. Serve over hot rice with additional soy sauce. Serves 6.

Mrs. Henry T. Clay
(Cater Snow)

BEEF WITH CARROT SAUCE
Family Dish

4 pounds lean roast	1 medium green pepper
salt and pepper to taste	1 small tomato, sliced
4 slices bacon, chopped	4 bay leaves
3 tablespoons oil	2 tablespoons vinegar
1 tablespoon sugar	3 tablespoons sour cream
1 medium onion, sliced	1 tablespoon flour
4-6 large carrots, sliced	pinch garlic (optional)

Salt and pepper meat. Put chopped bacon in frying pan; add oil and fry until golden. Add meat to pan and brown on all sides. Pour sugar in oil and brown. Add vegetables and bay leaves. Cover and simmer until 2 inches liquid have formed in pot. Pour vinegar over meat and simmer until tender. Take out meat and bay leaves. Put liquid and vegetables in processor and blend until smooth. Mix with sour cream and flour. Return to heat; bring to boil and pour sauce over sliced meat and serve. Serves 6.

BOLICHI (STUFFED EYE OF THE ROUND)

3-4 pounds eye of round roast, plus piece of suet	salt and pepper
1 chorizo sausage or Keilbasa polish sausage (or just under ½ pound)	tomato sauce (approximately ½ can or to consistency for stuffing)
1 medium slice cured ham	paprika
1 clove garlic, minced	3 tablespoons bacon drippings
1 medium mild onion, finely chopped	1 (10½ ounce) can consommé
½ green pepper, finely chopped	1 bay leaf
	4 whole cloves

Ask butcher to cut lengthwise pocket in center of beef, leaving opposite end closed. Grind together sausage and ham. Mix sausage, ham, garlic, onion, bell pepper and tomato sauce and stuff roast. Pack well but not too tightly. Secure open end with skewers or wire. Salt and pepper roast and sprinkle generously with paprika. Brown well in drippings over medium heat. Turn often to get even browning. When browned, add consommé, bay leaf and cloves to liquid. Cover and bake at 325°. Baste occasionally and cook about 3 hours or until meat is fork tender. Slice in thick servings and pass sauce. Serves 8-10.

Mrs. Toof A. Boone, Jr.
(Sylvia Wyllys)

CORNED BEEF-SAUERKRAUT CASSEROLE

1 ¾ cups sauerkraut, drained
½ pound thinly sliced corned
  beef
2 cups shredded Swiss cheese
3-5 tablespoons Thousand
  Island dressing
2 cups canned tomatoes

2 tablespoons butter or
  margaine
½ cup butter or margarine
1 cup crumbled rye wafers,
  seasoned
¼ - ½ tablespoon caraway seed

Preheat oven to 425°. Thinly layer sauerkraut in bottom of a greased casserole. Top with corned beef and Swiss cheese. Top with dressing and add tomatoes. Dot with 2 tablespoons butter or margarine. Melt ½ cup butter or margarine in saucepan. Add crumbled wafers and sauté. Add caraway seeds. Spread on top of casserole. Bake at 425° for 30 minutes.

Mrs. Rufus Dorsey Sams, III
(Sidney Tucker)

BEEF BRISKET

first cut of brisket, boneless (8
  ounces per person)
1 (2 ounce) package dry onion
  soup

3 tablespoons water
1 cup brown sugar
2 cups red wine
2-3 slices raw onion

Put brisket in Dutch oven and sprinkle with dry onion soup and 3 tablespoons water. Bake uncovered in 300° oven for 2 hours. Mix brown sugar and red wine. Pour over meat and add slices of onion. Cover and cook 2 more hours at 300°. Let cool and store in refrigerator. Before serving, skim all the fat from top and slice very thin. Put in a baking dish with sauce and reheat for 30-45 minutes or until hot. Serve over rice.

Mrs. Rush A. Peace
(Judy Robertson)

HORSERADISH CREAM
Great with Roast Beef

½ cup whipping cream
¼ cup prepared horseradish

1 tablespoon vinegar
½ teaspoon salt

Whip cream and add remaining ingredients. Serves 6-8.

Mrs. William A. Williams
(Ann Warlick)

CALF'S LIVER IN RED WINE

1 calf's liver, sliced
salt and pepper to taste
bacon, uncooked
2 tablespoons butter
1 cup sliced onion
½ cup sliced carrots
1 bay leaf
1 stalk celery

1 clove garlic, minced
parsley
thyme to taste
1 tablespoon flour
2 tablespoons fat
2 cups red wine
1½ cups water

Sauté carrots, onion, and celery in melted butter. Add parsley, thyme, bay leaf, and garlic. Place vegetable mixture in a casserole and sprinkle with 1 tablespoon flour. Salt and pepper liver, brown in 2 tablespoons fat. Place liver on top of vegetables in casserole and top each slice with a strip of bacon. Add wine and water to cover liver. Cover casserole and cook at 350° for 3 hours. Serve sauce over liver. Serves 4-6.

ROUND-UP CHILI
Serve on cold evening

2 tablespoons vegetable oil
3 pounds boneless chuck in
  1-inch cubes
2 garlic cloves, chopped
4 tablespoons chili powder
2 teaspoons ground cumin
3 tablespoons flour
1½ tablespoons ground
  oregano
2 (13¾ ounce) cans beef broth

1½ teaspoons salt
½ teaspoon pepper
1 (15½ ounce) can pinto beans,
  drained
2 ounces canned, chopped
  green chiles
4 cups cooked rice
1 (8 ounce) carton sour cream
2 limes, cut in wedges

Heat oil in heavy 4-quart pan over medium heat. Add beef, stirring frequently with a wooden spoon until brown. Lower heat and stir in garlic. Combine chili powder, cumin, and flour. Sprinkle meat with chili mixture, stirring until meat is coated. Crumble oregano over meat. Add broth and stir until liquid is well blended. Add salt and pepper. Bring to a boil stirring occasionally. Reduce heat and simmer 2 hours. Cool thoroughly, cover, refrigerate overnight. Reheat chili slowly and add beans and green chiles. Place cooked rice in serving bowls. Spoon chili mixture over rice and add 1 tablespoon sour cream on top of each serving. Garnish with lime wedges or squeeze over each chili portion. Pass French bread. Serves 8-10.

POLLY BERGEN'S CHILI

6 medium onions,
  finely chopped
6 medium green peppers,
  finely chopped
2 cloves garlic, minced
cooking oil
4 pounds ground round or
  chuck
4 (16 ounce) cans Italian-style
  tomatoes
4 (16 ounce) cans kidney
  beans, drained

2 (6 ounce) cans tomato paste
1 cup water
4 teaspoons salt
dash of pepper
1 teaspoon red wine vinegar
3 whole cloves
2 bay leaves
2 tablespoons chili powder or
  to taste
4 drops Tabasco
sugar

In a a large skillet, brown onions, peppers, and garlic in oil until golden. In a separate skillet, brown ground meat in batches. Separate meat with a fork and cook until all meat is browned. Drain off accumulated oil. Place onion, green pepper, garlic, and meat in a large pot. Add tomatoes, kidney beans, tomato paste, water, salt and pepper, vinegar, cloves, bay leaves, chili powder and Tabasco sauce. Cover and simmer over low heat for 1 hour. Add sugar to taste. Simmer uncovered for another hour. Remove cloves and bay leaves before serving. Serves 20.

Leftover idea: Mix 3 parts chili to 2 parts rice in a casserole. Cover with Parmesan cheese and bake in 350° oven for 45 minutes.

Mrs. Andrew W. Young
(Pamela Watkins)

BROWN SAUCE

½ cup beef fat
1 carrot, sliced
1½ cups diced onion
⅓ cup flour
2 quarts beef broth

1 bay leaf
2 sprigs parsley
¼ teaspoon thyme
3 tablespoons canned tomato
  sauce

Melt the fat in a heavy saucepan. Sauté the carrot and onion until browned. Sprinkle with the flour and stir until dark brown. Slowly add the broth, stirring constantly to boiling point. Add bay leaf, parsley and thyme. Cook over low heat 2 hours. Mix in the tomato sauce and cook 1 hour longer. Strain and season to taste. Use as a base for other sauces. Yields 5 cups.

BEEF CASSEROLE
A Family Favorite

1 pound ground beef
butter
1 (16 ounce) can tomato sauce
1 (8 ounce) package noodles
1 (3 ounce) package cream
  cheese

1 (8 ounce) carton sour cream
6 spring onions, chopped
  (optional)
grated Cheddar cheese

Brown beef in butter, add tomato sauce and simmer together for 2 minutes. Cook noodles according to directions on package until tender. Drain. While piping hot, mix in cream cheese, sour cream and onions. In a 2½-quart greased casserole, put 1 layer of noodle mixture, then 1 layer of meat mixture. Repeat layers, ending with a layer of noodles on top. Sprinkle with grated cheese. Bake in 350° oven for 30 minutes. Serves 6-8.

Mrs. Thomas F. Richardson
(Mary Anne Berg)

BASIC SPAGHETTI
Freezes well

1½ pounds ground round
3 tablespoons olive oil
1 large green pepper, chopped
1 large onion, chopped
3 tablespoons Worcestershire
  sauce
1(16 ounce) can tomatoes
2 (8 ounce) cans tomato sauce,
  plus 2 cans water
1 (8 ounce) can mushroom
  pieces, with juice

1 (10¾ ounce) can cream of
  mushroom soup
1 teaspoon chili powder
4 cloves garlic, crushed
¼ teaspoon oregano
1 teaspoon salt
⅛ teaspoon pepper
1 (8 ounce) package thin
  spaghetti
½ pound grated sharp cheese

Brown beef in olive oil. Add green pepper and onion, cooking until tender. Add all other ingredients except spaghetti and cheese. Cook slowly for 30 minutes. Cook spaghetti for a short time, rinse well and add to beef mixture. Put in 3-quart casserole dish. Sprinkle with cheese. Cover with foil and bake for 30 minutes at 350°. Remove foil to brown cheese under broiler before serving. Serves 8-10.

Mrs. Donald Beaty
(Ann Chandler)

SPAGHETTI

1 large onion, chopped
1 green pepper, chopped
1 stalk celery, chopped
1 clove garlic, mashed
1½ pounds ground meat
¼ cup butter or margarine
1 (1 pound 12 ounce) can
  tomatoes
1 (6 ounce) can tomato paste
1 teaspoon chili powder
1 teaspoon chopped parsley
1 clove
¼ teaspoon dry mustard

1½ teaspoons salt
cayenne to taste
½ teaspoon vinegar
½ cup red wine (optional)
½ grated carrot
1 (4 ounce) can button
  mushrooms or ¼ pound
  fresh sliced mushrooms
1 (2 ounce) bottle pimiento
  stuffed olives, halved
1 cup grated sharp cheese
  (optional)
1 package vermicelli

Brown onion, green pepper, celery and garlic in butter until just golden; add meat and lightly brown. Add all ingredients except mushrooms, olives, cheese and vermicelli. Cook slowly, being careful not to let burn, about 3 hours. Just before serving, add mushrooms, olives and cheese. Cook vermicelli according to directions. Either mix noodles with sauce and serve in tureen or put noodles on platter and cover with sauce. Serves 6-8.

Mrs. Andrew W. Young
(Pamela Watkins)

BRUNSWICK STEW

4-5 pound hen, cooked and
  ground, bones discarded
3-4 pound piece of lean pork,
  cooked and ground
2 (10¾ ounce) cans of
  tomatoes
⅔ cup Worcestershire sauce
1 (14 ounce) small bottle of
  catsup

3 large onions, chopped
6 large Irish potatoes,
  peeled and cubed
salt, pepper, chili powder to
  taste
1 (17 ounce) can whole kernel
  corn
1 (17 ounce) can English peas
  (optional)

Cook meats until they fall off the bone. Remove bones and save the broth. Grind meat until fine and add to potatoes and onions. Add all ingredients to the broth. Cook until thickened and serve.

Mrs. Marion H. Liles, Jr.
(Catharine Burns)

HAMBURGERS ROWNEY
A man's favorite topped with chutney

1½ pounds ground beef
1 egg, slightly beaten
2 tablespoons melted butter
⅔ cup bread crumbs
1 teaspoon salt
1 (3 ounce) package cream
  cheese, softened

1 tablespoon crumbled
  bleu cheese
1 teaspoon dry mustard
1 teaspoon horseradish
12 slices bacon, slightly
  cooked
salt and pepper

Combine beef, egg, butter, bread crumbs, and salt. Shape into 12 thin patties, using ⅓ cup mixture for each. Combine cheeses, mustard and horseradish. Top 6 patties with cheese leaving ½-inch margin for sealing. Cover with remaining patties and seal edges. Wrap 2 strips bacon around edges and secure with toothpicks. Broil 3 inches from heat 6-8 minutes. Season with salt and pepper. Turn and broil 4-6 minutes more. Season again. Try chutney to top hamburgers. Serves 6.

Mrs. Edgar Y. Mallary, III
(Lloyd Washington)

GROUND BEEF STROGANOFF

¼ cup margarine
¼ cup onion, chopped
1 clove garlic, chopped
2 (3-ounce) cans sliced
  mushrooms
1 pound ground beef
3 tablespoons lemon juice

3 tablespoons burgundy wine
1 (10½-ounce) can condensed
  beef consommé
1 teaspoon salt
¼ teaspoon pepper
¼ pound noodles
1 cup sour cream

Sauté mushrooms, garlic and onions in margarine. Add beef and cook until medium rare. Drain grease. Stir in lemon juice, burgundy, consommé, salt and pepper. Simmer for 15 minutes, uncovered. Stir in cooked noodles. Add sour cream prior to serving. Serves 6.

Mrs. John F. Rogers, Jr.
(Laura Bush)

HINTS

It requires 10 more minutes cooking time per pound for a boned or rolled roast than for one cooked with bones.

CATHERINE'S EVERYDAY MEAT LOAF

⅔ cup dry Herbal Pepperidge
  Farm bread crumbs
1 cup milk
1½ pounds ground beef
2 slightly beaten eggs

¼ cup grated onion
1 teaspoon salt
⅛ teaspoon pepper
½ teaspoon sage

SAUCE:
9 tablespoons brown sugar
¾ cup catsup

¾ teaspoon nutmeg
3 teaspoons dry mustard

Soak bread crumbs in milk. Add ground beef, eggs, onion and seasonings. Mix well. Place in greased loaf pan. Mix all sauce ingredients well, spreading one-third of sauce over top. Bake at 350° for 45 minutes to 1 hour. Don't overcook. Heat remaining sauce and serve with meat loaf. Serves 6.

Mrs. Grady A. Smith
(Anna Newton)

DELUXE MEAT LOAF

2 medium stalks celery,
  chopped
1 medium onion, minced
1 medium carrot, minced
2 strips bacon, finely diced
1 (4 ounce) can mushrooms,
  diced
1 medium green pepper, minced
½ teaspoon each of Ac'cent,
  celery salt, dry mustard and
  salt

2 tablespoons horseradish
¼ teaspoon each of garlic
  powder and pepper
1 tablespoon soy sauce
1 tablespoon Worcestershire
  sauce
1 cup milk
2 eggs
1 cup dry bread crumbs
1 pound lean ground chuck
1 (8 ounce) can tomato sauce

Combine all ingredients except beef and tomato sauce and mix well; let stand 30 minutes to 1 hour. Add beef, mix thoroughly. Spoon in 8 x 5 x 3-inch loaf pan. Bake at 350° for 1 hour and 15 minutes. Top with tomato sauce for last 15 minutes of baking time. Serves 6.

Mrs. Leo B. Huckabee
(Jane Odom)

PASTEL DE CHOCLO
Different and superb

¼ cup seedless raisins
5 tablespoons olive oil
2 pounds ground beef (round or sirloin)
4 cups coarsely chopped onion
¼ teaspoon finely chopped garlic
1 dried "Lontaka" chili, seeded and coarsely crushed with mortar and pastle
or
2 crumbled "Sequin" chili
2 teaspoons ground cumin seeds

1 teaspoon paprika
1½ teaspoons salt
¼ teaspoon freshly ground black pepper
½ cup sliced, pitted dark olives
3-3½ pound chicken, cut into 6-8 pieces
2 cups fresh kernel corn or 2 cups frozen corn, thawed
1 tablespoon milk
1 tablespoon sugar
2 chopped eggs

Soak raisins in ½ cup hot water for at least 10 minutes. In heavy 10-12 inch skillet, heat 2 tablespoons oil over high heat until a light haze forms above it. Reduce to moderate heat and add ground beef. Brown well, stirring with fork to break up large pieces. Stir in onions, garlic, raisins, chili, cumin, paprika, salt and pepper. Reduce heat to low. Cook uncovered 15 minutes, stirring occasionally. Transfer to a 4-quart casserole. Spread olives evenly over meat mixture. In a 10-12 inch skillet, heat 2 tablespoons oil over high heat, coating bottom evenly. Add chicken and brown on all sides quickly. Regulate heat to prevent burning. Cover and cook on low heat for 25 minutes. Arrange pieces on top of ground beef in casserole. Preheat oven to 350°. Place the corn and milk in blender or food processor and purée. Heat remaining 1 tablespoon of oil in small, heavy skillet and cook corn over moderate heat for 5 minutes, stirring constantly and regulating heat so it does not burn. The finished purée should have the consistency of thick cereal. Add chopped eggs over chicken. Pour corn purée over eggs in casserole and spread evenly to the sides of the dish. Sprinkle the top with sugar. Bake in the middle of oven for 30 minutes, then increase heat to 450° and bake for 10 minutes longer, or until top is golden brown. Serve hot from casserole. Serves 6-8.

Mrs. Gary C. Ertel
(Holly Akre)

HINTS

Casseroles containing sour cream should be heated in an oven no hotter than 325°. Sour cream curdles over high heat.

BEST MANICOTTI

FILLING:

½ cup butter
1 clove garlic, mashed
½ cup chopped onion
1 pound ground beef
1 (10 ounce) package frozen
chopped spinach, thawed
and drained

½ cup cottage cheese
2 eggs
1½ teaspoon Jane's crazy salt
12 manicotti shells, cooked

SAUCE I:

¼ cup butter, melted
¼ cup flour

2 chicken bouillon cubes
1½ cups milk
parsley

SAUCE II:

1 (15½ ounce) jar Ragu
spaghetti sauce with
mushrooms

2-2½ teaspoons sweet basil
grated Parmesan cheese

Filling: Sauté garlic and onion in butter. Add ground beef and brown. Remove from heat and add spinach, cottage cheese, eggs and crazy salt. Set aside. In the meantime, cook 12 manicotti shells. Drain and line a greased 3-quart casserole with shells. Fill each shell with ¼ cup filling. *Sauce I:* Blend flour and bouillon with melted butter. Stir in milk, parsley and heat mixture to boiling stirring constantly. Pour Sauce I over filled shells. Set aside. *Sauce II:* Mix sauce, pour over shells, sprinkle with Parmesan and bake at 350° for 30 minutes or until mixture is piping hot. Serves 6.

BEEF FILLETS WITH CHICKEN LIVER SAUCE

8 beef fillets, ¼-inch thick
4 tablespoons butter, divided
½ pound chicken livers
1 teaspoon salt
¼ teaspoon pepper

1 bay leaf
¼ teaspoon thyme
¼ cup dry sherry
¼ cup beef broth
2 tablespoons brandy

Cut fillets into strips. Melt 2 tablespoons butter and sauté livers. Add salt, pepper, bay leaf and thyme and sauté for 2 minutes. Discard the bay leaf and drain off liquid. Put livers, sherry and broth in the blender and purée. Return to the skillet and keep warm while preparing the beef. Melt remaining 2 tablespoons butter in another skillet and sauté fillets. Heat cognac and pour over beef. Carefully ignite. Transfer meat to a preheated serving dish and pour liver sauce over beef. Serves 6-8.

LASAGNE

1½ pounds lean ground beef or chuck
1 (28 ounce) can whole tomatoes
1 (12 ounce) can tomato paste
2 teaspoons garlic salt
1½ teaspoons oregano leaves
1 teaspoon basil leaves
olive oil
grated Cheddar cheese
3 medium onions, chopped
1 tablespoon chopped green pepper
2 cloves garlic, minced
dash Worcestershire sauce
cayenne pepper
2 cups creamed cottage cheese
½ cup grated Parmesan cheese
12 ounces shredded Mozzarella
1 (16 ounce) package lasagne noodles, cooked with olive oil and drained well

Preheat Dutch oven or large skillet over medium heat for 2 to 3 minutes. Add ground beef and brown about 5-7 minutes. Drain off fat. To browned beef, add tomatoes, broken up with fork. Stir in tomato paste, garlic salt, oregano leaves and basil leaves as well as onions, green pepper, Worcestershire sauce and minced garlic. Heat to boiling, stirring occasionally. Reduce heat to low and simmer uncovered for 20 to 30 minutes, or until mixture is consistency of spaghetti sauce. In small bowl, combine cottage cheese, and ½ cup Parmesan cheese. Set aside 1 cup of meat sauce and ½ cup Mozzarella. In ungreased lasagne pan, alternate layers of one-third each noodles, remaining meat sauce, remaining Mozzarella and cottage cheese. Start each layer with noodles. Spread reserved meat sauce over top. Sprinkle top with ½ cup Parmesan, reserved Mozzarella, and Cheddar cheese. Bake in preheated 350° oven, uncovered for 45 minutes. Let stand 15 minutes before cutting. Serves 8-10.

Mrs. Neil A. Struby
(Hazel Burns)

SAUCE CHASSEUR

2 tablespoons olive oil
½ pound mushrooms, sliced
4 tablespoons minced onion
½ cup dry white wine
2 tablespoons tomato paste
1½ cups Brown Sauce (See Index)
¼ teaspoon pepper
1 tablespoon butter
1 tablespoon minced parsley

Heat the oil in a saucepan. Sauté the mushrooms 5 minutes. Add onion and sauté 2 minutes. Mix in the wine and cook over low heat until reduced to half. Stir in tomato paste, brown sauce and pepper. Cook 5 minutes. Blend in butter and parsley. Serve with veal or beef. Yields 1½ cups.

HUNTER-STYLE BEEF GOULASH WITH NOODLES

2 pounds cubed stewing beef
4 tablespoons oil
1 cup thinly sliced onion
1 cup thinly sliced celery
1 cup green pepper strips
1 clove garlic, crushed
3 teaspoons paprika
1½ teaspoons salt

½ teaspoon pepper
1 bay leaf
2 tablespoons tomato paste
1 (10½ ounce) can undiluted
  beef bouillon
1 cup thinly sliced carrots
½ cup sour cream
egg noodles

In a deep, covered skillet, brown the beef in the oil. Remove the meat and, in the same oil, sauté for about 3 minutes the onion, celery, green pepper and garlic. Then stir in the paprika, salt, pepper, bay leaf, tomato paste, bouillon and carrots. Bring liquid to a boil, add the meat, reduce the heat and simmer covered 1½ to 2 hours or until the meat is quite tender. Just before serving time, heat thoroughly, keeping heat low while stirring in the sour cream. Serve over egg noodles. Serves 6.

Mrs. Charles F. Causey
(Alice Jackson)

CHEESEBURGER PIE
Children love it!

1 unbaked 9-inch pie shell
1 pound ground beef
¼ cup chopped onion
¼ teaspoon oregano
¼ teaspoon pepper

1 teaspoon salt
¼ cup chili sauce
¼ cup dry bread crumbs
1 (8 ounce) can tomato sauce

CHEESE TOPPING:
1 beaten egg
½ teaspoon each salt, dry
  mustard and Worcestershire
  sauce

¼ cup milk
2 cups grated cheese

Brown onion and ground beef. Add remaining ingredients. Mix well and pour into an unbaked pie shell. Mix topping ingredients well and spread over mixture. Bake at 425° until crust is golden and topping is bubbly. Cut into wedges to serve. Serves 6.

Mrs. William H. Greer, Jr.
(Kay Smith)

JOMSETA

5 small white onions, sliced
1 green pepper, sliced
2½ tablespoons margarine
2 pounds ground meat
¼ cup margarine
salt and pepper to taste
1 (10¾ ounce) can tomato
  soup
1 can water
1 (8 ounce) package broad
  noodles

1 (¾ ounce) can B 'n B
  mushrooms, reserving juice
1 (4 ounce) can ripe olives,
  sliced
½ cup chopped pecans
2 teaspoons Worcestershire
  sauce
2 cups grated cheese

Cook onions and pepper in 2½ tablespoons margarine until tender. Brown meat in ¼ cup margarine; salt and pepper to taste. Add soup, water and onion-pepper mixture and simmer slowly for about 1 hour. Cook noodles in salted water until tender. In large bowl, break up noodles. Add olives, nuts, meat mixture, mushrooms and 2 teaspoons Worcestershire sauce. Salt and pepper if needed. Pour into casseroles and bake at 350° until bubbly. Add grated cheese when mixture is thoroughly heated and bake until cheese melts. Makes 2 (1½-quart) casseroles. The casseroles can be frozen before adding grated cheese. Serves 10-12.

Mrs. Cubbedge Snow, Sr.
(Frances Cater)

ITALIAN CASSEROLE

1 pound ground chuck
salt and pepper to taste
2 tablespoons salad oil
1 medium eggplant, unpeeled,
  sliced
⅓ cup flour

¼ cup olive oil
2 (8 ounce) cans tomato sauce
½ teaspoon oregano
1 tablespoon Parmesan cheese
1 cup shredded Cheddar
  cheese

Season ground chuck with salt and pepper; shape into 6 patties. Brown patties in hot salad oil. Slice unpeeled eggplant into thick slices. Season with salt and pepper, coat with flour, and brown in olive oil. Place cooked eggplant slices in shallow 8 x 12-inch baking dish. Top each with a browned meat patty. Cover with tomato sauce. Sprinkle oregano and Parmesan cheese over all. Top with shredded Cheddar cheese. Bake at 300° for 35 minutes. Serves 6.

Mrs. Walker P. Johnson, Jr.
(Katherine Wilson)

SWEET-SOUR BEEF BALLS
WITH PINEAPPLE AND PEPPERS

1 pound ground beef	3 tablespoons cornstarch
1 egg	1 tablespoon soy sauce
1 teaspoon cornstarch	3 tablespoons vinegar
1 teaspoon salt	6 tablespoons water
2 tablespoons onion	½ cup sugar
dash of pepper	6 slices pineapple
1 tablespoon oil	3 large green peppers, cut in
1 cup pineapple juice	strips

Mix ground beef, egg, cornstarch, salt, onion and pepper. Form into small balls. Brown in small amount of oil and drain. To 1 tablespoon oil, add pineapple juice and cook over low heat a few minutes. Add mixture of cornstarch, soy sauce, vinegar, water and sugar. Cook until juice thickens, stirring constantly. Add meat balls, pineapple slices, and green pepper strips. Heat thoroughly. Serve hot with brown rice or noodles. Serves 6.

Mrs. Robert W. McAllister
(Anne Katherine Donnelly)

MARINADE SAUCE
Men love it

1½ cups salad oil	2 tablespoons dry mustard
¼ cup Worcestershire sauce	1 tablespoon black pepper
2¼ teaspoons salt	1½ teaspoons parsley flakes
½ cup vinegar	⅓ cup lemon juice
2 teaspoons garlic salt	1 teaspoon Ac'cent
¾ cup soy sauce	

Measure ingredients into a blender jar. Blend until contents are thoroughly mixed. The ingredients may be mixed in a shaker jar if no blender is available. Place steaks in a glass container. Pour sauce over steaks. Cover container and place in refrigerator 4-6 hours. Remove steak from sauce and cook on grill.

Mrs. Guy B. Eberhardt
(Melanie Roberts)

HINTS

Meat loaf will not stick to its pan if you put a strip of bacon at the bottom of the pan before placing meat loaf mixture in pan.

OSSO BUCCO BRAISED BEEF OR VEAL SHANKS

4 tablespoons butter
1½ cups chopped onion
½ cup chopped carrots
½ cup chopped celery
1 teaspoon garlic
6-7 pounds beef or veal shank or shin sawed—not chopped—into pieces, each 2½-inches long, and tied with string so meat will not fall off bone. (Be sure plenty of meat is on bone when purchased from butcher.)
salt
pepper

flour
½ cup olive oil
1 cup dry white wine
½ teaspoon dried basil
¾ cup beef or chicken stock
½ teaspoon dried thyme
3 cups drained whole canned tomatoes, chopped
6 sprigs parsley
2 bay leaves
Gremolata: 1 tablespoon grated lemon peel, 1 teaspoon chopped garlic, 3 tablespoons chopped parsley

Choose a heavy casserole or Dutch oven that has a tight cover and is just large enough to hold pieces of beef or veal shank standing up in 1 layer. Melt butter over moderate heat and when melted, add chopped onion, carrots, celery, and garlic. Cook stirring occasionally for 10-15 minutes. Remove from heat. Season meat-bones with salt and pepper, and then roll in flour. Shake off excess. In a heavy 10-12 inch skillet, heat 6 tablespoons olive oil until a haze forms over it. Brown meat-bones over moderately high heat 4 or 5 pieces at a time, adding more oil as needed. Transfer meat-bones to the casserole and stand side by side on top of vegetables. Preheat oven to 350°. Discard almost all fat from skillet. Pour in wine and boil over high heat until reduced to about ½ cup. Stir in basil, stock, thyme, tomatoes, parsley sprigs, and bay leaves and bring to a boil. Pour over meat-bones. Liquid should come halfway up the side of veal. Add more stock if necessary. Bring to boil on top of stove. Transfer to oven, cover and bake in lower third of oven. Cook 1 hour and 15 minutes. (Test meat for tenderness.) Remove casserole from oven when meat is tender and increase temperature to 450°. Transfer meat-bones to ovenproof platter. Place platter in top third of oven and bake 5-10 minutes until deep brown and glazed. Meanwhile, strain contents of casserole in sieve into a 2-3 quart saucepan. Boil the liquid over high heat stirring frequently until reduced to half original quantity. Pour reduced sauce over meat-bones and sprinkle top with Gremolata, which has been mixed together. Osso Bucco is traditionally served with rice or plain buttered noodles. Serves 6-8.

SHISH KEBAB WITH WILD RICE

1 (6 ounce) package long grain
  and wild rice
1 cup mayonnaise, divided
2 cups fresh mushroom slices
1 pound lamb, cut in 1½-inch
  cubes
1 cup cherry tomatoes

½ cup green pepper chunks
2 tablespoons chopped parsley
2 tablespoons chopped onion
1 tablespoon milk
¼ teaspoon salt
⅛ teaspoon garlic powder
⅛ teaspoon pepper

Prepare rice according to package directions, omitting margarine. Combine rice, ½ cup mayonnaise and mushrooms. Spoon into a 10 x 6-inch baking dish. Put meat, tomatoes and green peppers on skewers. Place skewers on top of rice. Bake at 350° for 40 minutes, turning kebabs once. Combine remaining ½ cup mayonnaise with last 6 ingredients and mix well. Serve sauce over kebabs. Serves 4.

Marinated beef cubes may be used instead of lamb. Also marinate the mushroom slices for extra flavor.

Mrs. Charles J. Cartwright
(Stella Blum)

VEAL CORDON BLEU

4 veal fillets, ⅛-inch thick
salt and pepper
Swiss cheese, thinly sliced
ham, very thinly sliced
flour

1 egg
Old London bread crumbs
6 tablespoons butter or
  margarine

Salt and pepper veal on both sides after pounding thin. Put slice of ham and Swiss cheese in each fillet and fold over. Dip in flour, egg and then bread crumbs. Refrigerate for at least 15 minutes before frying. Fry in butter or margarine about 4 or 5 minutes on each side. Serves 4.

Mrs. Edward P. Harper
(Suzanne Jones)

HINTS

When using food processor to shred cheese, use light pressure. Soft cheeses should be chilled. Hard cheeses are best processed at room temperature.

As an accompaniment to ham, spoon Major Grey's Chutney into a drained peach half. Broil 3-5 minutes.

VEAL PARMESAN

6 small, thin slices of veal
  (fresh or frozen)
¼ cup margarine

½ cup bread crumbs
½ cup grated Parmesan cheese
salt and pepper

Melt margarine. Pound each slice of veal on both sides with wooden hammer and season with salt and pepper. Mix bread crumbs and cheese in a small bowl. Dip each piece of veal in melted butter, then coat with cheese mixture. Place on ungreased shallow pan. Bake 30 minutes in 300° oven. Serves 4.

Mrs. Donald D. Comer
(Harriet Fincher)

POLISH LEG OF VEAL IN TOMATO SAUCE

leg of veal, boned and tied
2½ teaspoons salt
½ teaspoon freshly ground
  black pepper
2 tablespoons olive oil
1 cup thinly sliced onion

2 cloves garlic, minced
1 (29 ounce) can tomatoes,
  drained
1 teaspoon thyme
3 tablespoons minced parsley

Rub the veal with the salt and pepper. Heat the oil in a Dutch oven or heavy saucepan and brown the veal on all sides. Add the onion and garlic; cook until browned. Add the tomatoes and thyme. Cover and cook over low heat 2½ hours or until tender. Skim the fat from the gravy and stir in the parsley. Remove the strings, slice the veal, and serve the gravy in a sauceboat. Serves 8-10.

SPARERIBS WITH BOURBON

1 cup catsup
⅓ cup bourbon
¼ cup molasses
¼ cup vinegar
1 tablespoon lemon juice
1 tablespoon Worcestershire
  sauce

2 teaspoons soy sauce
2 teaspoons dry mustard
¼ teaspoon pepper
1 clove garlic, crushed
3 pounds lean spareribs

Several hours before baking, mix together all ingredients except ribs. Set aside. Place ribs in roasting pan and bake at 425° for 30 minutes. Pour off excess fat. Pour half of sauce over ribs. Bake at 325° for 45 minutes. Pour remaining sauce over ribs. Bake 45 more minutes. Serves 4.

NIW-GOO-YOK (SWEET AND SOUR PORK)

3 large green peppers
¾ cup oil
1 clove garlic
1 teaspoon salt
1 egg
2 tablespoons flour
½ teaspoon salt
1 pound lean pork, cubed
⅓ cup chicken broth

4 slices canned pineapple,
 cut up
1 tablespoon cornstarch
2 teaspoons soy sauce
¼ cup vinegar
¼ cup pineapple juice
¼ cup sugar
⅔ cup chicken stock

Cut each green pepper into 6 pieces. Cook in boiling water until almost tender, about 8 minutes. In 10-inch heavy frying pan, heat ¾ cup oil, garlic clove and 1 teaspoon salt. Make a batter by beating together 1 egg, 2 tablespoons flour and ½ teaspoon salt. Cut 1 pound lean pork into ½-inch cubes. Pour batter over pork and mix to coat each piece. Drop one piece at a time into hot oil and brown until golden. Pour out all but 1 tablespoon of oil, add ⅓ cup chicken stock and 4 slices pineapple, cut into 6 pieces each. Add the green pepper and pork. Cover and cook over low heat for 10 minutes. Blend cornstarch, soy sauce, vinegar, pineapple juice, sugar and chicken stock. Add to pork, pineapple, green pepper, stirring until thickened and hot, about 5 minutes. Serve over rice. Serves 4.

PORK CHOPS ITALIANO

8 pork chops
1 pound small fresh
 mushrooms
2 tablespoons oil
2 medium onions, chopped
1 clove garlic
4 large bell pepper strips

4 (8 ounce) cans tomato sauce
2 teaspoons salt
½ teaspoon pepper
1 bay leaf
2 tablespoons lemon juice
¼ teaspoon sage

Trim chops, salt and pepper, and brown. Drain fat. Place chops in large casserole, arranging mushrooms around chops. In large skillet, sauté onions, garlic and green peppers in oil until golden. Add tomato sauce, salt, pepper, bay leaf, lemon juice and sage. Simmer covered until vegetables are almost fork tender. Pour sauce over chops and add mushrooms. Cover and bake at 350° for 2 hours. Serves 8.

Mrs. D. Clark Ballard
(Nancy Johnson)

SAUSAGE CASSEROLE

1 bell pepper, diced
1 large onion, chopped
1 cup celery, diced
2-3 tablespoons olive oil
2 pounds hot or milk sausage
1 cup raw rice

4½ cups water
1 cup chopped, cooked chicken
2½ cups almonds, sliced
2 envelopes Lipton Chicken
    Noodle Cup-A-Soup

Sauté diced pepper, onion, and celery in olive oil. Remove and cook sausage. Drain. Bring soup, rice and water to boil. Add other ingredients and pour into large buttered casserole dish. Cover and cook at 350° for 45-60 minutes. Serves 6-8.

Mrs. Sidney E. Middlebrooks
(Susan Rau)

WEST INDIAN LEG OF LAMB
Serve with Chutney

1 leg of lamb
1 tablespoon salt
2 cloves garlic, sliced
½ cup strong coffee
½ cup orange liqueur, divided
1 tablespoon brown sugar
1 tablespoon molasses

½ teaspoon cinnamon
¼ teaspoon allspice
¼ teaspoon mace
salt to taste
1 tablespoon cornstarch
¼ cup water

Rub salt into lamb. Make slits and insert garlic slices. To make coffee sauce, combine coffee, ¼ cup orange liqueur, brown sugar, molasses and spices. Brush mixture on lamb. Roast at 325° for 25-30 minutes per pound. Baste frequently during cooking with coffee mixture. Combine cornstarch and water. Blend with drippings. Add water to correct consistency and cook over low heat until thickened and clear. Warm ¼ cup orange liqueur and pour over lamb. Ignite. Serve immediately with coffee sauce. Serves 8.

Mrs. Robert S. Mattox, III
(Glenda Banks)

PECAN-STUFFED HAM

7 pound boned, rolled ham
¼ cup butter
1 cup chopped onion
2 cups cornbread stuffing mix
½ cup chopped fresh parsley
1½ cups coarsely chopped
   pecans

1 egg, beaten
2 tablespoons prepared
   mustard
½ cup honey
2 tablespoons frozen orange
   juice concentrate, thawed

Sauté onion in butter and add stuffing mix, parsley, pecans, egg and mustard to make dressing. Fill ham cavity with dressing. Place ham in roasting pan and bake 1 hour at 325°. Mix honey and orange juice and baste ham. Continue baking 30 minutes. Let ham cool 30 minutes before slicing. Serves 8.

Mrs. Rufus Dorsey Sams, III
(Sidney Tucker)

HAM LOAF

MEAT LOAF MIXTURE:
2 pounds (4 cups) ground
   smoked ham
1 pound (2 cups) ground lean
   pork
1 cup Club cracker crumbs

1 tablespoon chopped onion
2 beaten eggs
1 cup milk
2 tablespoons chili sauce

GLAZE:
½ cup brown sugar
¼ cup vinegar

1 tablespoon dry mustard

Combine meat loaf ingredients and bake at 350° in a large greased loaf pan for 30 minutes. Mix ingredients for glaze in saucepan and boil for 1 minute. Pour over ham loaf and bake 1 more hour at 350°. Serve with the following sauce:

½ cup mayonnaise
½ cup sour cream
¼ cup prepared mustard
1 tablespoon chopped chives

2 tablespoons horseradish
1 tablespoon lemon juice
dash salt

Mix all above ingredients and pour over ham loaf or pass when serving.

HAM CASSEROLE

4 cups diced ham
8 hard-boiled eggs, quartered
2 (10 ounce) packages frozen
    artichoke hearts, thawed
½-1 pound fresh mushrooms
2 (10¾ ounce) cans cream of
    mushroom soup

1 tablespoon minced onion
¼ cup sherry
½ teaspoon garlic salt
1 cup grated sharp cheese

Butter a 3-quart casserole dish. Place ham, eggs and artichokes in casserole. Sauté mushrooms. Combine mushrooms with soup and other ingredients, and pour over artichoke-ham-egg-mixture. Sprinkle cheese on top. Bake at 400° for 30 minutes. Serve on Holland Rusk or in patty shells. Serves 8.

Mrs. Andrew W. Young
(Pamela Watkins)

HAM AND NOODLE EN KYATHION

4 ounces green egg noodles
⅓ cup chopped onion
⅓ cup chopped green pepper
½ pound fresh mushrooms,
    sliced
¾ cup butter

¼ cup sifted flour
1 teaspoon salt
¼ teaspoon pepper
1 quart milk
1 cup grated sharp cheese
3 cups cubed cooked ham

Preheat oven to 375°; grease ½-quart casserole. Cook noodles and drain. In large skillet, sauté onion, bell pepper and mushrooms in butter for 5 minutes. Add flour and seasonings. Stir until well blended. Add milk and cheese and simmer, stirring constantly until mixture thickens. Add noodles and ham and blend well. Place in casserole. Bake 20-25 minutes. Serves 6.

Mrs. James Linton Solomon
(Eden Persons)

MRS. GANDY'S COUNTRY HAM

country ham
1 cup vinegar

1 (16 ounce) box brown sugar

Soak ham for 1 hour then scrub well. Put ham in cold water to cover. Add 1 cup vinegar and 1 box of brown sugar. Simmer 20 minutes to the pound. Let cool and set in liquid overnight. Skin next morning. Score and decorate with pineapple, cloves, etc. Run in oven to warm before serving.

APPLE-FILLED HAM

1 (1 pound 6 ounce) can apple
   pie filling
⅓ cup seedless raisins

¼ cup chopped pecans
2 center cut ham slices,
   (½-inch thick)

GLAZE:

1 (10 ounce) jar currant jelly
¼ cup light corn syrup

2-3 tablespoons horseradish
¾ teaspoon dry mustard

Combine pie filing, raisins and pecans. Place one ham slice in baking pan. Spread filling on slice and cover with a second ham slice. Bake covered at 350° for 30 minutes. Baste with glaze. *Glaze:* Combine ingredients and bring to a boil. Baste ham every 10 minutes for ½ hour more cooking time. Serves 4-6.

BAKED HAM

1 (10-12 pound) ham
prepared mustard
¼ teaspoon ground cloves

1 cup prepared mustard
1 cup sherry
1 cup brown sugar

Rub surface of ham with mustard. Place ham in a roasting pan and bake at 300° for 20 minutes per pound. One hour before ham is done, remove it from oven. Discard all rind except that rind covering shank bone. Remove all excess fat and rub ham again with mustard. Dust cloves over ham. Combine mustard, sherry and brown sugar and baste ham. The last few minutes of cooking time, raise oven temperature to 450° to brown ham well.

TART HAM SAUCE

1 (12 ounce) jar apple jelly
1 (12 ounce) jar pineapple
   preserves

2½ ounces horseradish
½ ounce dry mustard (½ small
   container)

Melt all ingredients in a double boiler. Serve warm over ham. Refrigerate. Yields 2 pints.

Will keep indefinitely in refrigerator. Have served with ham and biscuits (fix your own) at cocktail party. Mixture stiffens when refrigerated. Can be served at room temperature. Also try ham sauce covering cream cheese as an hors d'oeuvre. Serve as a spread with crackers.

CHABLIS CREAM SAUCE FOR COUNTRY HAM

4 tablespoons butter
12 shallots, finely chopped
4 tablespoons flour
1½ cups chablis
2 tablespoons tomato paste

1 teaspoon salt
½ teaspoon freshly ground
    black pepper
1 cup heavy cream
2 egg yolks

Melt butter and add the shallots. Add flour and cook 3 minutes. Stir in chablis and continue stirring until thick. Add tomato paste and salt and pepper. Simmer 2 to 3 minutes. Stir in cream which has been mixed with egg yolks. Stir until thickened. Add more seasoning if desired.

BARBECUE SAUCE

¼ cup vinegar
½ cup water
¼ cup margarine
2 tablespoons sugar
1 tablespoon prepared mustard
1½ teaspoons salt
½ teaspoon black pepper

½ teaspon cayenne pepper
    (optional)
1 medium onion, thickly sliced
1 lemon, thickly sliced
½ cup catsup
2 tablespoons Worcestershire
    sauce

Combine all ingredients except catsup and Worcestershire in a saucepan and bring to a boil. Reduce heat and allow to simmer for 20 minutes. Add catsup and Worcestershire and bring to a boil again. Remove lemon and onion before storing. Serves 4-5.

Mrs. B. Michael Byrd
(Tip Barfield)
Similar recipe submitted by
Mrs. Peter M. Kramer
(Randall Huckabee)

POWDERED BARBECUE SAUCE

½ cup sugar
1 tablespoon seasoned salt
1 teaspoon paprika
¼ teaspoon garlic salt

1 teaspoon black pepper
½ teaspoon onion salt
½ teaspoon dry mustard

Combine all ingredients well. Sprinkle over beef, pork, or chicken before cooking.

VEGETABLES

BROCCOLI-ONION DELUXE

2 pounds fresh broccoli or 2
(10 ounce) packages frozen
cut broccoli
6 medium onions, quartered
8 tablespoons butter, divided
4 tablespoons flour
½ teaspoon salt

dash of pepper
2 cups milk
2 (3 ounce) packages cream
cheese
4 ounces (1 cup) shredded
sharp Cheddar cheese
2 cups soft bread crumbs

Cook broccoli according to directions. Drain. Cook onions in boiling salted water until tender; drain. In saucepan melt 4 tablespoons butter; blend in flour, ½ teaspoon salt and dash of pepper. Add milk; cook and stir until thick and bubbly. Reduce heat; blend in cream cheese until smooth. Place vegetables in 2½-quart casserole. Pour sauce over vegetables and mix lightly. Top with Cheddar cheese. Melt remaining butter; toss with bread crumbs. Bake casserole, covered at 350° for 30 minutes. Sprinkle crumbs around edge; bake uncovered for 30 minutes or until heated thoroughly. Serves 12.

Mrs. Derry Burns, Jr.
(Juliette Smith)

BLEU CHEESE BROCCOLI

3 (10 ounce) packages frozen
chopped broccoli, cooked
2 tablespoons margarine
2 tablespoons flour
½ teaspoon salt
1 cup milk

1 (3 ounce) package cream
cheese
1 wedge bleu cheese
½ cup cheese cracker crumbs
(optional)

Drain cooked broccoli; spread in casserole. Blend margarine, flour, salt and milk; cook until thickened, stirring constantly. Add cream cheese and bleu cheese; blend. Pour over broccoli; sprinkle with cheese cracker crumbs. Bake at 325° for 20-25 minutes. Serves 6-8.

Mrs. Alfred Lowe, Jr.
(Miriam Caskin)

HINTS

Add a pinch (⅛ teaspoon) of soda to green vegetables while cooking to retain color.

VEGETABLE MEDLEY

1 (16 ounce) can Chinese
vegetables
1 (16 ounce) can French cut
beans
1 (16 ounce) can LeSeur
English peas
1 (16 ounce) can cut asparagus
½ pound sharp cheese, grated
1½ (10¾ ounce) cans
mushroom soup
½ cup butter

1 (10 ounce) can water
chestnuts, sliced
½ cup chopped nuts
1 (12 ounce) can chopped
pimiento
3 hard-boiled eggs, grated
salt and pepper
1 cup crushed saltines
¼ cup melted butter
1 (3 ounce) can French fried
onion rings

Drain all vegetables. Mix vegetables, nuts, pimiento, eggs, salt, pepper, butter, soup, and cheese. Stir lightly. Place in 2 casseroles. Mix well. Mix crushed saltines and butter. Sprinkle on top of casseroles. Bake at 325° for 15 minutes. Lay onion rings on top. Bake 10 more minutes. Serves 20-24.

Mrs. Donald W. Rhame
(Alacia Lee)

ASPARAGUS WITH SHRIMP SAUCE

1½-2 pounds fresh asparagus
¼ cup butter
¼ cup flour
1 teaspoon salt
dash pepper (white pepper
preferable)

1 cup milk
1 cup half and half
1 tablespoon dry sherry
1½ cups cooked, peeled,
deveined shrimp
parsley sprigs to garnish

Prepare and cook asparagus until tender; drain. Melt butter in saucepan over low heat; blend in flour and seasonings. Slowly add milk and half and half, stirring constantly until smooth and thick. Add sherry. Stir. Carefully fold in shrimp; allow shrimp to heat through. Pour shrimp sauce over well drained, warmed asparagus. Garnish with parsley sprigs, if desired. Serves 6.

Mrs. G. Boone Smith, III
(Claire McCommon)

ASPARAGUS MILANESE

3-4 tablespoons unsalted
  butter, divided
2 pounds thin fresh asparagus,
  trimmed and cooked until
  tender

2 slices Mozzarella cheese
½ cup freshly grated Parmesan
  cheese

Preheat oven to 350°. Grease shallow baking dish with 2 tablespoons butter. Put cooked asparagus in dish, add cheese, and sprinkle with Parmesan. Dot with remaining 2 tablespoons butter. Bake 15 minutes. Serves 4.

Mrs. Timothy K. Adams
(Julie Bearden)

ZUCCHINI CASSEROLE

4 small zucchini squash, thinly
  sliced (2½-3 cups)
2 tablespoons chopped onion
3 tablespoons margarine or
  butter
2 tomatoes
1 tablespoon grated Parmesan
  cheese
1 teaspoon sugar
¾ teaspoon salt

½ teaspoon oregano
⅛ teaspoon garlic salt
⅛ teaspoon pepper
4 ounces Mozzarella cheese,
  grated
2 tablespoons margarine or
  butter
Pepperidge Farm stuffing
  (½-¾ cup)

Sauté zucchini and onion in margarine until limp. Place in oiled dish. Top with the 2 tomatoes which have been peeled and cut in wedges. Mix the Parmesan cheese, sugar, salt, oregano, garlic salt, and pepper and sprinkle over the tomatoes. Sprinkle with grated Mozzarella cheese. Top with 2 tablespoons margaine or butter mixed with Pepperidge Farm stuffing. Bake in 350° oven for 15-20 minutes. Serves 4-6.

Mrs. Ronald E. Robeson
(Carol Clark)

HINTS

Generally, vegetables that grow above the ground should be cooked uncovered. Those that grow underground should be cooked covered.

ZUCCHINI FRENCH STYLE

1 pound zucchini
2 tablespoons butter or
   margarine
1 tablespoon minced onion

¼ teaspoon instant garlic
¼ cup water
2 beef bouillon cubes
seasoned pepper

Wash zucchini, cut off ends, and cut in half crosswise. Cut halves into julienne sticks about ¼-inch wide. If zucchini is not to be cooked immediately, wrap in foil and refrigerate until needed. About 7 minutes before serving, melt butter in large skillet; add onion, garlic, water, crumbled bouillon cubes, and stir until melted. Add zucchini, then cook uncovered and quickly over high heat until tender crisp. When done, transfer zucchini to a serving dish and top with a sprinkle of seasoned pepper. Serves 4 to 5.

Mrs. Warren H. Thorpe
(Margaret Stum)

SQUASH SOUFFLÉ

2 pounds fresh cooked or 2
   (16 ounce) cans Margaret
   Holmes squash
3 tablespoons grated onion
1½ teaspoons salt
¼ teaspoon pepper

2 tablespoons sugar (may need
   1 tablespoon more sugar if
   onion is strong)
2 egg yolks (reserve whites)
¾ cup crushed cracker crumbs

WHITE SAUCE:
2 tablespoons butter
2 tablespoons flour

2 cups milk
2 egg whites

Drain squash thoroughly. To squash, add onion, salt and pepper, sugar, egg yolks, and cracker crumbs. Set aside. Make white sauce by mixing the butter, flour, and milk together, stirring until mixture thickens. Add squash mixture. Beat egg whites until stiff and fold carefully into mixture. Pour into 1½-quart casserole. Bake, covered, at 350° for 30 minutes. Serve immediately. Serves 8.

Mrs. D. Clark Ballard
(Nancy Johnson)

SQUASH WITH WHITE WINE

2 pounds yellow squash, sliced
1 cup chopped onion
1 teaspoon salt
1 (8 ounce) carton sour cream
⅓ cup grated Parmesan cheese

1¼ cups cubed Cheddar cheese
¼ cup dry white wine
¼ cup butter
salt and pepper to taste
buttered crumbs

Boil the squash and onion with the salt until barely tender. Drain and add sour cream, Parmesan cheese, Cheddar cheese, wine and butter. Salt and pepper to taste. Butter an 11-inch au gratin dish and pour squash mixture into dish. Top with buttered crumbs. Bake at 350° until bubbling hot and lightly browned, about 20-30 minutes. Serves 6.

Mrs. Derry Burns, Jr.
(Juliette Smith)

SQUASH CASSEROLE

3 cups thinly sliced cooked
  squash
1 cup grated medium sharp
  cheese
3 tablespoons chopped
  pimiento

2 eggs, well beaten
4 tablespoons chopped onion
3 tablespoons melted butter
1 cup scalded milk
1 cup saltine cracker crumbs
salt and pepper to taste

Combine all ingredients, except hot milk which is added last. Pour into greased 2-quart baking dish. Bake at 350° for 1 hour. Serves 8.

Mrs. Derry Burns
(Hazel Holmes)

BRUSSEL SPROUTS AU GRATIN

1 pound Brussel sprouts
2 tablespoons butter
2 tablespoons flour
2 cups milk
½ cup white wine

1 cup grated Monterey Jack
  cheese, divided
½ teaspoon salt
¼ cup bread crumbs

Cook brussel sprouts in small amount of boiling water. Drain. To make sauce, melt butter and add flour slowly. Add milk and wine. Stir until mixture thickens. Add ½ cup cheese and stir until melted. Add salt. Place brussel sprouts in a 2-quart greased dish. Cover with sauce. Top with remaining cheese and crumbs. Bake at 350° for 20 minutes. Serves 4.

AUSTRIAN CHEESE-STUFFED CAULIFLOWER

1 large head cauliflower,
  trimmed and washed
juice of ½ lemon
¼ pound Swiss cheese,
  cut into strips
salt and pepper to taste
	¼ cup melted butter or
	  margarine
	1 cup finely crushed
	  Pepperidge Farm herb
	  flavored stuffing mix

Soak cauliflower, head down, in cold salted water for 15 minutes. Cook in about 1 inch of boiling, salted water with the juice of ½ lemon until cauliflower is tender but still firm. (Cover the pot and check in 10 minutes.) Drain well. Place whole head in shallow baking pan. Press strips of cheese into cauliflower head. Sprinkle with salt and pepper. Mix butter and stuffing and press into cauliflower. Bake at 350° for about 20 minutes or until crumbs are lightly browned. Serves 6.

Mrs. Edgar Y. Mallary, III
(Lloyd Washington)

STUFFED ARTICHOKES

1 (10 ounce) package chopped
  spinach, cooked and drained
¼ cup minced onion
3 tablespoons butter
¼ cup sour cream
3 tablespoons grated Parmesan
  cheese, divided
	¾ teaspoon salt
	¼ teaspoon pepper
	dash of cayenne pepper
	2 (8 ounce) cans artichoke
	  bottoms
	grated Parmesan cheese

Cook spinach and drain. Sauté onion in butter until tender. Stir in spinach, sour cream, Parmesan, salt and peppers. Spoon mixture into artichoke bottoms. Place in shallow baking dish. Add water to barely cover bottom of baking dish. Sprinkle bottoms lightly with grated Parmesan and bake at 350° for 15 minutes. Serves 6-8.

Mrs. William W. Baxley, Jr.
(Charlene Carpenter)

HINTS

Noodles and spaghetti will not boil over if the cooking utensil is first rubbed on the inside with vegetable oil.

White onions are milder than yellow onions.

ARTICHOKE WITH MUSHROOM CASSEROLE

2 (12 ounce) cans artichoke
   hearts
1 (6 ounce) can sliced
   mushrooms
1 (1¾ ounce) envelope chicken
   gravy mix
dash thyme

dash marjoram
4 ounces Swiss cheese, grated
2-4 tablespoons dry white wine
Progresso seasoned bread
   crumbs

Preheat oven to 350°. Drain artichokes and mushrooms and layer in casserole. In meantime, prepare gravy according to directions. Add spices and grated cheese to mix well. Stir in wine to blend. Pour this mixture over artichokes and mushrooms. Top with seasoned crumbs. Bake uncovered 25-30 minutes. Serve 4 generously.

PAT HANSON'S SPINACH CASSEROLE

½ cup grated onion
½ cup butter
4 (10 ounce) packages frozen
   chopped spinach, cooked
1 pint sour cream
½ cup grated Parmesan
   cheese, divided

2 tablespoons lemon juice
¼ teaspoon garlic salt
6 artichoke hearts, chopped
1 cup buttered bread crumbs

Sauté onions in butter. Add spinach, sour cream, ¼ cup Parmesan cheese, lemon juice, garlic salt, and artichoke hearts. Pour into 2-quart casserole. Sprinkle over top with buttered crumbs and reserved ¼ cup Parmesan cheese. Bake at 350° until bubbly. Serves 12.

Mrs. Bruce J. Bishop
(Eleanor Richardson)

SAUSAGE-STUFFED PEPPERS

2 pounds ground pork
2 garlic cloves, finely chopped
1 teaspoon thyme
½ teaspoon cardamon
¼ teaspoon cumin

1½ teaspoons salt
½ teaspoon Tabasco
12 green peppers, using lower
   halves

Blend meat and seasonings and fry. Drain. Parboil green peppers 8 minutes in salted water. Drain and fill with sausage mixture. Arrange in an oiled baking pan. Bake at 350° for 25-30 minutes. Serves 10-12.

SEAFOOD STUFFED EGGPLANT

2 medium eggplants
1 large onion, chopped
4 tablespoons butter
1 pound shrimp
1 pound lump crab meat
½ to ¾ cup seasoned bread
    crumbs
2 eggs, beaten
1 teaspoon monosodium
    glutamate

1 teaspoon oregano
2 tablespoons chopped parsley
½ teaspoon salt
black pepper to taste
3 dashes Tabasco
1 tablespoon butter
paprika
grated Cheddar or Parmesan
    cheese (optional)

Slice eggplants in half and pan boil about 10 minutes. Remove from water, drain, cool slightly and scoop centers out of each half of eggplant. Place eggplant pulp in large mixing bowl and set aside. Sauté onion in butter and add to pulp. Add prepared shrimp and crab meat, bread crumbs, (reserving small amount for topping), beaten eggs, MSG, oregano, parsley, salt, pepper, and Tabasco. Mix well and fill eggplant shells. Arrange filled shells in shallow baking dish filled with ¼ cup water. Top each eggplant with remaining bread crumbs and butter; sprinkle with paprika. Top with grated cheese. Bake at 350° for 35-45 minutes and until top is golden. Serves 4.

Mrs. Ellsworth Hall, III
(Ann Bootle)

EGGPLANT PARMESAN

1 medium to large eggplant
1 egg
¼ cup white wine
bread or cracker crumbs
olive oil
1 (15 ounce) can tomato sauce

2 cloves garlic, finely chopped
½ teaspoon basil
½ pound Mozzarella cheese,
    sliced
½ cup grated Parmesan
    cheese

Peel and slice eggplant ⅜-inch thick. Beat egg and wine together. Dip eggplant slices in egg mixture, then in bread crumbs and brown in oil. Drain on paper towels. Simmer tomato sauce, garlic and basil together in saucepan 10-15 minutes. Layer half the eggplant, Mozzarella, Parmesan, and sauce in baking dish, then repeat in layers. Bake at 350° for 30 minutes. Serves 6.

Mrs. Bert Maxwell, III
(Mardi Barnes)

OKRA SUCCOTASH

1 pound okra, sliced
3 tablespoons bacon drippings
2 onions, chopped
3 cloves garlic, pressed
½ pound diced ham
1 (16 ounce) can tomatoes
1 cup butterbeans

1 cup corn
4 tablespoons butter
1 tablespoon sugar
½ teaspoon salt
½ teaspoon pepper
1 tablespoon minced celery

Sauté okra 10 minutes in bacon drippings. Add onions and garlic. Cook 5 minutes. Add remaining ingredients. Cook 20 minutes or until butterbeans are tender. Serves 6.

Mrs. William F. Ladson, Jr.
(Betty Sweet Simmons)

FRIED OKRA

1 pound okra, sliced
1 medium onion, finely
   chopped
2 tablespoons yellow cornmeal
2 tablespoons flour

½ teaspoon salt
¼ teaspoon pepper
⅓ cup milk
1 egg, beaten
oil

Combine all ingredients except oil. Drop by teaspoonfuls into hot oil. Press down with spatula. Remove from heat and serve when crust is golden brown. Serves 6.

CARROTS IN ORANGE SAUCE

1 (16 ounce) package small
   carrots
½ teaspoon salt
¼ cup butter
½ cup packed brown sugar

½ cup orange juice
1 tablespoon grated orange
   rind
⅛ teaspoon mace (optional)
2 teaspoons cornstarch

Scrape carrots lightly and cook 10 minutes in small amount boiling water. Drain and add ½ teaspoon salt and remaining ingredients, except cornstarch. Bring again to boil and simmer, covered for 20 minutes or until tender. Blend cornstarch with small amount of cold water and stir into mixture. Cook, stirring gently until mixture is clear and thickened.

Mrs. Stuart C. Davis, III
(Kay Lamar)

CARROT BALLS

1 pound carrots, cooked and
  mashed
2 eggs, well beaten

2 tablespoons flour
1 tablespoon melted butter
½ teaspoon salt

Combine all ingredients and mix well. Shape into 1-inch balls. Add more flour if necessary. Mixture will be sticky. Fry in deep vegetable oil. Drain. Serves 6.

Mrs. Jack R. Meadows
(Betty Norris)

CARROT CASSEROLE
Excellent

1 pound sliced carrots, cooked
  in salted water until tender
½ cup chopped onion
1 cup grated cheese

⅓ teaspoon salt
⅔ cup mayonnaise
1 teaspoon sugar
bread crumbs

Mix all ingredients well, except bread crumbs. Place in buttered baking dish. Top with buttered bread crumbs. Bake at 350° until bubbly. Serves 4.

Mrs. Fred J. Morgan
(Margaret Mitchell)

MOM'S CARROT RING

3 tablespoons butter
3 tablespoons flour
⅛ teaspoon white pepper
⅛ teaspoon dry mustard
1 teaspoon salt

pinch cayenne pepper
1 cup milk
3 eggs, separated
3 cups grated carrots

Melt butter in a saucepan. Stir in flour, white pepper, dry mustard, salt, and cayenne pepper. Add milk slowly. Heat and stir until thickened. Cool. Mix egg yolks with this cooled mixture. Add carrots. Beat egg whites until stiff and fold in. Pour into well-greased 2-quart ring mold. Set mold in hot water and bake at 350° for 1 hour. When done, invert mold on platter and serve. Fill the mold with hot peas and mushrooms. Serves 8-10.

Mrs. George Youmans
(Ann Dunlap)

FRENCH BEANS WITH CORN

1 (16 ounce) can French beans
1 (16 ounce) can shoepeg corn
½ cup chopped water chestnuts
1 (10¾ ounce) can cream of
  celery soup
½ cup grated sharp cheese
½ cup chopped onions
½ cup sour cream
½ cup slivered almonds,
  toasted
½ cup margarine
1 cylinder of (12 ounce) box
  Ritz crackers

Drain beans and corn. Mix with all other ingredients except margarine and crackers. Melt margarine and mix with crackers and sprinkle on top of casserole. Bake 40 minutes at 350°. Serves 6.

Mrs. Wilbur D. Owens, Jr.
(Betty Glenn)

TINY CORN FRITTERS

1 (17 ounce) can cream style
  corn
1½ cups cracker crumbs
1 large egg
½ teaspoon grated onion
salt and pepper to taste

Mix ingredients well the day before preparing. Drop by teaspoonfuls into hot oil and fry until brown. Drain on absorbent paper. Serves 6.

CORN SOUFFLÉ

¼ cup butter
¼ cup flour
⅔ cup milk
1 cup cream style corn
3 egg yolks, well beaten
½ teaspoon salt
¼ cup grated cheese
1 tablespoon chopped green
  pepper
3 egg whites, stiffly beaten

Melt butter, add flour, and blend well. Add milk and corn and cook until thickened. Remove from heat and add egg yolks, salt, cheese, and green pepper. Fold in beaten egg whites. Bake in greased 1½-quart baking dish at 325° for 45 minutes or until set. Serves 6-8.

Mrs. Donald W. Rhame
(Alacia Lee)

EULA'S FRIED CORN

¼ cup margarine
3 large ears tender corn, cut or
  grated, scraping cob
1 tablespoon cornstarch

1 teaspoon sugar
1 teaspoon salt
dash pepper
⅔ cup water

Melt margarine in iron skillet. Mix all ingredients in skillet and cook until mixture thickens, about 15 minutes. Serves 2-4.

Mrs. Andrew W. Young
(Pamela Watkins)

SNOW PEAS ORIENTAL

1 tablespoon soy sauce
½ teaspoon salt
½ teaspoon sugar
1 tablespoon oil
1 (10 ounce) package snow
  peas

½ pound fresh bean sprouts
¼ pound fresh mushrooms,
  sliced

Combine soy sauce, salt and sugar and set aside. Using a high flame, heat oil in skillet or Chinese wok. Add vegetables and stir fry 1 minute. Cover, lower heat and cook 2 minutes. Remove cover, raise heat, pour combined sauce over vegetables an stir fry 1 minute longer. Serves 4-6.

Mrs. Charles C. Corbin
(Margaret Oleson)

PARMESAN SAUCE

1 tablespoon butter
1 tablespoon flour
¼ teaspoon salt
dash pepper
dash paprika
dash dry mustard

1 cup milk
2 tablespoons Parmesan
  cheese
2 tablespoons sliced almonds,
  toasted

Melt butter. Blend in flour and seasonings. Add milk. Cook until mixture thickens. Add cheese and almonds and stir until cheese melts. Serve with vegetables. Yields 1 cup.

TOMATOES KILGROWSKI

4 large tomatoes
2 tablespoons butter
1 (10 ounce) box frozen,
  chopped spinach

⅓ cup grated Parmesan cheese
½ cup sour cream
salt
cayenne pepper

Core tomatoes. Cut about one-third of the way through in two places. Salt insides of tomatoes lightly. Drain. Cook spinach according to directions. Drain. Stir butter into spinach while hot and add cheese and sour cream. Mix thoroughly and season with salt and cayenne pepper to taste. Stuff tomatoes with spinach mixture. Sprinkle top with cheese. Heat for 15 minutes at 375°. If tomatoes have been prepared ahead of time and refrigerated, they may require longer cooking time. They should be thoroughly heated. Artichoke hearts can be added to mixture. Serves 4.

Mrs. J. Wilbur Coggins, Jr.
(Sue Moss)

RICE-STUFFED TOMATOES

8 medium tomatoes
2 tablespoons butter
⅓ cup chopped celery
¼ cup chopped onion
1 tablespoon flour
1 teaspoon salt
dash of pepper

1 cup chopped tomato pulp,
  drained
1 (2½ ounce) jar sliced
  mushrooms, drained
1 cup cooked rice
½ cup sour cream

Cut a thin slice off stem end of tomatoes. Scoop out pulp, leaving about ½-inch shell; reserve pulp. Turn tomatoes upside down to drain. In a 1½-quart saucepan melt butter; sauté celery and onion until tender. Blend in flour, salt, and pepper. Remove from heat and stir in tomato pulp, mushrooms and rice. Fold in sour cream. Fill tomatoes.* Place in 1½-quart oblong baking dish. Bake at 350° for 20 minutes. This can be prepared ahead of time, refrigerated and then brought to room temperature prior to cooking. Serves 8.

*Once cooked, the tomatoes are somewhat difficult to transfer to another dish without breaking, so plan to serve from dish in which they are cooked.

Mrs. Walker P. Johnson, Jr.
(Katherine Wilson)

FETTUCINI

1 (12 ounce) package wide
  noodles
1 cup heavy cream
3 tablespoons butter

¾ cup grated Parmesan cheese
dash salt, pepper to taste
chopped fresh parsley for
  garnish

Cook noodles according to package directions. Meanwhile, heat cream and butter in top of double boiler until butter melts. When noodles are cooked, drain and return to container in which noodles were cooked. Add cheese and cream mixture. Add dash of salt and pepper to taste and sprinkle with parsley and serve immediately. If it cannot be served immediately, cover with aluminum foil. Heat in 200° oven for 20-30 minutes before serving. Serves 6.

Mrs. Walter H. Bush, Jr.
(Ellen Love)

WILD RICE PARTY DISH

½ cup butter
1 cup wild rice
½ cup slivered almonds
2 tablespoons chopped onion

½ pound sliced mushrooms
1 teaspoon salt
2 tablespoons sherry
3 cups chicken broth

Combine all ingredients except broth in a heavy frying pan. Cook until rice is well coated, stirring frequently. Place in casserole with 3 cups chicken broth and cover. Refrigerate or freeze. When ready to serve, return to room temperature. Bake at 325° for 1 hour or more. Serves 6.

VARIATION: Add ⅔ pound sautéed sausage.

Mrs. Hugh Moss Comer
(Virginia Bateman)

WINE SAUCE
Good on Broccoli and Asparagus

¼-½ teaspoon curry powder
1 cup mayonnaise

1 teaspoon lemon juice
¼ cup dry white wine

Stir curry powder into mayonnaise. Stir in lemon juice and wine. Heat, but do not boil.

RED RICE
Good with Fried Seafood

6 strips bacon
2 onions, finely chopped
1 (6 ounce) can tomato paste
1½-2 cans water
3 teaspoons salt

2-3 teaspoons sugar
dash pepper
2 cups raw long grain rice
8 tablespoons bacon grease

Fry bacon; remove from pan; sauté onions in grease; add tomato paste, water, salt, sugar and pepper. Cook uncovered slowly about 10 minutes or until mixture measures 2 cups; then add it to rice in top section of steamer. Add the ½ cup remaining grease; steam for ½ hour; then add crumbled bacon and stir with fork. Cook 30-45 minutes longer. Serves 6-8.

Mrs. Samuel W. Popejoy
(Helen Farmer)

BROWN RICE
Good with Dove or Quail

1 cup butter
2 (10¾ ounce) cans beef
  consommé
2 (10¾ ounce) cans onion soup
1 (7 ounce) package long grain
  and wild rice mix (Comet or
  Uncle Ben's)

1 cup plain uncooked rice
1 (8 ounce) can mushrooms,
  drained

Melt butter in 2½-3 quart casserole. Add consommé, onion soup, and seasoning from wild rice package. Add rice and mushrooms. Stir. Bake uncovered in 325° oven for 1 hour. Serves 12-14.

Mrs. Frank W. Walthall, Jr.
(Janet Fortson)

MUSTARD SAUCE

1 egg, beaten
½ cup sugar
1 tablespoon flour
½ cup vinegar

½ cup beef bouillon
½ cup prepared mustard
¼ cup butter

Beat egg until light. Add sugar and flour. Set aside. Add vinegar and bouillon to mustard and add to first mixture. Cook in double boiler until mixture thickens. Add butter. Yields 1 pint.

ORIENTAL RICE CASSEROLE

1 (16 ounce) package long
  grain and wild rice mix
1 cup chopped onion
1 cup chopped celery
3 tablespoons butter
2 tablespoons soy sauce

1 (3 ounce) can sliced
  mushrooms
1 (8 ounce) can sliced water
  chestnuts
⅓ cup slivered almonds,
  toasted

Cook rice according to package directions. Sauté onion and celery in butter until tender. Add all remaining ingredients. Mix well. Bake in 1½-quart casserole at 350° for 20 minutes. Serves 8.

Mrs. William W. Baxley
(Stella Cater)

ST. PAUL'S RICE

1 pound mild pork sausage
1 large bell pepper, chopped
1 large onion, chopped
2 stalks celery, chopped

1 (3.5 ounce) box Lipton
  chicken noodle soup mix
1 cup rice
4½ cups water

Brown sausage. Add bell pepper, onion, and celery. Drain grease. Boil the soup mix, rice and water for 7 minutes. Combine with sausage mixture. Pour mixture in greased casserole. Bake in covered dish for 1 hour at 350°. For garnish, top casserole with grated cheese or slivered almonds. Serves 8.

Mrs. Andrew W. Young
(Pamela Watkins)

BUTTER BEANS WITH PECANS

2 cups cooked butter beans
1 beef bouillon cube
½ cup boiling water
½ cup chopped pecans
1 medium onion, chopped

dash Worcestershire sauce
½ cup grated mild Cheddar
  cheese
⅓ cup soft bread crumbs
2 tablespoons butter

Line a greased casserole dish with cooked butter beans. Add the bouillon cube to water and stir until dissolved. Add water to beans with pecans, onion, Worcestershire, and grated cheese. Toss lightly to blend. Sprinkle top with bread crumbs. Dot with butter. Bake at 350° for 30 minutes. Serves 4.

CHILI RICE CASSEROLE

4 cups cooked ranch rice
1 cup chopped onion
¼ cup margarine
1 (16 ounce) carton sour cream
1 cup cream style cottage
  cheese

½ teaspoon salt
⅛ teaspoon pepper
2 (4 ounce) cans green chiles,
  drained and chopped with
  seeds
2 cups grated Cheddar cheese

Cook rice according to package directions. In skillet, sauté onion in margarine. Remove from heat. Stir in hot rice, sour cream, cottage cheese, salt and pepper. Toss lightly to mix well. Layer half of rice mixture in a greased 2-quart casserole dish, then half the chiles; sprinkle with half the cheese. Repeat. Bake uncovered at 375° for 25 minutes. Serves 8.

Mrs. Carl C. Schuessler
(Lynn Mercer)

WINE RICE

1 cup raw rice
1 cup chopped fresh tomatoes
½ cup chopped onion
1 pound fresh mushrooms,
  sliced
chicken broth
½ cup red wine

2 teaspoons salt
¼ teaspoon pepper
1 cup Le Sueur peas, drained
½ cup butter
½ cup grated Parmesan
  cheese

Put first 4 ingredients in a skillet. Add chicken broth equal to amount liquid called for on rice package minus ½ cup. Add wine, salt and pepper. Mix well. Cover 30-40 minutes on low heat or until liquid is absorbed. Stir in peas, butter, and Parmesan. Serves 8.

SOUR CREAM HOLLANDAISE SAUCE

1 (8 ounce) carton sour cream
juice of one lemon
2 egg yolks

½ teaspoon salt
¼ teaspoon paprika

Mix all ingredients together. Stir *over* hot water in a double boiler until thickened.

Mrs. James E. Carpenter, Jr.
(Patricia Reynolds)

CELERY AND APPLES INDIA
Good with Poultry or Lamb

3 cups celery, sliced diagonally
¼ cup chicken stock or water
¾ teaspoon salt, divided
1⅓ cups unpeeled apples,
  sliced ¼-inch thick

3 small white onions, sliced
¼ cup butter or margarine
1¼ teaspoons curry powder
1 teaspoon sugar

Place celery, stock or water, and ½ teaspoon salt in medium-size saucepan. Bring to boiling point. Cover and cook 3 or 4 minutes or until celery is crisp tender. Drain. Set aside. In a large frying pan, sauté apples and onions in butter or margarine with curry powder and remaining salt for 5 minutes or until apples are tender. Add celery and sugar. Cook 1 or 2 minutes. Serves 6.

Mrs. Gary C. Ertel
(Holly Akre)

NELL SAMS' CHESTNUT AND OYSTER DRESSING

2 pounds chestnuts, chopped,
  boiled tender
3 (1 pound) loaves bread
½ cup butter
2½ cups chopped onion
3 cups chopped celery
3 cloves garlic, minced

6 tablespoons parsley
½ cup butter
2 tablespoons basil
1 tablespoon marjoram
1 teaspoon sage
salt and pepper to taste
24 small oysters

To prepare chestnuts: remove shells and skins from chestnuts by making V-shaped cut in flat side of each nut. Spread on cookie sheet and coat with salad oil. Put pan in 450° oven for 10 minutes. Cool. Remove shells and skins. Coarsely chop chestnuts and boil in water until tender. Drain, set aside, and cool. To prepare dressing, remove crusts from bread and pick bread apart into small flakes. Cook onion, celery and garlic in butter until lightly colored. Empty contents of skillet over bread and mix. Add chestnuts and parsley and toss. Melt ½ cup butter in skillet in which onion and celery were cooked. Add basil, marjoram and sage. Cook over low heat for 1 minute. Add to bread and toss. Add salt, pepper, and oysters and toss. Stuff neck and body cavity. Sew up cavities and truss.

CELERY CASSEROLE

3 cups diced celery
¼ cup slivered almonds
½ cup sliced water chestnuts
½ cup mushrooms
5 tablespoons butter
3 tablespoons flour

1 cup chicken broth
¾ cup half and half
½ cup grated Parmesan
  cheese
½ cup bread crumbs
melted butter

Parboil celery 5 minutes in salted water. Drain and place in a casserole dish with almonds, water chestnuts and mushrooms. Make white sauce by mixing butter and flour slowly with broth and half and half. Stir in the celery mixture. Combine cheese and crumbs and sprinkle on top. Drizzle melted butter on top of crumbs. Bake at 350° for 20-30 minutes. Serves 6-8.

Mrs. Robert M. Boone
(Nell Chambless)

CHEESE CARAWAY POTATOES

4 large potatoes, peeled, and
  thinly sliced
8 ounces Mozzarella cheese,
  shredded
½ small onion, finely diced
1 (13 ounce) can evaporated
  milk

2 eggs, beaten
1½ teaspoons caraway seed
1 teaspoon salt
¼ teaspoon pepper
2 tablespoons butter

Cook potatoes in small amount boiling salted water. Drain, reserving ½ cup cooking water. In 2-quart casserole, alternate layers of potatoes and cheese, sprinkling onion between each layer. Combine ½ cup cooking water, milk, eggs, caraway seed, salt and pepper. Pour over potatoes. Dot with butter. Bake at 350° for 30 minutes. Serves 6.

HASH BROWN POTATO CASSEROLE

2 pounds frozen hash brown
  potatoes
½ cup melted butter
1½ teaspoons salt
2 cups grated Cheddar cheese
½ cup chopped onion

1(16 ounce) carton sour cream
1 (10¾ ounce) can cream of
  chicken soup
1 teaspoon lemon pepper
  seasoning

Mix all ingredients together. Place in a buttered casserole and bake at 350° for 45 minutes. Serves 10 to 12.

PRALINE YAM CASSEROLE

4 medium yams, cooked
2 eggs
½ cup firmly packed dark
   brown sugar, divided

⅓ cup melted butter, divided
1 teaspoon salt
½ cup chopped pecans
pecan halves

ORANGE SAUCE:
⅓ cup sugar
1 tablespoon cornstarch
⅛ teaspoon salt
1 teaspoon grated orange peel
1 cup orange juice
2 tablespoons lemon juice

2 tablespoons butter
1 tablespoon Grand Marnier (or
   orange liqueur)
3 dashes Angostura bitters

Mash yams in large bowl. Beat eggs, ¼ cup sugar, 2 tablespoons melted butter and salt. Pour into 1-quart casserole. Arrange pecan halves in pattern over top or sprinkle with chopped pecans; sprinkle with remaining ¼ cup sugar and drizzle with remaining melted butter. Bake uncovered at 375° for 20 minutes. Serve with warmed orange sauce. *Orange Sauce:* Blend sugar, cornstarch, and salt in saucepan. Add grated orange peel, orange juice, and lemon juice. Bring to a boil over medium heat stirring constantly until sauce is thickened. Remove from heat and stir in butter, Grand Marnier, and Angostura bitters. Serves 6.

Mrs. Ray C. Pearson
(Judye Wynne)

GOURMET POTATOES

6 medium potatoes, cooked
   peeled, shredded
2 cups shredded sharp
   Cheddar cheese
¼ cup butter

1½ cups sour cream (room
   temperature)
⅓ cup chopped onion or chives
1 teaspoon each salt and
   pepper

Cook potatoes in skin. Cool, peel and shred. Combine cheese and butter in saucepan over low heat. Stir until almost melted. Remove from heat and blend in sour cream, onion, salt and pepper. Fold gently into potatoes, and pour mixture in a greased 2-quart casserole. Bake at 350° for 30-35 minutes. Serves 6.

Mrs. Allen King
(Blanch Redding)

POTATOES AMANDINE

4 cups fresh cooked, mashed
   potatoes (about 6 large
   potatoes)
2 cups cream style cottage
   cheese, sieved
¾ cup sour cream

3 tablespoons grated onion
3 teaspoons salt
¼ teaspoon white pepper
¼ cup melted butter or
   margarine
½ cup toasted slivered almonds

Mash potatoes well (add no milk or butter). Mix potatoes, sieved cottage cheese, sour cream, onion, salt and pepper. Spoon into shallow, buttered 2-quart casserole and brush surface with melted butter. Bake at 350° for about 30 minutes or until surface is browned lightly. Sprinkle with almonds. Serves 6.

Mrs. William P. Brooks
(Veronica White)

SWEET POTATO SOUFFLÉ

3 cups cooked, mashed sweet
   potatoes
1 cup sugar
½ cup milk

⅓ cup butter
2 eggs, slightly beaten
1 teaspoon vanilla extract

TOPPING
1 cup shredded coconut
1 cup chopped pecans
1 cup brown sugar

⅓ cup flour
⅓ cup melted butter

Combine first 6 ingredients. Put mixture in a greased 1-quart casserole. Mix together coconut, pecans, brown sugar, flour, and melted butter. Sprinkle this topping on casserole and bake 20 minutes at 400°.

Mrs. Kenneth W. Dunwody
(Pauline Hinkle)

HINTS

To crisp french fries, peel and slice and soak in cold water refrigerated overnight.

SWEET POTATO CASSEROLE

3 cups cooked sweet potatoes,
  drained
1 cup sugar (or to taste)
2 eggs
1 teaspoon vanilla extract (or
  ½ cup bourbon)

½ cup evaporated milk
½ cup butter or margarine
1 teaspoon cinnamon (optional)

TOPPING:
1 cup brown sugar
⅓ cup flour

⅓ cup melted butter
1 cup chopped pecans

Mix hot potatoes with remaining ingredients, reserving topping ingredients. Place in a greased casserole. To make topping, mix sugar and flour with butter; fold in nuts. Spread mixture on top of potatoes. Place casserole in oven and bake for approximately 30 minutes at 350° or until mixture is firm.

Mrs. Robert W. McAllister
(Anne Katherine Donnelly)

MUSHROOMS
Good with Steak

3 tablespoons butter
½ cup water
2 beef bouillon cubes
1 pound whole mushrooms,
  washed and drained

salt and pepper to taste
Worcestershire sauce
  (dash or two)

In saucepan, melt butter. Add water and dissolve bouillon cubes. Stir in mushrooms and remaining seasonings. Cover and cook 10-15 minutes.

VARIATION: Add 1 tablespoon sherry.

Mrs. Joseph A. Wall
(Patricia Hammock)

HINTS

For a glossy finish to sautéed mushrooms, add a little lemon juice to the butter.

WALNUT-STUFFED MUSHROOMS

18 medium whole mushrooms
4 tablespoons corn oil
   margarine
½ cup chopped walnuts
¼ cup chopped onion
1 clove garlic, minced

¼ cup fresh bread crumbs
1 tablespoon chopped parsley
¼ teaspoon ground black
   pepper
2 pinches ground cayenne
   pepper

Remove stems from mushrooms. Chop 1 cup stems, set aside. In large skillet, melt 2 tablespoons corn oil margarine over medium heat. Sauté walnuts and remove from skillet. Melt remaining margarine in skillet. Mix in mushroom stems, onion and garlic and sauté. In medium bowl, combine walnuts, mushroom stem mixture, bread crumbs, parsley, pepper and cayenne pepper. Mix well. Place mushroom caps on broiler rack. Stuff each cap with filling. Bake at 350° for 15-20 minutes or until done. Serves 6.

Mrs. Paul S. Gillespie
(Elise Hartman)

JEROME'S MUSHROOMS

1 pound large whole
   mushrooms
1 medium onion, chopped
6 saltines, crumbled
½ cup bread crumbs
¼ cup grated Parmesan
   cheese
thyme to taste

oil
basil to taste
salt and pepper to taste
1 tablespoon chopped almonds
1 (10 ounce) package chopped
   spinach, cooked and drained
½ cup vermouth

Wash and dry mushrooms and remove stems. Chop the stems and sauté with onions in oil. Add crumbled crackers, bread crumbs, Parmesan cheese, pinch of thyme and basil, salt and pepper to taste, almonds, and spinach. Mix well. Stuff mushrooms. Place in shallow pan and pour in vermouth. Bake at 325° for 15 to 20 minutes. Do not overcook. Serves 4-6.

Mrs. H. Jerome Strickland
(Joyce Henderson)

HINTS

For fluffier rice, add 1 teaspoon lemon juice to each quart of cooking water.

VIDALIA ONION PIE
Brunch dish

8 slices bacon	salt and pepper
1 large onion	¼ cup grated Swiss cheese
3 tablespoons flour	¼ cup grated Parmesan
2 eggs, beaten	cheese
1 cup milk	1 pie shell, unbaked

Fry bacon and sauté onion in bacon drippings. Crumble bacon and mix with sautéed onion. Sprinkle flour over mixture. Beat eggs and add milk. Stir in bacon and onion. Season with salt and pepper. Sprinkle cheeses over bottom of pie shell. Cover with milk mixture. Bake at 350° for 1 hour. Serves 4-5.

Mrs. Warren C. Grice
(Mary Joe Vandiver)

VIDALIA ONION CASSEROLE

4 cups Vidalia onions,	1 cup bread crumbs
cut into rings	½ cup grated cheese
¼ cup butter	grated Parmesan cheese

SAUCE:

2 tablespoons butter	⅓ cup sherry
2 tablespoons flour	⅔ cup chicken broth

Sauté onions in butter until translucent. Remove from skillet and place in 2-quart casserole. Make a sauce of butter, flour, sherry and chicken broth. Cook until thickened. Pour sauce over onions. Top with bread crumbs and grated cheese. Sprinkle with Parmesan cheese. Cook 30 minutes at 350°. Serves 4-6.

Mrs. Cathey A. Smith
(Bonnie Johnson)

HINTS

Refrigerate onions before chopping to lessen fumes.

To remove skins from tomatoes, plunge one at a time into boiling water 30 seconds.

PARSLEYED CUCUMBERS
Good with Fish or Veal

5-6 cucumbers
salt
pinch of sugar
2 tablespoons white wine
  vinegar

3 tablespoons butter
2 tablespoons chopped parsley
salt and pepper

Peel, seed and cut cucumbers into uniform shapes. Place in a colander and sprinkle with salt, sugar and vinegar. Let them drain about 30 minutes. Remove and pat dry. Plunge them into rapidly boiling water. Return water to boil and cook about 1 minute, depending on size and shape. Drain, refresh with cold water and pat dry. Can prepare ahead to this point. Melt butter in a sauté pan and add cucumbers. Toss until heated. Sprinkle with parsley. Correct seasoning with salt and pepper and serve immediately. Serves 8-10.

Mrs. Thomas H. Lowe
(Maribeth Wills)

HERB BUTTER

2 cups butter or margarine
1 tablespoon Worcestershire
  sauce
1 tablespoon garlic
juice of ½ lemon
1 teaspoon anchovy paste

3 tablespoons chopped parsley
1 tablespoon paprika mixture (6
  teaspoons salt, 1 teaspoon
  white pepper and 1 teaspoon
  paprika)

Whip butter. Whisk in remaining ingredients. Shape into 1-inch thick sticks, wrap in waxed paper and freeze. (Also freezes beautifully in small ramekins.)

Delicious on fish, steaks, breads and vegetables.

Mrs. Kenneth D. Sams
(Harriet Newton)

HINTS

Adding salt to water while cooking corn *only* toughens the corn. Add ½ cup milk and 1 teaspoon sugar to water to make corn tender.

APPLE CASSEROLE

3-6 apples, peeled, cored, sliced
¾ cup sugar
½ cup margarine, melted

1 cup oatmeal
¼ cup brown sugar
⅓ cup flour

Place apples and sugar in a buttered casserole. Top with a mixture of the margarine, oatmeal, brown sugar, and flour. Bake for 1 hour at 350°. Serves 4-6.

Mrs. Ronald E. Robeson
(Carol Clark)

VARIATION: Add ½ teaspoon cinnamon and dash nutmeg

APRICOT CASSEROLE

4 (16 ounce) cans peeled
  apricot halves, drained
1 (16 ounce) box light brown
  sugar

1 (16 ounce) box Ritz crackers,
  crumbled
butter

Grease casserole and line bottom with a layer of drained apricots. Sprinkle brown sugar, then crumbled crackers on top of apricots. Generously dot casserole with butter chips. Repeat, ending with crackers and top with butter. Cook uncovered for 1 hour at 300°. Serves 12.

Mrs. M. Edwin Everett, Jr.
(Helen Birdsey)

HOT SPICED FRUIT WITH ORANGE MARMALADE

1 (16 ounce) can sliced
  peaches, drained, reserving
  juices
1 (17¾ ounce) can pear halves,
  sliced, drained, reserving
  juices
1 (15½ ounce) can pineapple
  chunks, drained, reserving,
  juices

½ cup orange marmalade
2 tablespoons margarine
1 (3-inch) cinnamon stick
¼ teaspoon ground nutmeg
¼ teaspon ground cloves

Drain fruit, reserving ½ cup syrup from each. Combine syrups, marmalade, margarine and spices in a medium saucepan; bring to a boil and boil 3 minutes. Reduce heat; stir in fruit, and simmer 20 minutes. Serves 8-10.

CURRIED FRUIT

1 cup pitted Bing cherries,
  drained
2 cups sliced peaches, drained
1 (16 ounce) can sliced
  pineapple, drained
1 (16 ounce) can apricots,
  drained

3 medium ripe bananas, sliced
¾ cup brown sugar
3 tablespoons cornstarch
2 tablespoons curry powder (or
  to taste)
⅓ cup butter

Drain fruit and cut in large pieces. Add bananas. Combine brown sugar, cornstarch and curry. Add melted butter to mixed fruit, then add sugar mixture. Toss lightly. Turn into a buttered casserole. Bake 350° for 40 minutes. Serves 8-10.

HONEY BAKED APPLES

4 cooking apples, cored
¼-½ cup honey
¼ cup raisins

¼ cup chopped almonds
4-6 teaspoons brown sugar

Peel top half of each apple and core. Mix honey, raisins, almonds, and brown sugar together. Fill apples. Put filled apples in casserole filled ½-inch with water to prevent sticking. Bake at 300° for 45 minutes or until caramelized. Serves 4.

BLENDER HOLLANDAISE

3 egg yolks
1 teaspoon salt
¼ teaspoon pepper

dash cayenne
2 tablespoons lemon juice
½ cup melted butter

In the blender, place egg yolks, salt, pepper, cayenne, and lemon juice. Blend briefly, then slowly add butter, and continue blending until sauce begins to thicken. Season to taste with small amounts of salt, pepper or lemon juice.

The addition of finely chopped parsley, dried tarragon, shallot or onion (any combination) turns this Hollandaise into a Sauce Bearnaise.

Mrs. Eugene C. Dunwody
(Susan Foxworth)

CAKES

BEST CHOCOLATE CAKE

CAKE:

¾ cup cocoa
1⅛ cups hot coffee
¾ cup butter
2¾ cups sugar
¾ cup sour cream

1½ teaspoons vanilla extract
3 cups sifted flour
¾ teaspoon soda
¾ teaspoon salt
5 egg whites (reserve yolks)

FILLING

⅓ cup flour
pinch salt
½ cup sugar, divided
1⅓ cups hot milk

2 egg yolks
1 cup heavy cream, whipped
1 teaspoon vanilla extract

ICING:

¼ cup soft butter
2 cups confectioners' sugar
3 squares chocolate, melted

2½ teaspoons hot coffee
3 egg yolks, beaten

Preheat oven to 350°. Mix cocoa and coffee. Cool. Cream butter and sugar. Mix and sift dry ingredients three times. Add to batter and mix well. Add sour cream, vanilla extract, and cocoa-coffee mixture. Fold in stiffly beaten egg whites. Bake in 3 greased pans at 350° for 35-40 minutes. Cool. For filling, in a saucepan, mix the flour, salt, half of the sugar and milk. Cook until thick. Combine egg yolks and the remaining sugar and add to the mixture, cooking until thick. Cool and add cream and vanilla extract. Spread between cake layers. For icing, mix butter and sugar. Add remaining ingredients. Ice cooled cake.

Mrs. Wilbur I. Tucker
(Elizabeth Conner)

CHOCOLATE ICING

3 cups confectioners' sugar
¼ cup hot water
1 egg
½ cup soft butter

4 (1 ounce) squares
unsweetened chocolate,
melted

Blend all ingredients and ice cooled cake.

Mrs. James L. Solomon
(Virginia McCook)

CHOCOLATE CINNAMON CAKE

2 cups sugar
2 cups flour
¼ teaspoon salt
½ cup butter
½ cup Crisco or margarine
1 cup water

4 tablespoons cocoa
½ cup buttermilk
2 eggs, beaten
1 teaspoon soda
1 teaspoon vanilla extract
2 teaspoons cinnamon

ICING:
½ cup butter
4 tablespons cocoa
6 tablespoons milk
1 (16 ounce) box confectioners'
  sugar

1 teaspoon vanilla extract
1 cup chopped nuts (optional)

Sift together sugar, flour and salt. Bring butter and Crisco to boil in a saucepan with water and cocoa. Blend buttermilk, eggs, soda, vanilla extract and cinnamon in large bowl. Add flour mixture to buttermilk mixture. Then add chocolate mixture and beat. Pour mixture in 10 x 15-inch pan. Cook at 400° for 20 minutes. For icing, bring butter, cocoa, and milk to boil. Add confectioners' sugar and vanilla extract. Add nuts, if desired. Pour over warm cake.

Mrs. James G. Wilcox, Jr.
(Betty Wilson)

NUT CAKE

6 eggs, beaten
4 cups flour
2 cups sugar
1 cup butter
2 teaspoons baking powder

¾ cup milk
½ cup brandy or wine
1½ whole nutmegs, ground
1 quart shelled pecans
1 quart raisins (1½ pounds)

Preheat oven to 250°. Beat eggs. Sift baking powder into flour. Cream flour, sugar and butter. Add milk. Pour brandy over nutmeg. Mix all, except nuts and raisins. Flour nuts and raisins and fold into batter. Pour batter into greased and floured tube pan. Steam 4 hours covered with foil at 250° placing pan of water on bottom rack of oven. Makes 1 (5 pound) cake.

Mrs. Corinne C. Barfield
(Corinne Cole)

HINTS

If a cake browns too quickly, place a pan of warm water on the oven rack above it.

SEVEN LAYER CHOCOLATE CAKE

1½ cups butter
2 cups sugar
1 teaspoon vanilla extract

6 eggs
3 cups sifted flour

FILLING:
1 (12 ounce) package chocolate
   chips
¼ cup hot water
½ cup butter

4 egg yolks, beaten
3 tablespoons confectioners'
   sugar
1½ tablespoons rum extract

FROSTING:
4 tablespoons margarine
1 cup packed brown sugar
¼ cup evaporated milk

3 tablespoons cocoa
½ teaspoon vanilla extract

Let butter and eggs reach room temperature. Whip butter until fluffy, add sugar slowly. Add vanilla extract. Add eggs; one at a time, whipping each egg in until the mixture is even. Slowly fold in flour. Bake in a greased and floured tube pan at 350° for 1 hour until done. Cool in pan for 15 minutes, then turn out onto a rack to cool thoroughly. Cut a vertical notch in the side of the cake to use as a guide for re-stacking; then slice the cake horizontally into 7 layers. Put the layers back together with filling. Then cover with icing. For filling, melt chocolate chips and butter with water in top of a double boiler. Stir in beaten egg yolks and keep stirring until thickened. Remove from boiler, add sugar and extract; cool by setting it down into bowl of cold water. Spread on cake after thoroughly cooled. For frosting, boil ingredients for 2 minutes. Beat with wire whisk until smooth. Frost top and sides of cake.

Ms. Betty Moseley Ramsbottom
(Betty Moseley)

GERMAN CHOCOLATE ICING

1 cup evaporated milk
1 cup sugar
3 egg yolks, slightly beaten
½ cup butter

1 teaspoon vanilla extract
1⅓ cups frozen coconut
1 cup chopped pecans

Mix all ingredients except coconut and pecans; cook over medium heat stirring constantly for 12-15 minutes until mixture resembles a custard. Cool and add coconut and pecans. Spread on two 9-inch layer cakes.

WHITE CHOCOLATE CAKE

¼ pound white chocolate
½ cup boiling water
1 cup butter or margarine
2 cups sugar
4 eggs, separated
2½ cups flour

1 teaspoon soda
1 tablespoon vanilla extract
1 cup buttermilk
1 cup Angel Flake coconut
1 cup broken pecans

FROSTING:
1 (8 ounce) package cream
   cheese, room temperature
½ cup butter or margarine
1 teaspoon vanilla extract

1 (16 ounce) box confectioners'
   sugar
1 tablespoon milk

Melt white chocolate in boiling water; set aside to cool. Cream butter and sugar; add egg yolks and beat; add chocolate and vanilla extract. Add flour and soda, alternating with buttermilk. Mix well. Fold in stiffly beaten egg whites, coconut and pecans. Grease and flour pans. Bake at 350° about 20-25 minutes. For frosting, mix all ingredients together. Frost cooled cake. Makes four 9-inch layers or three 8 x 8 inch.

Mrs. Charles F. Rehberg, Jr.
(Nancy Rowland)

ITALIAN CREAM CAKE

½ cup softened butter
2 cups sugar
½ cup shortening
5 eggs, separated
1 teaspoon soda

1 cup buttermilk
2 cups sifted flour
1 cup Angel Flake coconut
1 teaspoon vanilla extract

Cream butter, sugar and shortening. Add egg yolks, beating after each addition. Dissolve soda in buttermilk and add alternately with flour to egg mixture. Add coconut, fold in stiffly beaten egg whites, and add vanilla extract. Pour into three 8-inch greased and floured cake pans. Bake 350° for 25-30 minutes. Cool cakes.
Ice with cream cheese icing found on page 257.

Mrs. Rufus Dorsey Sams, III
(Sidney Tucker)

MILKY WAY CAKE

8 (1¾ ounce) Milky Way candy
  bars
1½ cups butter, divided
2 cups sugar
4 eggs, well beaten
2½ cups flour

¼ teaspoon baking soda
1¼ cups buttermilk
1 teaspoon vanilla extract
1 cup chopped pecans
confectioner's sugar

ICING:
2½ cups sugar
1 cup evaporated milk
½ cup butter
1 cup marshmallow cream

1 (6 ounce) package chocolate
  chips
1 cup chopped pecans

Melt Milky Way bars with ½ cup butter. Cool; cream remaining butter with sugar and to it add beaten eggs and cooled chocolate mixture. Sift flour and baking soda together. Alternating, add flour and buttermilk to batter. Add vanilla extract and pecans. Grease pans and dust with confectioner's sugar. Bake in three 9-inch cake pans 30-45 minutes at 325°. For icing, combine sugar and evaporated milk. Cook to soft ball stage. Remove from heat. Add butter, marshmallow cream, and chocolate chips, stirring until all have melted. Add pecans. Ice cooled cake between layers and on top.

Mrs. William W. Williams
(Ann Warlick)

SPICE COFFEE CAKE
Best when warm

2 eggs
1 cup mayonnaise
1 (18½ ounce) box Duncan
  Hines spice cake mix

1(16 ounce) can whole-berry
  cranberry sauce
confectioners' sugar

Mix eggs, mayonnaise and cake mix. Fold in cranberry sauce. Bake in two 13 x 9 x 2-inch pans at 325° for 25-30 minutes. Dust cake with confectioners' sugar.

Mrs. John H. Morgan
(Louise Mooney)

SHARON'S RUM CAKE

1 (18½ ounce) package Duncan Hines yellow cake mix
1 (3¾ ounce) package instant vanilla pudding

4 eggs
¾ cup Mazola oil
¾ cup rum

TOPPING
½ cup chopped pecans
½ cup cherries, drained and halved

¾ cup butter
¾ cup light brown sugar

Mix cake ingredients and blend at medium speed. For topping ingredients, melt butter and sugar together. Stir in cherries and nuts. Pour topping mixture into Bundt pan, cover with cake mixture, and bake at 325° for 40-60 minutes. Let stand 3 minutes before removing from pan. Serves 8.

Mrs. Edgar Y. Mallary, III
(Lloyd Washington)

COCONUT-SOUR CREAM LAYER CAKE

1 (18½ ounce) package butter-flavored cake mix
2 cups sugar
1 (16 ounce) carton sour cream

1 (12 ounce) package frozen coconut, thawed
1½ cups whipped topping, thawed

Prepare cake according to directions on package making two 8-inch cake layers. When layers are cool, split each layer in half. Combine sugar, sour cream and coconut. Chill. Reserve 1 cup sour cream mixture for frosting. Spread remainder on layers. Combine reserved sour cream mixture with whipped topping. Spread on tops and sides of cake. Refrigerate 3 days before serving.

VARIATIONS OF ICING: 1½ cups sugar, 1 (8 ounce) carton sour cream, and 18 ounces frozen coconut. Mix sugar and sour cream together. Add coconut. Allow mixture to sit for 15 minutes before icing one 8-inch layer cake or 9-inch layer cake.

Mrs. William W. Williams
(Ann Warlick)

WALDORF ASTORIA CAKE

2 cups sugar
2 teaspoons baking powder
2 cups cake flour
1 teaspoon salt
½ cup butter, softened
2 eggs, beaten

4 squares unsweetened
  chocolate, melted
1½ cups milk
2 teaspoons vanilla extract
1 cup finely chopped nuts

ICING:
1 (16-ounce) box confectioners'
  sugar
½ cup butter, softened
1 egg, beaten
2 squares unsweetened
  chocolate, melted

1 teaspoon lemon juice
1 teaspoon vanilla extract
3 or 4 tablespoons evaporated
  milk
1 cup chopped nuts

Preheat oven to 375°. Grease and flour two 9-inch cake pans. Set aside. Sift dry ingredients together. Cream butter and sugar. Add melted chocolate and well beatened eggs. Alternately add milk and dry ingredients. Add vanilla and nuts. Pour into greased cake pans. Cook for 25-30 minutes at 375°. Do not overcook. For icing, cream confectioners' sugar and butter. Add egg, chocolate, lemon juice and vanilla extract. Add 3 or 4 tablespoons of milk until frosting is soft enough to spread. Add nuts and spread.

Mrs. Steve L. Wilson
(Gena Ware)

CARAMEL ICING

½ cup margarine
1 cup firmly packed brown
  sugar
⅓ cup milk

2 cups confectioners' sugar
1 teaspoon vanilla extract
1 cup chopped nuts

Melt margarine in heavy skillet. Add brown sugar. Cook over low heat 2 minutes, stirring constantly. Add milk and continue to cook. Stir until mixture comes to boil. Remove from heat and let cool about 10 minutes. Add confectioners' sugar. Stir until right consistency to spread. Add vanilla extract and nuts. Cool 5 minutes and spread on your favorite yellow cake recipe. Frosts 2-layer cake.

Mrs. Henry T. Clay
(Cater Snow)

ORANGE SLICE CAKE
Freezes well

1 cup butter
2 cups sugar
4 eggs
½ cup buttermilk
1 teaspoon soda
3½ cups flour
1 pound dates, chopped

1 pound orange slice candy,
  chopped
2 cups chopped nuts
1 (3½ ounce) can flaked
  coconut
1 cup fresh orange juice
2 cups confectioners' sugar

Cream butter and sugar until smooth. Add eggs one at a time, beating well after each addition. Dissolve soda in buttermilk and add to creamed mixture. Place flour in a large bowl and add dates, orange slices and nuts. Stir to coat each piece. Add flour mixture and coconut to the creamed mixture. This makes a very stiff dough that should be mixed with your hands. Pour into 2 loaf pans that have been greased and floured. Bake at 250° for 2½ to 3 hours. Combine orange juice and confectioners' sugar and pour over hot cakes. Let stand in pan overnight. When removed from pans, seal in foil to enhance flavor.

Mrs. Linton M. Solomon, Jr.
(Eleanor Anthony)

SURPRISE CAKE

1 cups chopped raisins
1 cup water from raisins
½ pound hot pork sausage,
  uncooked
2 cups light brown sugar

1 teaspoon soda
1 teaspoon cinnamon
1 teaspon baking powder
2½ cups flour
1 cup finely chopped nuts

PENUCHE ICING:
½ cup butter
1 cup packed brown sugar
¼ cup milk

1¾ to 2 cups sifted
  confectioners' sugar

Cover raisins with water and cook for 20 minutes. Mix all other ingredients, except water. Add water from raisins. Bake in 2 lightly greased and floured round 9-inch cake pans at 350° for about 45 minutes. When cake is cool, ice wiht Penuche Icing. For icing, melt butter in saucepan. Add brown sugar. Boil over low heat for 2 minutes, stirring constantly. Add milk and bring to a boil. Cool to lukewarm and gradually add confectioners' sugar. Place pan in ice water and stir until spreading consistency. Serves 8-10.

LANE CAKE

1 cup butter
2 cups sugar
3¼ cups flour
¾ teaspoon salt
3½ teaspoons baking powder

½ cup milk
½ cup evaporated milk
1 teaspoon vanilla extract
8 egg whites, beaten

FILLING:
8 egg yolks, beaten
1 cup sugar
½ cup butter, softened
1 cup chopped pecans

2 cups grated coconut
1 cup chopped raisins
½ cup whiskey

Cream butter and sugar thoroughly. Sift flour, salt and baking powder 3 times. Add small amounts of flour to creamed mixture alternately with milk, beating until smooth after each addition. Add vanilla extract. Beat egg whites until fluffy (not dry) and fold in. Grease three 9-inch layer cake pans lightly and line bottoms with waxed paper. Bake in preheated 350° oven for 25 minutes. For filling, combine nuts, coconut, raisins, and whiskey and let soak. Beat yolks until light. Gradually add sugar and softened butter and beat well. Cook in top of double boiler until slightly thickened, stirring constantly. Fold nut-whiskey mixture into egg mixture. Alternate layers of cake and filing. After assembling cake in layers with filling, ice cake with your favorite white icing.

DOROTHY'S ANGEL FOOD CAKE

1¼ cups sifted Swans Down
   cake flour
½ cup sugar
1½ cups or 12 egg whites
   (at room temperature)

1¼ teaspoons cream of tartar
¼ teaspoon salt
2 teaspoons vanilla extract
1⅓ cups sugar

Measure sifted flour, add ½ cup sugar, and sift 4 times. Combine egg whites, cream of tartar, salt and vanilla extract in large bowl. Beat at high speed until soft peaks form. Sprinkle in remaining sugar (1⅓ cups) in 4 additions, beating until blended. Sift in flour mixture in 4 additions. Bake in ungreased 10-inch tube pan at 350° for 35 to 40 minutes. Cool cake upside down in pan.

Mrs. Ralph G. Newton, Jr.
(Harriet Adams)

FIVE-FLAVOR CAKE
Great!

1 cup butter
½ cup vegetable shortening
3 cups sugar
5 eggs, well beaten
3 cups flour
½ teaspoon baking powder

1 cup milk
1 teaspoon rum extract
1 teaspoon coconut flavoring
1 teaspoon butter flavoring
1 teaspoon lemon extract
1 teaspoon vanilla extract

GLAZE:
1 cup sugar
½ cup water
1 teaspoon coconut flavoring
1 teaspoon rum extract

1 teaspoon butter flavoring
1 teaspoon lemon extract
1 teaspoon almond extract
1 teaspoon vanilla extract

Preat oven to 325° for cake. Cream butter, shortening, and sugar until light. Add beaten eggs; combine flour and baking powder. Add dry ingredients to creamed sugar mixture alternating with milk. Add flavorings and extracts. Pour into greased 10-inch tube pan, bake 1½ hours at 325°. Combine glaze ingredients; bring to a boil; stir until sugar dissolves; pour mixture over warm cake while still in tube pan. Serves 12-15.

MARSHMALLOW APPLESAUCE CAKE

2¾ cups unsifted flour
2 cups sugar
1½ teaspoons baking soda
1½ teaspoons salt
¼ teaspoon baking powder
1 teaspoon ground cinnamon
½ teaspoon ground cloves
½ teaspoon ground allspice

½ cup soft shortening
2 eggs
2 cups unsweetened
  applesauce
1 cup walnut halves
20 large marshmallows
  (¼ pound)

Sift together flour, sugar, soda, salt, baking powder and spices. Add soft shortening, eggs and applesauce. Beat until smooth and well blended. Stir in walnuts. Pour into greased and floured 13 x 9 x 2-inch pan. Press whole marshmallows into batter pressing through to bottom of pan (makes 4 to 5 rows). Bake in moderate 350° oven about 50 minutes. Serves 20.

Mrs. Charlotte S. Watson
(Charlotte Selman)

SHERRY CAKE

1 (18½ ounce) box yellow
    cake mix
1 (3¾ ounce) box instant
    vanilla pudding
¾ cup oil
¾ cup cream sherry

1 tablespoon butternut
    flavoring
4 eggs
¼ cup sugar
1 teaspoon cinnamon
2 teaspoons nutmeg

ICING:
1 cup sifted confectioners'
    sugar
2 tablespoons milk

½ teaspoon vanilla extract
½ teaspoon sherry

Mix cake mix and pudding. Add oil, sherry and butternut flavoring.
Add eggs one at a time mixing well, but do not over-beat. Mix
together sugar, cinnamon, and nutmeg. Grease bundt pan and put
in one-third batter, sprinkle with one-third sugar-cinnamon-nutmeg
mixture. Repeat with remaining batter and sugar-cinnamon-nutmeg
mixture. Bake at 350° for 40-45 minutes. Mix icing ingredients
together and spoon over warm cake.

Mrs. Wilbur I. Tucker
(Elizabeth Conner)

PINEAPPLE CAKE

2½ cups sifted self-rising flour
4 eggs, separated
2 cups sugar
1¼ cups salad oil
1 (15 ounce) can crushed
    pineapple drained well,
    reserving juice

2 tablespoons hot water
1½ teaspoons cinnamon
1 cup chopped nuts

GLAZE:
4 tablespoons pineapple juice
¼ cup margarine

½ (16 ounce) box
confectioners' sugar

Combine flour, egg yolks, sugar and oil. Add pineapple, water and
cinnamon. Beat egg whites stiff. Fold into mixture. Add nuts. Bake
in greased tube pan for 1 hour at 325°. Mix glaze ingredients and
pour over cake while hot and still in pan. Punch holes in cake and
let glaze seep into cake.

Miss Ann Word Thornton

WONDERFUL BANANA CAKE

BANANA FILLING:
4 large bananas
3 tablespoons butter, softened
¼ cup sugar

3 tablespoons dry sherry
¼ teaspoon nutmeg

CAKE:
2 cups sugar
½ cup butter
4 egg yolks
1 teaspoon vanilla extract
2½ cups sifted flour

2 teaspoons baking powder
¼ teaspoon salt
¾ cup milk
4 egg whites, beaten with
    pinch salt

FROSTING:
1 cup heavy cream

2 tablespoons confectioners'
    sugar

In shallow baking dish, bake 4 large bananas, *unpeeled*, in 350° oven for 25-30 minutes or until soft. Cool and then peel bananas and mash them with butter until smooth. Stir in sugar, sherry and nutmeg. Refrigerate filling while you prepare the cake. Cream sugar and butter until fluffy. Add egg yolks, one at a time, beating well after each addition. Add vanilla, combine flour, baking powder and salt. Add to sugar, butter, egg yolk mixture alternately with ¾ cup milk, one-third at a time. Beat egg whites and pinch of salt until stiff. Fold into yolk mixture. Divide batter between 2 buttered and floured 9-inch cake pans and bake 350° for 25-30 minutes, or until done. Cool in tins 5 minutes, then invert on cake racks and cool completely. Half with serrated knife. Place one layer, cut side up on cake plate. Spread with one-third banana mixture. Top with second layer and continue to layer cake and banana mixture, ending with layer of cake. Frost cake with 1 cup cream whipped with 2 tablespoons confectioners' sugar, or to taste. Chill 3 hours.

SEAFOAM ICING
Great for Spice Cakes

1½ cups light brown sugar
2 egg whites

⅓ cup water
pinch salt

Cook ingredients in double boiler for 7 minutes or until icing is desired spreading consistency. Ice a 2-layer cake.

Mrs. Leo B. Huckabee
(Jane Odom)

FRESH APPLE CAKE
Moist!

1½ cups cooking oil
2½ cups sugar
3 eggs, well beaten
2 teaspoons vanilla extract
3 cups sifted flour
1 teaspoon soda

1 teaspoon salt
1 teaspoon each cinnamon,
   nutmeg, cloves
3 cups chopped apple
1 cup chopped nuts

GLAZE:
½ cup butter or margarine
1 cup brown sugar
¼ cup undiluted evaporated
   milk

1 teaspoon vanilla extract

Mix oil and sugar. Add eggs and vanilla extract. Add flour, soda, salt, cinnamon, nutmeg and cloves. Fold in apple and nuts. Bake in greased, floured tube pan at 350° for about 1 hour. For Glaze, melt butter, adding sugar and milk and continue cooking at a rolling boil for 1 minute. Add vanilla extract. Cool and pour over cake.

Mrs. John F. Rogers, Jr.
(Laura Bush)

PLUM CAKE

2 cups self-rising flour
2 cups sugar
1 teaspoon cinnamon
1 teaspoon nutmeg
1¼ teaspoons allspice

1 cup Wesson oil
2 (4¾ ounce) jars baby food
   plums
3 eggs, well beaten
2 cups chopped pecans

GLAZE:
1 cups confectioners' sugar

juice of one lemon

Sift flour, sugar and spices together. Add oil, plums and eggs. Mix well. Add pecans. Pour into greased bundt pan. Bake at 350° for 1 hour. Cool for 15 minutes. Glaze with 1 cup confectioners' sugar and juice of 1 lemon which have been mixed together.

Ms. Patricia Hardeman Lewis
(Patricia Hardeman)

STRAWBERRY CAKE

1 (3 ounce) package strawberry
  gelatin
½ cup very warm water
1 (18½ ounce) box white cake
  mix

¾ cup vegetable oil
½ of (10 ounce) package
  strawberries, thawed
4 eggs

ICING:
1 (16 ounce) box confectioners'
  sugar
½ cup margarine

½ of (10 ounce) package
  strawberries, thawed

Dissolve gelatin in water and cool. Add mix, oil, strawberries, and eggs. Beat until blended. Pour into tube pan. Bake at 350° for 1 hour to 1 hour and 15 minutes. For icing, cream margarine and sugar. Add strawberries and juice, a little at a time, while blending until desired consistency. Ice cooled cake. Serves 20-25.

Mrs. H. Lowry Tribble, Jr.
(Susan Terry)

HOLIDAY EGGNOG CAKE

CAKE:
1 (18½ ounce) package Duncan
  Hines yellow cake mix
1 cup canned eggnog
¼ cup vegetable oil

3 eggs
2 tablespoons rum
¼ teaspoon nutmeg

ICING:
1 (8 ounce) package cream
  cheese, softened
1 (16 ounce) package
  confectioners' sugar, sifted

1½ teaspoon eggnog
few drops yellow food coloring
dash nutmeg

Preheat oven to 350°. In large bowl, combine cake mix, eggnog, vegetable oil, eggs, rum and nutmeg. Beat at medium speed 3 minutes. Pour into 3 well-greased and floured 8-inch square pans. Bake 20 minutes at 350°. Cool 10 minutes. Remove from pans. Cool completely. Frost with cream cheese icing. For icing, beat softened cream cheese until fluffy. Gradually beat in sifted confectioners' sugar. Add eggnog, ½ teaspoon at a time, and a few drops yellow food coloring. Add a dash of nutmeg and ice cake. Makes one 8-inch square cake.

EGGNOG FROSTED CAKE

1 angel food cake
½ cup butter, softened
2 cups confectioners' sugar
2 egg yolks
1 teaspoon vanilla extract
¼ teaspoon nutmeg
2 tablespoons sherry and
  2 tablespoons whiskey or 4
  tablespoons Scotch

5 tablespoons coffee cream
1½ cups whipping cream,
  whipped
nutmeg for garnish

Cut cake into 4 layers with serrated knife. Cream soft butter with sifted sugar until fluffy. Blend in 1 egg yolk at a time. Stir in vanilla extract, nutmeg, liquor and coffee cream. Spread on cake layers and reassemble cake. Whip heavy cream and ice cake. Sprinkle with nutmeg. Refrigerate for at least 6 hours. Serves 12.

Mrs. Robert A. Clark, Jr.
(Helen Walker)

TWO HUNDRED-FIFTY DOLLAR CAKE

½ cup butter
2 cups sugar
4 squares chocolate, melted
2 eggs, well beaten
1½ cups milk

2 cups flour
2 teaspoons baking powder
pinch salt
2 teaspoons vanilla extract
1 cup chopped nuts

ICING:
½ cup butter
2 squares chocolate
1 egg
1½ cups confectioners' sugar

pinch salt
1 teaspoon vanilla extract
1 tablespoon lemon juice
1 cup chopped nuts

Cream butter and sugar well. Add melted chocolate and well-beaten eggs. Sift dry ingredients. Add alternately with milk. Add vanilla extract and nuts. Pour batter into 3 layer cake pans and bake in 350° oven. For icing, melt butter and chocolate. Add beaten egg, sugar, vanilla extract and lemon juice. Mix well. Add nuts. Spread on cake.

Mrs. Oliver C. Bateman
(Mary Jane Gosline)

CARROT CAKE
A large, moist cake!

1½ cups salad oil
2¼ cups sugar
4 eggs
3 cups flour
2 teaspoons baking powder
2 teaspoons baking soda
½ teaspoon salt

2 teaspoons cinnamon
1 teaspoon nutmeg
½ teaspoon allspice
3 cups grated carrots
1 teaspoon vanilla extract
1 cup chopped nuts

Blend salad oil and sugar. Add eggs and blend. Sift flour, baking powder, baking soda, salt, cinnamon, nutmeg, allspice into mixture. Blend. Add grated carrots (Food processor can be used.) Add vanilla extract and nuts. Blend. Pour batter into 2 greased and floured 9-inch cake pans. Cook at 350° about 40-50 minutes. When cool, ice with cream cheese icing or orange glaze.

Mrs. William W. Williams
(Ann Warlick)

CREAM CHEESE ICING

1 (8 ounce) package cream
cheese, softened
½ cup butter, softened
1 (1 pound) box confectioners'
sugar

2 teaspoons vanilla extract
1 cup chopped nuts

Cream butter and cream cheese. Add sugar, vanilla extract and nuts. Blend well. Ice cooled carrot or apple cake. Refrigerate iced cake.

Mrs. William W. Williams
(Ann Warlick)

SIMPLE POUND CAKE

2 cups sugar
1 cup butter
6 eggs

2 cups flour
1 teaspoon vanilla extract

Mix sugar and butter until creamy. Add eggs, beating one at a time. Then add flour very slowly to batter. Beat until mixture is creamy. Add vanilla extract. Pour into a greased tube or loaf pan. Bake at 300° for 1 hour.

Mrs. G. Phelps Wade
(Joyce Waits)

OATMEAL CAKE

1 cup quick oats
½ cup butter
1¼ cups boiling water
1 cup sugar
1 cup brown sugar
2 eggs, beaten

1⅓ cups sifted flour
½ teaspoon salt
1 teaspoon soda
1 teaspoon nutmeg
1 teaspoon cinnamon

TOPPING:
¼ cup butter
1 cup brown sugar
¼ cup evaporated milk

1 cup flaked coconut
1 cup chopped pecans

Pour boiling water over oats and butter. Allow to stand 20 minutes. Add remaining cake ingredients. Bake for 35-45 minutes at 350° in buttered 1½ quart pyrex dish. Mix and simmer all topping ingredients to melt butter and dissolve sugar. Spread over cake. Brown under broiler.

Mrs. Thomas L. Bass
(Patricia Walker)

CHOCOLATE POUND CAKE

1 cup butter plus ½ cup
  shortening
3 cups sugar
5 eggs
3 cups cake flour

½ teaspoon baking powder
½ cup cocoa
¼ teaspoon salt
1¼ cups milk
1 tablespoon vanilla extract

Cream butter and shortening, add sugar and beat until light. Add eggs one at a time, beating after each addition. Sift flour, baking powder, cocoa, and salt. Add dry ingredients alternately with milk. Add vanilla extract before last flour. Bake in a greased and floured tube pan 1 hour and 15 minutes at 325°.

Mrs. Alex R. Mitchell
(Eyleen Jackson)

VARIATION FOR A COCONUT POUND CAKE: Omit chocolate and substitute 1 teaspoon vanilla extract, 1 teaspoon coconut flavoring. (Superior Brand Coconutti), and 1 teaspoon almond extract for the 1 tablespoon vanilla extract.

BROWN SUGAR POUND CAKE
From Mrs. Charley Farmer

1 cup butter
½ cup Crisco shortening
1 (16 ounce) box light brown
  sugar
5 large eggs
3 cups cake flour
½ teaspoon salt

1 teaspoon baking powder
¼ teaspoon soda
1 cup milk
1 teaspoon vanilla extract
1 teaspoon almond extract
½ cup chopped pecans
  (optional)

ICING:
1 (16 ounce) box light brown
  sugar
½ cup margarine

1 (5⅓ ounce) can evaporated
  milk

Cream butter, shortening and sugar. Add eggs, one at a time, beating well. Add sifted dry ingredients alternately with milk. Add extracts and nuts. Pour into greased and floured 10-inch tube or bundt pan. Bake at 325° for 50 minutes, then at 350° for 20 minutes longer. For icing, combine ingredients and cook until boiling, stirring constantly. Continue cooking for 2 minutes. Cool and beat well. Ice cake.

Mrs. J. Wilbur Coggins, Jr.
(Sue Moss)

SOUR CREAM POUND CAKE

1 cup butter
3 cups sugar
6 eggs
3 cups flour
¼ teaspoon salt

¼ teaspoon baking soda
1 (8 ounce) carton sour cream
1 teaspoon vanilla extract
2 tablespoons bourbon

Cream butter and sugar. Add eggs one at a time, beating well after each addition. Add dry ingredients which have been sifted together, alternating with sour cream. Add vanilla extract and bourbon. Bake in a greased and floured tube pan or two 9 x 5-inch loaf pans at 325° for approximately 1 hour.

Mrs. Donald K. Ream, III
(Liz Daves)

MOTHER'S DARK FRUIT CAKE

1½ cups real butter
1 pound sugar
4½ cups flour (use 3⅓ cups
   in cake and 1 cup to dredge
   fruit and nuts)
10 eggs, separated
2 pounds raisins, chopped
1 (15-ounce) box currants,
   chopped
1 pound citron, chopped
½ cup molasses
1½ cups chopped pecans
½ pound almonds, chopped
½ pound crystallized
   cherries, cut up
1 tablespoon ground cinnamon
1 tablespoon ground cloves
1 tablespoon ground nutmeg

Cream butter and sugar well. Separate eggs and add yolks, one at a time, beating well after each addition. Add half of 3½ cups flour, spices and whites of eggs that have been well beaten. Add molasses and remainder of flour. Mix well. Add dredged fruit and nuts. Grease three 9 x 5 x 3-inch loaf pans and line with brown paper. Pour mixture into pans and bake 2 hours, 15 minutes in 275° preheated oven. Cool 30 minutes on racks, remove carefully from pans, and peel off brown paper. Brush warmed loaves with bourbon. Continue brushing loaves with bourbon every other day for 2 more weeks.

Ingredients will mix better at room temperature.

Mrs. Leo B. Huckabee
(Jane Odom)

FUDGE CUPCAKES

1 cup flour
1¾ cups sugar
4 eggs
4 squares semi-sweet chocolate
1 cup margarine
1½ cups chopped pecans
1 teaspoon vanilla extract

Combine flour, sugar and eggs; blend by hand but do not beat. Melt chocolate and butter in a saucepan; stir in nuts. Combine sugar mixture, chocolate mixture and vanilla extract; blend but do not beat. Pour into paper-lined muffin tins, and bake at 325° for 30 minutes. Yields 2 dozen cupcakes.

Mrs. Andrew W. Young
(Pamela Watkins)

HINTS

To scald milk without scorching, rinse pan in cold water before using.

PUMPKIN-ORANGE CAKE

1½ cups sugar
½ cup shortening
2 eggs
1 cup canned pumpkin
½ of (6 ounce) can orange
   juice concentrate, thawed
   (or ⅓ cup)
¼ cup milk

1⅔ cups flour
1 teaspoon baking powder
½ teaspoon baking soda
1 teaspoon ground cinnamon
½ teaspoon ground allspice
½ teaspoon ground nutmeg
¼ teaspoon ground cloves
½ cup currants or raisins

FLUFF FROSTING:
3 tablespoons flour
1 cup milk
1 teaspoon vanilla extract

¾ cup sugar
½ cup butter
½ cup pecan halves

In large mixing bowl, beat together the sugar and shortening until light. Add eggs. Add pumpkin, orange juice concentrate, and milk. Stir together the flour, baking powder, soda and spices. Add to pumpkin mixture, beating until smooth. Stir in currants or raisins. Spread batter in 2 greased and floured 8-inch round cake pans. Bake in 350° oven for 30 to 35 minutes, or until cake tests done. Cool in pans 10 minutes; turn out and cool on wire rack. To make frosting: Blend together in a small saucepan flour and milk. Cook and stir until bubbly. Cool to room temperature, about 1 hour. Stir in vanilla extract. Beat together the sugar and butter until light and fluffy. Gradually beat in cooled milk mixture. Spread between cake layers; frost sides and top. Garnish with pecan halves.

FIG CAKE

½ cup butter, softened
1 cup sugar
3 eggs
½ teaspoon vanilla extract
2 cups flour
1 teaspoon soda
1 teaspoon cinnamon

1 teaspoon nutmeg
1 teaspoon cloves
1 cup buttermilk
1½ cups chopped fig preserves
½ cup chopped nuts
½ cup coconut
1 cup chopped raisins

Cream butter and sugar. Add eggs one at a time. Stir in vanilla extract. Combine flour, soda and spices and add to creamed mixture alternately with buttermilk. Add remaining ingredients and bake in a greased and floured bundt pan at 350° for 50 minutes.

TOFFEE CRUNCH CAKE

2 cups flour
1 (9.9 ounce) package coconut
   almond or coconut pecan
   frosting mix
½ cup firmly packed brown
   sugar

½ cup butter, softened
1 teaspoon salt
1 teaspoon soda
1 cup buttermilk
1 teaspoon vanilla extract
1 egg

TOPPING:
3 (1¼ ounce) Heath candy bars,
   crushed

¾ cup reserved crumb mixture

Preheat oven to 350°. Grease (not oil) 9 x 13-inch pan. Lightly spoon flour into measuring cup, level off. In large bowl, combine first 4 ingredients, blend at low speed until crumbly. *Reserve ¾ cup of mixture for topping.* To remaining mixture, add salt, soda, buttermilk, vanilla extract and egg. Beat 1 minute at medium speed. Pour into greased pan. Combine Topping ingredients and sprinkle over batter. Bake 20-30 minutes or until toothpick inserted in center comes out clean.

SWEET POTATO CAKE

CAKE:
2 cups sugar
1 teaspoon cloves
1 teaspoon cinnamon
1 teaspoon allspice
1 teaspoon nutmeg
1 teaspoon salt
2 teaspoons baking powder
¼ cup cocoa

1 cup butter
4 eggs, separated
2 cups flour
1 cup cooked mashed sweet
   potatoes
½ cup chopped pecans
1 teaspoon vanilla extract

ICING:
2 cups sugar
1 cup milk
2 oranges, rind and juice
1 lemon, rind and juice

1 grated fresh coconut
1 cup chopped golden raisins
1 teaspoon cornstarch
1 cup chopped pecans

Blend spices and sugar together. Add salt, baking powder and cocoa. Mix well. Add butter and mix well. Add yolks, then flour and potatoes. Fold in beaten whites and pecans. Add vanilla extract and bake in two 8-inch pans at 350° for 30 minutes. Allow to cool and remove from pans. Mix all icing ingredients in a saucepan and cook, stirring constantly until thick. Remove from heat and spread on cake while warm.

PIES

SHERRY CHIFFON PIE
From the Frances Virginia Tea Room

PIE CRUST:

2½ cups graham cracker crumbs

2 tablespoons soft butter
2 tablespoons sugar

FILLING:

1 tablespoon Knox gelatin
1½ tablespoons cold water
½ cup canned evaporated milk
¼ cup cold water
3 egg yolks

10 tablespoons sugar, divided
4 egg whites
5 tablespoons pale dry Sherry or rum
whipped cream

To make crust, mix crumbs, butter and sugar together and press into two 8-inch pie plates. To make filling, soak together gelatin and cold water. Mix canned milk, water, egg yolks and sugar and cook to custard consistency. Add gelatin mixture and dissolve. Add 5 tablespoons pale dry sherry or rum. When mixture has cooled, fold in 4 egg whites, beaten to a peak, with 5 tablespoons sugar. Pour mixture into crusts and chill. Serve topped with whipped cream. Yields 2 (8-inch) pies.

Mrs. William L. Young
(Nancy Whitaker)

GRASSHOPPER PIE

25 large marshmallows
⅔ cup half and half
4 tablespoons Crème de Menthe liqueur
4 tablespoons Crème de Cocoa liqueur

1 cup whipping cream, whipped
graham cracker crust
chocolate bits for topping

Heat marshmallows and half and half in double boiler until melted. Cool. Fold in liqueurs. Next fold in whipped cream. Pour into graham cracker crust. Top with chocolate bits. Freeze. Serves 6-8.

Mrs. Robert J. Edenfield
(Margaret King)

PEPPERMINT PIE

CRUST:
1½ cups chocolate cracker
  crumbs

¼ cup softened butter

FILLING:
1½ cups milk
1 envelope unflavored gelatin
½ cup sugar
¼ teaspoon salt

4 eggs, separated
1 cup crushed peppermint
  candy (or 1 teaspoon
  peppermint flavoring)

Mix chocolate cracker crumbs and butter; pack mixture firmly into pie pan. Mix milk, gelatin, sugar and salt in heavy saucepan. Add egg yolks and beat with a rotary beater until well blended. Cook and stir over low heat until thick and the consistency of custard. Add crushed candy or peppermint flavoring. Chill until slightly thickened. Beat egg whites until they stand in soft peaks. Fold into gelatin mixture. Spoon into pie shell and chill thoroughly before serving. Add grated chocolate to top of pie or whipped cream if desired. Serves 6-8.

Mrs. Arthur P. Barry
(Texas Roughton)

CHOCOLATE PEPPERMINT PIE

1 cup M & M plain candies
2 tablespoons butter
2 tablespoons water
2 (3½ ounce) cans flaked
  coconut

3 pints peppermint ice cream
chocolate sauce

CHOCOLATE SAUCE:
1 cup M & M peanut candies
½ cup half and half

¼ cup light corn syrup
⅛ teaspoon cream of tartar

Place candies, butter and water in heavy saucepan. Cook over low heat for 10 minutes until mixture is melted and smooth. Add coconut. Press on bottom of buttered 9-inch pie plate. Chill until set. Spoon peppermint ice cream into shell. Pour chocolate sauce over ice cream. For chocolate sauce, combine candies, ¼ cup half and half, corn syrup and cream of tartar in small saucepan. Cover. Place over low heat for 10 minutes, uncover, stir and heat until chocolate is melted and smooth. Chill. Add remaining half and half for desired consistency. Makes 1¼ cups sauce. Serves 6-8.

PECAN PIE
Easy and Delicious

3 whole eggs, beaten
¼ cup melted butter
½ cup sugar
dash salt

1 teaspoon vanilla extract
1 cup chopped pecans
1 (9-inch) unbaked pie shell
1 cup light corn syrup

Beat eggs and add butter, sugar, salt, corn syrup and vanilla extract. Place chopped pecans in bottom of unbaked pastry shell. Pour mixture on top of nuts. Nuts will rise to top to form a crusted layer. Bake at 350° for 50-60 minutes. Serves 6-8.

Mrs. Jack K. Lasseter
(Camille Caskin)

VARIATION: Add ¼ cup rum instead of vanilla extract.

PEANUT BUTTER ICE CREAM PIE
Prepare ahead of time

18 squares of graham crackers, crushed
¾ cup chopped salted peanuts
¼ cup sugar

¼ cup melted butter or margarine
½-¾ teaspoon almond extract, if desired

FILLING:
½ cup whipping cream, whipped
1 quart Breyers vanilla ice cream, softened

½ cup chunky peanut butter
chocolate sauce (optional)

Combine cracker crumbs, peanuts, sugar, butter, and extract if desired. Pat into a 9-inch pie pan and bake 8 minutes at 375°. Chill. For filling, whip cream. Mix peanut butter with softened ice cream and fold whipped cream into mixture. Spoon into crust. Freeze until firm (about 5 hours). Serve with homemade chocolate sauce, if desired. Serves 10-12.

This filling and crust can be made in your food processor.

Mrs. Ray C. Pearson
(Judye Wynne)

BLACK BOTTOM ICE CREAM PIE
Make Ahead

CRUST:

1½ cups crushed gingersnaps
¼ cup confectioners' sugar

⅓ cup melted butter

FILLING:

1 cup chocolate ice cream,
  softened

1 quart vanilla ice cream,
  softened

SAUCE:

1 (6 ounce) package semi-sweet
  chocolate morsels

½ cup whipping cream

For crust, combine gingersnaps, confectioners' sugar and melted butter. Mix well and press into a 9-inch pie pan. Spread chocolate ice cream in bottom of crust and freeze until firm. Meanwhile, make a sauce by combining chocolate morsels and whipping cream in a saucepan. Heat until morsels are melted, stirring constantly. Remove from heat. Cool, spread one half of the cooled sauce over the chocolate ice cream. Freeze until set. Spoon softened vanilla ice cream over sauce. Freeze until firm. Drizzle remaining sauce over frozen pie. Freeze again and serve as a frozen pie. Yields 9-inch pie.

CRUMB-TOPPED APPLE PIE

2-2¼ cups apples, peeled,
  cored and sliced
1 cup sugar, divided
1 (9-inch) unbaked crust
1 teaspoon cinnamon
¾ cup flour
⅓ cup butter

OPTIONAL:
1 teaspoon lemon rind
2 tablespoons sugar
¼ cup warm rum

Mix apples with ½ cup sugar and 1 teaspoon cinnamon and pour into crust. To make crumb topping, mix ½ cup sugar with ¾ cup flour and cut in butter. Sprinkle topping evenly over apples. Bake at 450° for 10 minutes, reduce heat to 350° and bake for 40 minutes more. Mix optional ingredients in saucepan and flame. Pour over individual servings. Yields 9-inch pie.

Mrs. Thomas L. Bass
(Patricia Walker)

KEY LIME PIE

CRUST:
1 (8½ ounce) box chocolate
wafers

½ cup unsalted butter or
margarine, melted

FILLING:
1 (14 ounce) can sweetened
condensed milk
1 tablespoon grated lime rind
⅓ cup fresh lime juice
3 eggs, separated
3-4 drops green food coloring

¼ teaspoon salt
1 cup heavy cream, whipped
2 tablespoons sugar
1 tablespoon dark rum
shaved chocolate
1½ teaspoons lime rind

Place wafers in strong plastic bag and crush finely with rolling pin. Add melted butter or margarine; blend well. Press mixture firmly to sides and bottom of 10-inch pie plate. Bake at 350° for 10 minutes. Cool on rack for 30 minutes. Mix milk, lime juice, 1 tablespoon lime rind and beaten egg yolks. Add coloring, mix. Beat egg whites and salt until stiff (but not dry). Fold gently into milk mixture. Chill 30 minutes. Top with whipped cream to which you have added sugar and rum; sprinkle with shaved chocolate and remaining 1½ teaspoons lime rind.

Mrs. E. Baxter Evans
(Maida Ragan)

DATE-MACAROON PIE
Easy and Good

3 egg whites
1 cup sugar
1 teaspoon baking powder
12 saltine crackers, finely
crushed

12 dates, chopped
1 teaspoon almond extract
1 cup chopped pecans
½ pint cream, whipped

Beat egg whites, sugar and baking powder until stiff. Combine all other ingredients except cream, and fold in egg whites. Pour into 9-inch pie pan. Bake at 350° for 45 minutes. Top with whipped cream and serve.

Mrs. Madge Webb Birdsey
(Madge Webb)

FRESH STRAWBERRY PIE

2 pints fresh strawberries,
  divided
1 cup sugar
2 tablespoons cornstarch
½ cup water

2 tablespoons butter
1 cup whipping cream, whipped
3 tablespoons sugar
1 (9-inch) baked pie shell

Wash strawberries. Line bottom of baked pie shell with 1 pint strawberries. Mash remaining strawberries and combine with sugar. Mix water and cornstarch and add to mashed strawberries. Bring to a boiling point, lower heat and allow mixture to boil 2 minutes in a rolling boil. Remove from heat; add butter to mixture; cool. Spoon over strawberries in the cooked pie shell. Whip cream with 3 tablespoons sugar. Spoon over top. Refrigerate 3 to 4 hours before serving. Serves 6-8.

Mrs. William W. Williams
(Ann Warlick)

PUMPKIN CHIFFON PIE

1¼ cups canned or fresh
  pumpkin
½ cup sugar
½ cup milk
½ teaspoon cinnamon
½ teaspoon nutmeg
¼ teaspoon ginger
¼ teaspoon salt

4 beaten egg yolks
1 envelope unflavored gelatin
¼ cup cold water
½ pint whipping cream
½ cup sugar
3 egg whites, beaten until stiff
  with ½ teaspoon salt
1 (9-inch) baked pie shell

Combine pumpkin, sugar, milk and spices. Add to beaten egg yolks. Cook mixture in a double boiler 5-6 minutes until thickened stirring almost constantly. Dissolve gelatin in cold water and add to hot mixture. Cool in refrigerator until partially set. Whip ½ pint whipping cream and ½ cup sugar together, adding half to cooled pumpkin mixture. Add egg whites and salt that have been beaten until stiff. Mix well and pour into cooled pie shell. Add other half of whipped cream as topping. Serves 8.

Mrs. Harold E. Causey
(June Farmer)

HINTS

To maintain egg quality, store the egg with the larger end up.

CHOCOLATE CINNAMON PIE

2 eggs, separated
½ teaspoon vinegar
¼ teaspoon salt
¼ teaspoon cinnamon
½ cup sugar
¼ cup water
1 (6 ounce) package semi-sweet
  chocolate bits, melted

½ pint whipping cream
¼ cup sugar
1 (9-inch) baked pie shell
toasted slivered almonds,
  to garnish

To make meringue, beat egg whites, vinegar, salt and cinnamon. Continue beating until whites are stiff. Pour mixture into baked pie shell. Bake at 325° for 15-18 minutes. Remove from oven. Beat egg yolks; add water and chocolate bits. Pour half of chocolate mixture over cooked meringue. Cool. Beat whipping cream with ¼ cup sugar. Put half of whipped cream - sugar mixture over cooled chocolate that is in meringue. Add remaining whipped cream to other chocolate mixture and spread on top. Refrigerate overnight. Serves 7.

Mrs. W. Thomas Moody, III
(Mary MacGregor)

OLD FASHIONED LEMON PIE
A man's delight

½ cup butter
1 cup sugar
2 whole eggs
2 egg yolks

6 tablespoons fresh lemon juice
1-2 teaspoons grated lemon
  rind
1 (9-inch) baked pastry shell

MERINGUE:
2 egg whites
¼ teaspoon cream of tartar
⅛ teaspoon salt

¼ teaspoon vanilla extract
¼ cup sugar

Cream butter and sugar together in top of double boiler. Add whole eggs, egg yolks and lemon juice, mixing thoroughly. Place over hot water, stirring constantly. Cook until mixture thickens. Stir in lemon rind. Chill. Pour into cooled, baked pastry shell. Top filling with meringue, made by combining egg whites, cream of tartar, salt and vanilla extract. Beat until frothy, then add sugar gradually until stiff peaks form. Bake in hot 400° oven for 7 minutes or until meringue peaks are golden brown. Serves 6-8.

Dr. Robert H. Jones

FROZEN LEMON MERINGUE PIE

6 tablespoons melted butter
grated peel of 1 lemon
⅓ cup lemon juice
⅛ teaspoon salt
1 cup sugar
2 eggs

2 egg yolks
1 pint vanilla ice cream,
  softened
1 (9-inch) baked pie shell or
  graham cracker crust

MERINGUE:
3 egg whites

3 tablespoons sugar

Melt butter. Add grated lemon peel, lemon juice, salt and sugar. Stir. Combine slightly beaten 2 whole eggs and 2 egg yolks with sugar mixture and cook over boiling water, beating constantly until thick and smooth. Cool. Smooth 1 pint vanilla ice cream in pie shell. Freeze. Top with half of lemon butter sauce. Freeze. Repeat vanilla layer. Freeze. Repeat lemon butter sauce. Freeze. Top with meringue, made by beating egg whites with sugar until stiff peaks form. Brown lightly in a hot 400° oven. Freeze.

Mrs. W. Cobb Matthews
(Marguerite Baxter)

VARIATION: For crust, crumble 20 chocolate wafers. Mix and toss with ¼ cup melted butter. Press into pie shell. Bake at 350° for 8 minutes.

LEMON CHESS PIE

2 cups sugar
4 eggs
1 tablespoon flour
1 tablespoon white corn meal
¼ cup milk

¼ cup melted butter
¼ cup lemon juice
2 teaspoons grated lemon rind
1 (9-inch) unbaked pie shell
whipped cream (optional)

Combine sugar and eggs. Set aside. In a separate bowl, toss together flour and corn meal. Add to sugar and eggs. Add milk, melted butter, lemon juice and lemon rind to sugar-flour mixture. Pour into unbaked 9-inch pie shell. Bake 50-60 minutes at 350°. Corn meal rises to form crust. Top with whipped cream if desired. This makes a good deal of pie filling and you may have enough to fill several tart shells. Serves 6-7.

Mrs. R. C. Souder, Jr.
(Jacqueline Lamm)

PECAN FUDGE PIE

½ cup butter
3 squares unsweetened
  chocolate
4 eggs
3 tablespoons white corn syrup

1½ cups sugar
¼ teaspoon salt
1 teaspoon vanilla extract
1 cup chopped pecans
1 (9-inch) pie shell

Melt butter and chocolate in top of double boiler and cool slightly. Beat eggs until light. Beat syrup, sugar, salt and vanilla extract into the eggs. Add pecans, then add chocolate mixture to sugar mixture. Mix thoroughly and pour into pie shell. Bake at 350° for 25-35 minutes. Top should be crusty and filling set, but soft inside. Top with whipped cream or ice cream. Serves 6-8.

Mrs. Daniel L. Pike
(Chandler Jones)

CHERRY PIE MARNIER

2 cups tart cherries, reserving
  juice
1 tablespoon Cherry Marnier
  liqueur
½ teaspoon almond extract

¾ cup sugar
1½ tablespoons flour
1½ tablespoons cornstarch
1 tablespoon butter
2 (9-inch) unbaked pie shells

Mix together cherries, juice, Cherry Marnier liqueur and almond extract and pour in 1 unbaked pie shell. Sprinkle dry ingredients over cherry mixture and dot with butter. Cover with second crust in which steam vents have been cut. Brush the top of crust with cream so it will brown evenly. Bake at 425° for 25 minutes. Top with vanilla ice cream or scoops of whipped cream. Serves 6-8.

ORANGE COCONUT PIE
Different and Delicious

1½ cups sugar
½ cup butter
3 whole eggs
rind of 1 orange, grated

1 (3½ ounce) can Angel Flake
  coconut
1 (9-inch) unbaked pie shell
¼ cup orange juice

Cream sugar and butter. Add eggs, beating well after each addition. Add orange juice, grated orange rind and coconut. Pour into an unbaked pie shell and bake at 350° for 45 minutes or until pie filling is firm.

CHOCOLATE MUD PIE

1 (8 ounce) package chocolate wafers
½ cup melted butter
1½ pints coffee ice cream, softened

⅓ cup cocoa
⅔ cup sugar
1½ cups heavy cream, divided
3 tablespoons butter
1 teaspoon vanilla extract

Crush wafers and mix in melted butter. Press into bottom and on sides of 9-inch pie pan. Bake at 375° for 10 minutes. Cool completely. Carefully spread coffee ice cream into crust. Freeze until firm, about ½ hour. In a 2-quart saucepan, over medium heat, heat cocoa, sugar, ½ cup cream and butter until mixture is smooth and boils. Remove from heat; stir in vanilla extract. Cool slightly, pour over ice cream and freeze until firm approximately 1 hour. Just before serving, garnish with remaining whipped cream. Serves 8.

Mrs. M. Warren Reid, Jr.
(Kristin Nading)

JAPANESE FRUIT PIE
Great!

½ cup melted margarine
1 cup sugar
2 eggs
3 tablespoons milk

1 teaspoon vanilla extract
½ cup coconut
½ cup golden raisins
½-1 cup chopped pecans

Beat margarine, sugar and eggs well. Add milk and vanilla extract. Beat well again. Fold in coconut, raisins and pecans. Pour in unbaked 9-inch pie shell. Bake at 350° for 40 minutes. Serves 6-8.

Mrs. William W. Kidd
(Judy Lee)

RASPBERRY PIE

1 (9-inch) unbaked pie shell
½ cup slivered almonds
3 egg whites, beaten stiff
1 tablespoon lemon juice
1 teaspoon almond extract

1 cup sugar
1 (10 ounce) package frozen raspberries, thawed
1 cup whipping cream, whipped

Press almonds into pie shell and bake at 450° for 12 minutes. Set aside to cool. Beat egg whites until stiff peaks form. Add lemon juice, almond extract and sugar. Fold in raspberries and whipped cream. Spoon into pie shell and freeze 4 to 6 hours. Serves 8.

PATTY SHELLS

8 ounces cream cheese
1½ cups butter or margarine

3 cups flour

Cream the cream cheese and butter. Add flour and mix well. Chill before placing in molds. Press mixture to line the sides of miniature patty shell molds. Bake at 350° for about 15 minutes or until shells are golden. Yields approximately 6 dozen.

Mrs. John E. Oswald
(Melissa Ruth Johnson)

PERFECT PIE CRUST

1½ cups flour (Wondra)
¼ cup chilled unsalted butter,
    cut into 1-inch cubes

¼ cup chilled Crisco shortening
¼ teaspoon salt
¼ cup cold water

In a blender or food processor, blend the flour, butter, shortening and salt until the mixture is crumbly. Add cold water and mix until dough comes clean from bowl and forms a ball. Flatten dough in 8-inch circle, cover in plastic wrap and place in refrigerator for 30 minutes. Preheat oven to 400°. Place dough on lightly floured surface and roll to desired size. To bake, prick sides and bottom of pie shell with a fork. Bake 25 minutes. If recipe calls for an unbaked shell which will be filled before baking, do not prick dough. For a 2-crust pie, double the recipe. Makes 1 (8-9 inch) pie crust.

Mrs. Alex R. Mitchell
(Eyleen Jackson)

FLAKY PASTRY

5 cups flour
1 tablespoon brown sugar
¼ teaspoon baking powder
1½ teaspoons salt

2 cups Crisco shortening
1 tablespoon vinegar
1 egg, beaten
water

Sift together dry ingredients. Cut shortening into sifted ingredients until mixture is crumbly. Combine vinegar and egg and add enough water to yield 1 cup liquid. Add water to dry ingredients and blend well. Form mixture into a ball. Divide dough and roll out onto floured pastry board. For a pie shell, baked pricked pastry for 12-15 minutes at 450°. Yields approximately 6 (9-inch) crusts.

COOKIES
AND
CANDY

CHOCOLATE MACAROONS
Very moist

1 (6 ounce) package semi-sweet
  chocolate bits
2 egg whites
¼ teaspoon salt

¼ cup sugar
1 (7 ounce) package coconut
2 teaspoons vanilla extract

Melt chocolate bits and let cool. Beat whites until stiff. Add salt and sugar to egg whites, adding sugar gradually. Pour chocolate into meringue and fold in coconut and vanilla extract. Drop by teaspoonfuls on a greased baking sheet. Bake at 325° for 13-15 minutes. Yields 2 dozen.

MATILLE'S DATE BALLS

1 (8 ounce) box chopped dates
1 cup brown sugar
½ cup butter
½ (3½ ounce) can coconut

1 cup chopped nuts
2 cups Rice Krispies
confectioners' sugar

Place the dates, sugar, butter and coconut in a large boiler and cook 6 minutes, while stirring constantly. Remove from heat and add the nuts and Rice Krispies. Make into balls and roll in confectioners' sugar. Yields approximately 40 balls.

Mrs. Charles F. Causey
(Alice Jackson)

MOM'S COCONUT MACAROONS

2 cups moist shredded coconut
½ cup sweetened condensed
  milk

1 teaspoon vanilla extract

Combine coconut and milk; add vanilla extract and mix well. Drop by teaspoonfuls, 1 inch apart, on a greased cookie sheet. Bake in 350° oven 10 minutes or until delicately browned. Remove from cookie sheet at once. Yields 2 dozen.

Mrs. Albert S. Hatcher, III
(Deryl Howington)

OATMEAL LACE COOKIES
For Children Bakers!

½ cup melted butter
1 cup sugar
1 cup quick oats
2 tablespoons flour

¼ teaspoon baking powder
¼ teaspoon salt
1 egg, beaten
½ teaspoon vanilla extract

Mix first 3 ingredients. Sift together the flour, baking powder and salt. Add beaten egg and vanilla extract. Drop by ½ teaspoon or less on cookie sheet covered with aluminum foil. Allow plenty of room as cookies spread out flat. Cook 350° for 7 - 8 minutes until golden brown. Watch carefully. Remove from cookie sheet and peel cookies off foil. Let cool flat, not stacked. Yields 48 cookies.

Mrs. William W. Williams
(Ann Warlick)

TOLL HOUSE OATMEAL COOKIES

1 cup butter or margarine
¾ cup brown sugar
¾ cup sugar
2 unbeaten eggs
1 teaspoon hot water
1 teaspoon vanilla extract
1½ cups flour

1 teaspoon salt
1 teaspoon soda
1 cup chopped nuts
1 (12 ounce) package chocolate
    chips
2 cups oatmeal

Cream butter or margarine; add both sugars. Mix in eggs, one at a time, vanilla extract, and hot water. Sift flour, salt and soda. Add nuts, chocolate chips and oatmeal. Drop by teaspoonfuls on lightly greased pan and bake at 375° 8 to 10 minutes. Yields 6 - 7 dozen cookies.

Mrs. Ferdinand V. Kay
(Laurie Shannon)

HINTS

Shortening is easily measured in cold water. If ½ cup is needed fill a cup ½ full of water and add shortening until level is 1 cup.

ORANGE SLICE COOKIES

1 cup flour
1 teaspoon baking powder
1 cup chopped orange slice
  candy

1 cup chopped pecans
1 cup packed dark brown sugar
2 eggs, slightly beaten
1 cup confectioners' sugar

Sift flour and baking powder together and add to orange slice candy and pecans which have been mixed together. Mix brown sugar and eggs and add to flour mixture. Spread in a greased 9-inch square Pyrex dish. Bake at 325° for 30 minutes. Let cool, cut into squares, and roll in confectioners' sugar. Yields 16 square cookies.

Mrs. William H. Greer, Jr.
(Kay Smith)

PECAN COOKIES
Easy and Good

1 cup melted butter
1 cup light brown sugar
1 cup pecan halves

1 package (22) whole graham
  crackers

Mix butter and sugar. Boil 2 minutes - do not stir. Add pecans and cool slightly. Arrange graham crackers on teflon pan. Pour mixture over graham crackers arranging pecans. Bake at 350° for 10 minutes. Cool and remove from pan.

Mrs. J. Stuart Windt
(Margaret Smenner)

POTATO CHIP COOKIES

1 cup butter
½ cup sugar
1 teaspoon vanilla extract

1½ cups sifted flour
½ cup crushed potato chips

Cream butter and sugar. Add vanilla extract, flour and chips. Drop by teaspoonfuls on ungreased cookie sheet. Bake at 350° for 10-14 minutes. Yields 4 dozen.

CONGO COOKIES

2¾ cups sifted flour
½ teaspoon salt
2½ teaspoons baking powder
⅔ cup butter
1 (1 pound) box brown sugar
3 eggs

1 cup chopped nuts
1 (6 ounce) package chocolate
  bits
1 teaspoon vanilla extract
1½ teaspoons maple flavoring

Sift together flour, salt and baking powder. Set aside. Melt butter and add brown sugar. Stir until well mixed and allow to cool slightly. Add eggs one at a time, beating well after each addition. Add dry ingredients; then nuts, chocolate bits, vanilla extract, and maple flavoring. Mix well and pour into greased 10½ x 15½ x ¾-inch pan. Bake at 350° for 35 minutes. Cut into squares. Yields 3 dozen.

Mrs. Edgar Y. Mallary, III
(Lloyd Washington)

DATE COOKIES

36 whole pitted dates
36 pecan or walnut halves
¼ cup butter or margarine
  softened
¾ cup packed light brown
  sugar

1 egg
½ cup sour cream
1¼ cups flour blended with
  ¼ teaspoon salt, ¼ teaspoon
  baking powder and
  ½ teaspoon baking soda

ICING:
¼ cup butter or margarine
1 cup confectioners' sugar

½ teaspoon vanilla extract
1 tablespoon hot water

Slit dates and stuff with nuts. Set aside. Beat butter and sugar. Add egg and beat until light colored. Blend in sour cream, then stir in flour mixture. Drop stuffed dates one at a time in batter and with metal spatula, swirl batter around date to coat. Drop by teaspoonfuls on greased cookie sheet. Bake in center of preheated 350° oven 12-14 minutes or until golden. Spoon a little icing over each cookie, then cool on racks. For icing, heat butter or margarine until light brown, stir in confectioners' sugar, vanilla extract and hot water until smooth. Yields 36.

Mrs. John C. Edwards
(Peggy Schmitt)

CHOCOLATE BUTTERSWEETS

½ cup butter or margarine
½ cup confectioners' sugar
¼ teaspoon salt

1 teaspoon vanilla extract
1¼ cups flour

CREAMY NUT FILLING:
1 (3 ounce) package cream
cheese, softened
1 cup sifted confectioners'
sugar
2 tablespoons flour

1 teaspoon vanilla extract
½ cup chopped nuts
¼ cup flaked coconut

CHOCOLATE FROSTING:
½ cup semi-sweet chocolate
morsels
2 tablespoons butter or
margarine

2 tablespoons water
½ cup sifted confectioners'
sugar

Cream butter and sugar. Add salt and vanilla and beat well. Stir in flour. Shape dough into 1-inch balls and place on ungreased cookie sheet. Use index finger and press a hole in center of each ball. Bake at 350° for 12-15 minutes until very lightly browned. For filling, combine all ingredients and stir well. While cookies are still warm, fill center with 1 teaspoon of Creamy Nut Filling. For frosting, combine chocolate morsels, butter and water in small saucepan and melt over low heat stirring constantly. Remove from heat and add confectioners' sugar. Beat until smooth. If frosting is too thick, add a few drops of water. Cool cookies completely. Spread on Chocolate Frosting. Yields 3 dozen.

Mrs. Cubbedge Snow, Jr.
(Edyth McKibben)

CORNFLAKE KISSES

3 egg whites
1 cup sugar
2 teaspoons vanilla extract

½ teaspoon almond extract
3½ cups Frosted Flakes
1 cup chopped pecans

Beat egg whites until stiff. Gradually add sugar and extracts. Fold in Frosted Flakes and pecans. Drop by teaspoonfuls on a cookie sheet lined with waxed paper. Bake at 250° for 40 minutes. Yields 4 dozen.

VARIATION: substitute ½ teaspoon black walnut flavoring for the almond extract.

CARROT COOKIES

¾ cup shortening
1 cup sugar
1 cup cooked, mashed carrots
2 cups flour
¼ tablespoon salt

2 teaspoons baking powder
½ teaspoon lemon extract
½ teaspoon vanilla extract
grated rind of an orange
1 egg

ICING:
1 cup confectioners' sugar
orange juice and grated orange
  rind

2 tablespoons melted butter

Cream shortening and sugar. Add remaining ingredients. Drop by teaspoonfuls on an ungreased cookie sheet. Bake at 375° for 15 minutes. For icing, mix all ingredients well to obtain desired consistency. Ice cooled cookies. Yields 3-4 dozen.

BEVERLY ADAMS' CHESS CAKE

CRUST:
1 (18.5 ounce) box yellow cake
  mix

½ cup margarine, softened
1 egg

FILLING:
1 (1 pound) box confectioners'
  sugar
2 eggs

1 (8 ounce) package cream
  cheese

For crust, mix ingredients together. Pack in a well-greased 13 x 9 x 2-inch pan to make crust. For filling, mix ingredients together and pour over crust. Bake 30 minutes in 350° oven that has been preheated. Cut into squares. Serves 12-15.

Mrs. William A. Snow, Jr.
(Jean Lamar)

HINTS

To determine the age of an egg, put the egg in cold water. If the egg lies on its side, it is very fresh; if it is at an angle it is at least 3 days old; and if it stands on end it is 10 days old.

To make egg yolks beat more quickly, add 1 teaspoon water.

MOLASSES CRISPS

1½ cups lightly salted butter or margarine
4 cups flour
4 teaspoons baking soda
1 teaspoon salt
2 teaspoons ground cinnamon

1 teaspoon ground cloves
1 teaspoon ground ginger
2½ cups sugar
½ cup dark molasses
2 large eggs

Melt butter in large saucepan; remove from heat and let cool. Sift flour with baking soda, salt, cinnamon, cloves and ginger. To the melted, cooled butter add 2 cups of the sugar, the molasses and eggs and beat well. When smooth and thick, stir in flour mixture about 1 cup at a time. When dough is well mixed, cover and chill 2 hours or longer. Heat oven to 375°. Roll dough into small balls, using about 1½ teaspoons dough for each. Roll balls in remaining ½ cup sugar and place 2 inches apart on ungreased baking sheets. Bake for about 10 minutes until cookies are a dark golden brown. Remove from oven and let cookies cool about 2 minutes on the baking sheet before removing to a wire rack to cool completely. To have them chewy, cook cookies for 5-6 minutes. For crisp cookies, cook for 10 minutes. Yields about 12 dozen.

Mrs. E. Baxter Evans
(Maida Ragan)

CREAM CHEESE CRESCENTS

2 cups butter
1 pound cream cheese
4 egg yolks

4 cups flour
confectioners' sugar

NUT FILLING:
4 egg whites, beaten
½ cup sugar

1 pound ground pecans
drop vanilla extract

Cream butter, cream cheese and egg yolks. Add flour to make dough. On a board, dusted with confectioners' sugar, roll out cream cheese dough. In the meantime, for filling, beat whites and add sugar, pecans and extract. Spread filling over dough and cut into 2-inch squares. Roll into crescents. Bake at 350° for 20-25 minutes.

Mrs. Leo A. Erbele
(Josephine Phelps)

LEMON PECAN SLICES

1 cup flour
½ cup melted butter
2 eggs, beaten
1½ cups brown sugar
½ cup grated coconut
1 cup chopped pecans

2 tablespoons flour
½ teaspoon baking powder
½ teaspoon salt
1 teaspoon vanilla extract
1½ cups confectioners' sugar
lemon juice

Combine the 1 cup flour with the butter to make a smooth paste. Spread the paste in a 9 x 13-inch pan. Bake it at 350° for 12 minutes. Combine the eggs, brown sugar, coconut, pecans, flour, baking powder, salt, and vanilla extract. Spread the mixture on top of the paste. Bake at 350° for 25 minutes. When cool, spread with the confectioners' sugar thinned to desired consistency with lemon juice. Cut into oblong slices. Makes about 24 (1 x 2 inch) bars.

VARIATION: Add ½ cup more coconut and eliminate lemon icing and you have coconut bars.

Mrs. Charles F. Causey
(Alice Jackson)

M & M PARTY COOKIES
Children's Favorite

1 cup shortening
1 cup brown sugar
½ cup sugar
2 teaspoons vanilla extract
2 eggs

2¼ cups flour
1 teaspoon soda
1 teaspoon salt
½ to ¾ pound plain M & M
    candies

Cream shortening and sugars. Beat in vanilla extract and eggs. Sift flour, soda, and salt; then add to above mixture. Mix in candies. (Some candies can be saved and placed on top of cookies before cooking.) Drop by teaspoonfuls on ungreased cookie sheet. Bake at 375° for 10 - 12 minutes. Yields 3 dozen.

Mrs. T. Alfred Sams, Jr.
(Sydney Hollis)

HINTS

Sifted flour means to sift flour before you measure.

DANISH PASTRY APPLE BARS

2½ cups sifted flour
1 teaspoon salt
1 cup shortening
1 egg yolk
milk

1 cup crumbled corn flakes
8-10 tart, diced, apples
¾-1 cup sugar
1 teaspoon ground cinnamon
1 egg white, beaten

ICING:
1 cup confectioners' sugar,
    sifted

4 teaspoons milk

Combine flour and salt, and cut in shortening. Beat egg yolk and add enough milk to make ⅔ cup liquid, then stir into flour mixture. On floured surface, roll out half the dough into a rectangle. Fit into bottom and sides of a 15½ x 10½ x 1-inch pan. Sprinkle with crumbled corn flakes and top with apples. Combine sugar and cinnamon and sprinkle on top. Cover with remaining dough. Seal and cut slits in top crust. Beat egg white and brush on top. Bake 50 minutes in 375° oven. While warm, ice with mixture of confectioners' sugar and milk. Serves 10-12. Mrs. Robert J. Edenfield
(Margaret Caroline King)

LEMON CRUMBLE SQUARES

⅔ cup softened butter
1 cup firmly packed brown
    sugar
1 cup old fashioned oats
1 teaspoon baking powder
½ teaspoon salt

1½ cups flour
1 (15 ounce) can sweetened
    condensed milk
½ cup lemon juice
2 egg yolks
1 teaspoon grated lemon rind

Cream butter and brown sugar; stir in oats and dry ingredients. Mix until crumbly. Spread half of mixture in greased 13 x 9 x 2-inch pan, packing firmly. Combine sweetened condensed milk, lemon juice, egg yolks, and lemon rind; let stand 1 minute to thicken. Spread over crumb crust; sprinkle with remaining crumb mixture. Bake at 350° for 25 minutes. Cool 15 minutes in pan. Chill in refrigerator until firm. Cut into 1¾-inch squares. Better if kept in refrigerator and served cold. Yields 2 dozen.

Mrs. Andrew Young
(Pamela Watkins)

HINTS

Raisins should be heated slightly before adding to batter to distribute raisins more evenly.

DREAM BARS

CRUMB CRUST:

½ cup softened butter   ½ cup brown sugar
1 cup flour

FILLING:

1½ cups brown sugar   ¼ teaspoon salt
2 eggs, beaten   1 cup coconut
1 teaspoon vanilla extract   1 cup chopped nuts
2 tablespoons flour   1 cup chopped dates
½ teaspoon baking powder

To make crumb crust, mix butter, flour and brown sugar until crumbly and pat into shallow 8 x 15-inch pan. Bake at 350° for 15 minutes. Remove and cool. Mix brown sugar, beaten eggs and vanilla extract together. Sift flour, baking powder, and salt and add to brown sugar mixture. Fold in coconut, nuts and dates. Bake at 350° 15-20 minutes. Do not overcook. Cool in pan and cut into squares. Yields 50 bars.

Mrs. John C. Edwards
(Peggy Schmitt)

G'S APRICOT BARS
A tart cookie

⅔ cup dried apricots   ¼ teaspoon salt
½ cup soft butter   1 cup light brown sugar
¼ cup sugar   2 eggs
1 cup sifted flour   ½ teaspoon vanilla extract
⅓ cup flour   1 cup chopped pecans
½ teaspoon baking powder   confectioners' sugar

Cover apricots with water and boil 10 minutes. Drain and chop. Preheat oven to 350°. Grease an 8 x 8 x 2-inch pan. Mix butter, granulated sugar, and sifted flour until crumbly. Pack into greased pan and bake 25 minutes or until lightly browned. Sift the remaining dry ingredients. Beat eggs and add to the dry ingredients; then add apricots, vanilla extract, and pecans. Spread the mixture over the crust and bake 30 minutes. Cool and cut into bars and roll in confectioners' sugar. Yields about 32 bars.

Mrs. Wilbur I. Tucker
(Elizabeth Conner)

JAM BARS

1 cup butter
¾ cup sugar
3 egg yolks
3 cups cake flour (regular flour subtract 2 tablespoons each cup)

½ teaspoon baking powder
1 teaspoon vanilla extract
1 cup chopped nuts
1 (10 ounce) jar of strawberry jam (more if desired)
3 stiffly beaten egg whites

Cream butter and sugar; then add egg yolks, flour, baking powder and vanilla extract. Mix well and pat dough lightly into 10 x 12-inch pan. Spoon jam over dough. Lightly sprinkle with flour, then cover with ½ cup chopped nuts. Cover this with 3 stiffly beaten egg whites and top this with ½ cup more nuts. Bake a 325° for 1 hour. Cool and cut in bars. Yields approximately 4 dozen.

Mrs. Walter M. Massey, III
(Carlene Kollmar)

FRUIT BARS

1 (1 pound) box light brown sugar
1 cup butter
4 eggs
2 cups flour
3 cups chopped pecans

1 pound candied red cherries, chopped
1 pound candied red and green pineapple, chopped

Cream brown sugar and butter. Add eggs one at a time; then add flour. Sprinkle nuts on bottom of 13 x 9 x 2-inch greased and floured pan. Pour batter over nuts. Place chopped fruits on top of batter. Bake 1 hour at 350°. Yields 36 bars.

Mrs. Carl C. Schuessler
(Lynn Mercer)

HINTS

Egg whites beat faster and stiffer if done one at a time in a bowl barely wider than the beater. A teaspoon of cold water added to whites during beating will almost double the volume.

Do not use an aluminum pan to beat egg whites. The whites will discolor and not obtain proper volume.

CHEW CAKES

1 (1 pound) box light brown
   sugar
½ cup softened margarine
3 eggs

2 cups self-rising flour
1 teaspoon vanilla extract
1 cup chopped pecans
confectioners' sugar

Cream sugar and margarine. Add eggs and beat well. Blend in flour and then add vanilla extract and nuts. Bake in a well-greased 13 x 9 x 2-inch pan at 300° for 45 minutes. Cookies will fall. When cool sprinkle with sugar and cut in squares. Yields 2½ dozen.

Mrs. Mason Clisby
(Emtelle Mason)

VARIATION: Add 1 cup coconut or 1 teaspoon almond extract instead of vanilla extract.

LEMON BARS

1¾ cups flour
⅓ cup confectioners' sugar
1 cup butter
4 eggs

2 cups sugar
⅓ cup lemon juice
¼ cup flour
½ teaspoon baking powder

ICING: (Optional)
2 tablespoons soft butter
1½ cups confectioners' sugar

2 or 3 tablespoons lemon juice

In a large bowl, sift flour and confectioners' sugar. Cut in butter until mixture resembles corn meal. Press into 13 x 9 x 2-inch pan. Bake 20-25 minutes at 350°. Beat together eggs, sugar, and lemon juice until sugar dissolves. Sift ¼ cup flour and baking powder and add to egg mixture. Beat at low speed until sugar dissolves. Pour over baked crust. Bake an additional 25 minutes at 350°. Combine butter and confectioners' sugar. Mix lemon juice into mixture until smooth. Spread on cooled lemon bars. Yields 24 squares.

Mrs. W. Henry Dodd
(Bowman Hanson)

HINTS

Meringues can be reheated in slow oven for 15 minutes if they become soggy.

MACADAMIA NUT-RUM BARS

COOKIE CRUST:
½ cup butter, room
   temperature
¼ cup sugar
1 cup flour

FILLING:
2 eggs, slightly beaten
1¼ cups packed brown sugar
2 tablespoons flour
½ teaspoon salt
¼ teaspoon baking powder
1 cup flaked coconut
1 cup Mauna Loa Bits or
   chopped macadamia nuts
1 teaspoon vanilla extract
1 tablespoon Jamaican rum

FROSTING:
2 tablespoons butter, room
   temperature
1¼ cups confectioners' sugar
   (sift before measuring)
1 tablespoon milk or half and
   half
½ teaspoon vanilla extract
1 teaspoon rum

Mix crust ingredients together at medium speed until thoroughly blended. Press mixture evenly over bottom of 9 x 13-inch or 8 x 10-inch cake pan. Bake at 350° for 15 to 20 minutes until just beginning to brown. Remove from oven. Stir filling ingredients together until well blended and spread over crust. Bake 15 to 20 minutes at 350° until firm and golden brown. Beat together frosting ingredients until smooth. Add a little more milk and/or rum if necessary to make a good spreading consistency. Spread over cooled bars. May be cut into 32 or 48 bars.

Mrs. Frank W. Walthall, Jr.
(Janet Fortson)

APRICOT BALLS

3 cups coconut
1 cup chopped nuts
1 (14 ounce) can sweetened
   condensed milk
1 teaspoon vanilla extract
1 (6 ounce) box dried apricots,
   cut in small pieces
confectioners' sugar

Mix all ingredients. Form into 1-inch balls and roll in confectioners' sugar when ready to serve. Freezes well. Yields 40 balls.

DELICIOUS BROWNIES

½ cup butterscotch pieces
¼ cup butter
¾ cup flour
⅓ cup firmly packed brown
  sugar
1 teaspoon baking powder
¼ teaspoon salt

1 egg
½ teaspoon vanilla extract
1 (6 ounce) package semi-sweet
  chocolate pieces
¼ cup chopped nuts
1 cup small marshmallows

Preheat oven to 350°. Grease bottom and sides of 9-inch pan. Melt butterscotch pieces with butter. Cool to warm, then add flour, brown sugar, baking powder, salt, egg, and vanilla extract. Mix well. Fold in chocolate pieces, nuts and marshmallows. Spread in 9-inch pan. Bake at 350° for 20-25 minutes. Mixture will appear soft when it is removed from oven, but it will firm up when it cools. Yields 36 bars.

DOUBLE-FROSTED BROWNIES
Rich!

5 (1 ounce) squares
  unsweetened chocolate,
  divided
½ cup butter
2 eggs

1 cup sugar
1 teaspoon vanilla extract
½ cup flour mixed with
  ¼ teaspoon salt and
  ½ cup chopped nuts

FROSTING:
1½ cups sugar
⅓ cup butter

½ cup half and half
1 teaspoon vanilla extract

Preheat oven to 350°. Melt 2 squares chocolate and butter in heavy saucepan; cool. In bowl, beat eggs until blended; add sugar and mix well. Stir in chocolate mixture, vanilla extract and flour mixture. Spread in greased 11 x 7 x 1½-inch pan. Bake for 20-25 minutes. Cool in pan on rack. For frosting, mix sugar, butter and half and half in medium saucepan. Bring to boil; then cook over moderate heat *WITHOUT* stirring until soft-ball stage (236° on candy thermometer). Cool in pan of cold water until lukewarm. Add vanilla extract. Beat until creamy and of spreading consistency. Spread brownies with frosting. Melt remaining 3 squares of chocolate and spread over frosting. Chill several hours until firm. Bring to room temperature and cut into squares. Yields 15 squares.

Mrs. John D. Reeves
(Lee Buford)

CHOCOLATE PEPPERMINT BROWNIES
Freezes Well

COOKIE:

2 squares unsweetened chocolate
½ cup butter
2 eggs
1 cup sugar

¼ teaspoon peppermint extract
½ cup flour
pinch salt
½ cup chopped nuts

FROSTING:

1 cup confectioners' sugar
2 tablespoons butter
1 tablespoon evaporated milk

½ teaspoon peppermint extract
drop or two green food coloring

GLAZE:

2 squares unsweetened chocolate

2 tablespoons butter

Melt chocolate and butter; add eggs which have been beaten with sugar; stir in remaining cookie ingredients and bake in a buttered 9-inch square pan at 350° for 15 minutes. Cool. Mix frosting ingredients; spread on brownies and chill. Melt chocolate and butter for glaze and spread over iced brownies. Store in refrigerator. Yields 2½ dozen small squares.

Mrs. William W. Williams
(Ann Warlick)

MACADAMIA NUT BALLS
Wonderful!

1 cup butter
½ cup sugar
1 teaspoon vanilla extract
2¼ cups sifted flour

¼ teaspoon salt
1 cup finely chopped macadamia nuts
confectioners' sugar

Preheat oven to 350°. Cream butter and beat in sugar and vanilla extract. Sift flour with salt and stir into first mixture. Stir in nuts. Shape into 1-inch balls and place on ungreased baking sheet. Bake at 350° for 12 minutes or until slightly brown. Roll warm cookies in confectioners' sugar. Yields 3½ dozen.

ROSETTES

BATTER:
2 eggs, beaten
2 teaspoons sugar
¼ teaspoon salt

1 cup milk
1 cup flour
1 tablespoon lemon extract

RICHER BATTER:
2 whole eggs
1 egg yolk
⅔ cup heavy cream

½ cup sugar
1 cup flour

Mix ingredients of either batter and beat until smooth. Chill batter thoroughly. Heat rosette iron in skillet set at 375° for 3 minutes. Drain and dip into batter to within ¾ inch of top of mold. Fry rosette until golden. Remove. Sift confectioners' sugar on both sides of rosettes. Store in a tin box. Serve with sherbet scoops.

CHOCOLATE PRETZELS

1 cup softened butter
1 cup sugar
1½ teaspoons grated lemon
   peel
3 egg yolks

1 cup ground almonds
¼ teaspoon almond extract
2¼ cups sifted flour (sift
   before measuring)

GLAZE:
2 (6 ounce) packages semi-
   sweet chocolate pieces

¼ cup light corn syrup
½ cup light cream

Combine butter, sugar and lemon peel. Beat until fluffy and smooth. Add yolks, one at a time, beating well after each addition. Add almonds and extract. Gradually add flour to mix well. Refrigerate dough 1 hour. Meanwhile, make chocolate glaze. In top of double boiler, combine chocolate pieces, corn syrup and cream. Cook until chocolate is melted and mixture is smooth. Remove from heat. Preheat oven to 350°. Grease baking sheet. Form dough into balls (1 tablespoon dough). Form each ball into a roll 8 inches long. Shape into pretzels. Bake 10-12 minutes at 350° or until pretzel cookies are golden. Glaze warmed cookies. Let glazed cookies set before placing in refrigerator to store. Yields 4 dozen.

HINTS

When sending cookies by mail, pack them in popped popcorn to prevent breakage.

PEANUT BUTTER CUP TARTS

36 Reeses' miniature peanut butter cups

1 (15 ounce) roll refrigerated peanut butter cookie dough

Refrigerate candies, so wrappers will peel off easily. Unwrap each. Follow slicing instructions on cookie dough and quarter each slice. Place each piece in a greased miniature muffin cup. Bake in 350° oven 8-10 minutes or until cookies puff up. Remove frm oven and immediately push a candy cup into each cookie filled muffin cup. The cookie will deflate and come around the candy. Let pan cool. Then refrigerate until shine leaves the chocolate. Remove from refrigerator and lift each tart from the cup, with the tip of a knife. Yields 3 dozen cookies.

Can also use chocolate kisses instead of Reeses' peanut butter cups.

Mrs. W. Tyler Evans, Jr.
(Sarah Halliburton)

PECAN-RAISIN TARTS

CREAM CHEESE PASTRY:

1 (3 ounce) package cream cheese, softened

1 cup flour
¼ cup butter

To make pastry, blend softened cream cheese with flour and butter. Line small ungreased tins with cream cheese pastry.

FILLING:

½ cup butter
1 cup sugar
2 egg yolks
1 teaspoon vanilla extract

1 cup chopped pecans
1 cup raisins
2 egg whites, beaten stiff

Blend filling ingredients in order folding in egg whites last. Fill tart shells. Bake 20 minutes at 375°. Yields 48 small tarts.

Mrs. Wilbur I. Tucker
(Elizabeth Conner)

HINTS

The volume of egg whites is increased when the eggs are at room temperature.

ENGLISH TOFFEE

2 cups butter
2 cups sugar
2 tablespoons white corn syrup
6½ tablespoons water

2 cups finely chopped nuts
11-12 ounces grated milk
   chocolate

To make toffee, cook all ingredients except nuts and chocolate to the hard crack stage (290°). Do not overcook. Coat 2 long pieces of aluminum foil with non-stick spray and then coat a second time with margarine. Line a cookie sheet with foil. Sprinkle foil with one third of nuts. Pour toffee over nuts, sprinkle with one half of the shredded chocolate, then sprinkle with another one third of nuts. Press other piece of oiled foil on top and turn over. Remove foil, sprinkle on remaining chocolate. Then cover with remaining nuts. Replace foil and press lightly. Allow candy to harden at least 12 hours. Remove foil and break into pieces.

EXCELLENT DIVINITY

3 cups sugar
1 (1 pound) box light brown
   sugar
1½ cups water

1 cup light Karo syrup
2 egg whites, stiffly beaten
2 cups broken nuts
1 teaspoon vanilla extract

Using a heavy saucepan, dissolve sugars, water and syrup over medium heat. Boil until candy thermometer reaches 236°; pour one half of syrup slowly, beating all the while, over the stiffly beaten whites. Cook remainder of syrup to 252°. Then beat into whites. Add nuts and vanilla extract and continue beating until gloss of candy lessens and will stand up in peaks. When firm, drop by teaspoonfuls on waxed paper. Mixture sets up quickly. Yields 100 pieces.

Mrs. Leo B. Huckabee
(Jane Odom)

HINTS

To check cooking thermometers for accuracy, place thermometers in boiling water and if thermometer reaches 212°, it is accurate.

ELIZABETH'S BOURBON BALLS

2 (1 pound) boxes + 1¾ cups
  confectioners' sugar
½ teaspoon cream of tartar
1 teaspoon salt
1 cup softened margarine

½ cup sweetened condensed
  milk
2 cups finely chopped pecans
6 tablespoons bourbon

COATING:
2 (8 ounce) boxes semi-sweet
  chocolate

2 ounces paraffin

Mix first 7 fondant ingredients well in a large bowl; mixture may be stiff. Cover tightly and refrigerate overnight, or for up to a week. Bourbon flavor will intensify after refrigeration. Remove about one-third of the fondant from the refrigerator and shape into ¾-inch balls. To make coating, melt both boxes of chocolate with the paraffin in the top part of a double boiler over hot water. Mix well. Remove from heat, but keep top of double boiler over pan of hot water. With a spoon, dip cold fondant balls into melted chocolate until coated; then place on waxed paper. Fondant balls must be cold to coat properly. If chocolate becomes thick, return to double boiler to heat briefly. Follow the same procedure with remaining fondant. Yields about 150 (¾-inch) balls.

Mrs. N. Tyrus Ivey
(Cathy Ewing)

MARTHA WASHINGTON CANDY

2 pounds confectioners' sugar
2 pounds candied or preserved
  cherries
1 quart chopped pecans
1 (7 ounce) package finely
  grated or Angel Flake coconut

1 (14 ounce) can sweetened
  condensed milk
2 teaspoons vanilla extract
4 ounces paraffin
2 (12 ounce) packages semi-
  sweet chocolate morsels

Mix first 6 ingredients together well. Shape into small balls. Place on waxed paper. Put toothpick in each; chill. Melt paraffin and chocolate; keep warm. Dip each in chocolate; place on clean waxed paper. Chill again; pull toothpick out shortly after chocolate cools. Keep refrigerated.

Mrs. William W. Williams
(Ann Warlick)

BUCKEYES

1 cup softened butter or
  margarine
1½ (1 pound) boxes
  confectioners' sugar
1 (12 ounce) jar crunchy peanut
  butter

2 (6 ounce) packages chocolate
  morsels, melted
2 ounces paraffin

Soften butter. Knead with hands all ingredients except chocolate and paraffin. Roll into 1-inch balls and refrigerate for at least 1 hour. Melt chocolate morsels and paraffin. Put peanut butter balls on toothpick and dip in chocolate mixture until half covered. Yields 4 dozen.

Mrs. E. Max Crook
(Susan McNeill)

RUM BALLS

3 tablespoons corn syrup
½ cup rum
3 cups finely rolled vanilla
  wafers

1 cup confectioners' sugar
1½ cups finely chopped nuts
1½ teaspoons cocoa (optional)

Mix syrup and rum together; then add remaining ingredients. Shape into 1-inch balls, roll in confectioners' sugar. Store in airtight containers. Yields about 40 balls.

Mrs. Robert F. Hatcher
(Georgia Williams)

SUGARED NUTS

½ cup brown sugar
¼ cup sugar
½ cup sour cream

dash of salt
3 cups whole pecans

Combine sugars and sour cream and stir over medium heat until sugar is dissolved. Boil to soft ball stage (238° on candy thermometer). Add salt. Remove from heat, add nuts and stir until they are coated. Pour onto waxed paper and separate nuts carefully. They will harden after several minutes. Yields 3 cups sugared nuts.

Mrs. N. Tyrus Ivey
(Cathy Ewing)

ORANGE BALLS
Children love to make!!!

2½ cups crushed vanilla
   wafers
½ cup melted margarine or
   butter

¼ cup orange juice
   concentrate
1 cup confectioners' sugar

Mix together all ingredients except confectioners' sugar. Roll into small balls. Let balls set up at least 30 minutes then roll in confectioners' sugar. Yields 2 dozen.

Mrs. J. Richard Johnson
(Lyn Law)

PRALINES

1½ (3 ounce) packages
   butterscotch pudding (not
   instant)
1½ cups sugar

¾ cup brown sugar
¾ cup evaporated milk
1½ tablespoons butter
2¼ cups pecan halves

Combine first 5 ingredients, cook and stir over low heat until sugars dissolve. Add pecans and bring to full boil. Stir until soft ball stage is reached (236°). Remove from heat and beat until candy thickens. Drop by teaspoonfuls on waxed paper. Form patties in 2-inch diameter. Put a pecan half on each patty to decorate. Yields 32 patties.

WHITE CHOCOLATE FUDGE

2 cups sugar
1 cup evaporated milk
½ cup butter
8 ounces white almond bark
   candy
1 cup tiny marshmallows

½ cup flaked coconut
½ cup chopped almonds,
   toasted
1 teaspoon vanilla extract
whole almonds to garnish
   (optional)

Butter sides of a 3-quart saucepan. Add sugar, evaporated milk and butter. Cook over medium heat to soft ball stage (236°), stirring frequently. Remove from heat. Add almond bark and marshmallows; heat until melted. Quickly stir in coconut, almonds and vanilla extract. Pour into a buttered 10 x 6 x 1½-inch dish. Cut when cool. Yields 2 pounds.

FANTASY FUDGE

3 cups sugar
¾ cup margarine
⅔ cup (5½ ounce can) evaporated milk
1 (12 ounce) package semi-sweet chocolate pieces

1 (7 ounce) jar marshmallow creme
1 cup chopped nuts
1 teaspoon vanilla extract

Combine sugar, margarine and milk in a heavy 2½ quart saucepan. Bring to a full rolling boil, stirring constantly. Continue boiling 5 minutes, still stirring constantly to prevent scorching. Remove from heat; stir in chocolate pieces until melted. Add marshmallow creme, nuts and vanilla extract; stir until well blended. Pour into greased 13 x 9-inch pan. Cool at room temperature; cut in squares. Yields approximately 3 pounds.

Mrs. Lelia J. Horton
(Lelia Jones)

FUDGE CANDY (MICROWAVE)

⅓ cup cocoa
1 (1 pound) box confectioners' sugar
8 tablespoons butter

¼ cup milk
1 tablespoon vanilla extract
½ cup broken pecans (optional)

Mix cocoa and sugar. Add butter. Cook in microwave on high for 2 minutes. Beat in milk and vanilla extract. Stir in broken pecans, if desired. Pour into buttered 8 or 9-inch round pan. Refrigerate 1 hour or place in freezer for 20 minutes.

Mrs. Crawford B. Edwards
(Mildred Taylor)

MINTED WALNUTS

¼ cup light corn syrup
1 cup sugar
½ cup water
10 marshmallows

1 teaspoon essence of peppermint
3 cups walnut halves

Mix syrup, sugar and water and bring to a boil. Cook to soft ball stage (236°). Remove from heat. Add marshmallows and peppermint. Stir until marshmallows are dissolved. Add walnuts. Stir until coated. Pour onto waxed paper. Separate walnuts with fork while hot. Yields 3 cups.

BUTTERY CASHEW BRITTLE

2 cups sugar	1 cup butter or margarine
1 cup light corn syrup	3 cups cashews
½ cup water	1 teaspoon baking soda

In 3 quart saucepan, combine sugar, corn syrup, and water. Cook and stir until sugar dissolves. Bring syrup to boiling; blend in butter or margarine. Stir frequently after mixture reaches the thread stage (230°). Add cashews when the temperature reaches the soft-crack stage (280°) and stir constantly until temperature reaches the hard-crack stage (300°). Remove from heat. Quickly stir in soda, mixing thoroughly. Pour onto 2 buttered baking sheets or 2 buttered 15½ x 10½ x 1-inch pans. As the candy cools, stretch it out thin by lifting and pulling with 2 forks from edges. Loosen from pans as soon as possible; turn candy over. Break up. Yields 2½ pounds.

CANDIED GRAPEFRUIT PEEL

2 large white grapefruit	½ cup white corn syrup
sectioned	1 cup water
1 cup sugar	sugar to coat peel

Prepare peel by cutting grapefruit into 4 sections. Remove the white membrane. Cover peel with water; bring to a boil and boil 10 minutes. Drain. Repeat 3 times. Cut peel into thin strips. In a large saucepan, cook the sugar, corn syrup and water over low heat until sugar dissolves. Add peel and boil gently for about 45 minutes until syrup is absorbed. Drain in a colander. Roll peels, a few at a time, in sugar on waxed paper. Place the peels in single layers on a cookie sheet covered with waxed paper. Dry for about 2 days, uncovered. Store in tight container. Makes about 60 thin-sliced strips and keeps well.

Cutting the strips thinly avoids the very bitter taste. Also, don't skimp on the boiling steps in fresh water, which also removes the too bitter taste.

Mrs. Alexander H. S. Weaver
(Adele Burgin)

HINTS

If candy will not harden add 1 tablespoon corn syrup to mixture and cook longer.

DESSERTS

APPLE CRISP
Very good

1 cup sugar
3 tablespoons flour
1 teaspoon ground cinnamon
¼ teaspoon ground nutmeg
⅛ teaspoon ground cloves

¼ teaspoon salt
6-7 cups peeled, sliced cooking
   apples
butter

TOPPING:
½ cup firmly packed brown
   sugar

1 cup flour
½ cup butter or margarine

Combine sugar, flour, spices and salt in a large bowl. Add apples and stir to coat well. Let stand for 30 minutes. Spoon apples into a greased 10-inch pie plate or 9-inch square pan and dot with butter. Make topping by combining brown sugar and flour. Cut butter into small pieces and work into flour mixture until crumbly. Sprinkle topping over apples. Bake at 400° for 50 minutes. Serve warm with ice cream. Serves 6-8.

Mrs. Charles J. Cartwright
(Stella Blum)

BRANDIED APPLE FRITTERS

6 apples, cored and sliced
¼ cup brandy
⅛ teaspoon cinnamon
1 egg, separated
2 teaspoons sugar
½ cup milk

1 cup flour
½ teaspoon salt
1½ teaspoons baking powder
confectioners' sugar to dust
   fritters

Pare apples. Cut into ½ inch slices and cut out cores. Pour brandy and cinnamon over apples. Cover to marinate several hours. To the beaten egg yolk, add sugar, milk, sifted dry ingredients, and the marinade. Fold in stiffly beaten egg white. Dip apple slices in batter. Lower into hot fat. Fry until delicately brown. Drain on absorbent paper. Sprinkle with sifted confectioners' sugar. Serve hot. Serves 8.

APPLE SOUFFLÉ

1 cup milk	1 tablespoon apricot preserves
¼ teaspoon salt	pinch cinnamon
4½ tablespoons instant tapioca	3 egg yolks
	1 tablespoon rum
¾ cup sugar	3 egg whites
2 red apples, peeled and grated	whipped cream
1 tablespoon water	

In top of double boiler, combine milk, salt and tapioca. Cook until thick and smooth. Add the sugar and continue cooking until sugar dissolves. Set aside to cool. In separate pan, combine apples, water, preserves and cinnamon. Cook until soft. Add yolks to milk mixture, one at a time. Add rum. Fold apple mixture into milk mixture. Beat whites until stiff. Fold into apple mixture. Pour into a 1-quart greased soufflé dish. Place in a pan of water and bake at 350° for 1 hour. Serve immediately. Top with whipped cream. Serves. 6.

ORANGE SOUFFLÉ

2 envelopes unflavored gelatin	juice of 2½ oranges
½ cup cold water	(or 1½ cups orange juice)
½ cup boiling water	1 cup sugar
1 pint whipping cream, whipped	3 egg yolks

SAUCE:

½ teaspoon unflavored gelatin	¼ cup sugar
2 tablespoons cold water	1 teaspoon vanilla extract
1 pint whipping cream	2 tablespoons brandy
3 egg yolks, beaten	4 tablespoons sherry

Let gelatin stand in water for ½ hour, then add boiling water, stir until dissolved. Mix orange juice and sugar; add beaten egg yolks. Stir gelatin into mixture. Fold in the whipped cream lightly and hastily. Turn into soufflé dish and refrigerate to congeal. Serve with sauce. For sauce, cover gelatin with water, let stand for 1 hour. Heat cream in double boiler. Beat yolks and sugar until very light and add to cream, stirring until it thickens. Add gelatin. When cool, add vanilla extract, brandy and sherry. Top soufflé with shaved chocolate. Serves 6.

Mrs. Margaret H. Duncan
(Margaret Haley)

SOUFFLÉ FROID au CHOCOLAT

2 squares unsweetened
 chocolate
½ cup confectioners' sugar
1 cup milk
1 envelope unflavored gelatin,
 softened in 3 tablespoons
 cold water

¾ cup sugar
1 teaspoon vanilla extract
¼ teaspoon salt
2 cups heavy cream, whipped

Melt chocolate squares over hot water. When melted, stir in confectioners' sugar, mixing well. Heat milk just enough so that film shows on surface, then stir into the melted chocolate slowly and thoroughly. Cook, stirring constantly, until mixture reaches the boiling point. Do not boil. Remove from heat and mix into it the softened gelatin, sugar, vanilla extract and salt. Place in the refrigerator and chill until slightly thickened. Then beat mixture until it is light. In a separate bowl, beat heavy cream until it holds a slope. Then fold into the chocolate mixture and pour into a 2 quart soufflé dish. Chill 2-3 hours in refrigerator or until ready to serve. Serves 8.

Mrs. W. Henry Dodd
(Bowman Hanson)

CHOCOLATE DELIGHT

1 cup flour
¾ cup melted butter or
 margarine
½ cup chopped pecans
1 (8 ounce) package cream
 cheese
1 cup confectioners' sugar

3 cups whipped cream, divided
2 (3.5 ounce) packages instant
 chocolate pudding mix
3½ cups milk
1 teaspoon vanilla extract
nuts to garnish

Crust: Mix flour, melted butter and pecans and spread in bottom of 9 x 13-inch greased Pyrex dish. Bake 15 minutes at 350°. Set aside to cool. For first layer, mix cream cheese, confectioners' sugar and 1½ cups whipped cream and spread on crust. For second layer, mix pudding, milk and vanilla extract and spread on first layer. For third layer, cover with remaining whipped cream (1½ cups). Sprinkle nuts on top. Spread each layer as you prepare it. Place in refrigerator overnight. Serves 12-14.

Mrs. Phillip H. Beard
(Mickey Windt)

APRICOT TORTE
Very rich

CAKE:

3 cups sifted flour
¾ cup sugar
½ teaspoon salt

1 cup sweet butter
1 egg

FILLING:

2 cups ground pecans
1½ cups confectioners' sugar
1 teaspoon brandy

1 (16 ounce) carton sour cream
1 teaspoon vanilla extract

TOPPING:

strained apricot preserves

confectioners' sugar

Preheat oven to 350°. Lightly flour backs of six 9-inch layer cake pans. Combine dry ingredients in large bowl. Add cold butter into mixture using fingers to mix well. Break egg into mixture and mix well. Form dough into ball. Divide ball into 6 equal parts. Roll each into 9-inch circle and place on inverted pans. Bake 10 minutes or until edges just begin to brown. Let layers cool and remove with broad spatula. Combine pecans, sugar, brandy, sour cream and vanilla extract and stir until smooth. Spread over each cake layer except top layer and press together gently. Spread top layer with a thin coating of apricot preserves and sprinkle with confectioners' sugar. Cut into thin wedges to serve. Keep refrigerated. Serves 10-12.

Mrs. Lee B. Murphey
(Judith Meier)

RUM AND SOUR CREAM SAUCE

1 (16 ounce) carton sour cream
1½ cups dark brown sugar
2 tablespoons rum

1 teaspoon cinnamon
½ teaspoon nutmeg

Mix all ingredients together and serve over strawberries or blueberries.

HINTS

Toast grated coconut in a heavy skillet over medium heat until it begins to brown, 3-4 minutes. A delicious topping on fresh fruit or ice cream.

TIPSY TRIFLE

2 dozen ladyfingers
2 dozen almond macaroons
and sherry enough to
saturate them
¼ pound blanched almonds,
sliced lengthwise

1 quart boiled custard, bought
or homemade
1 cup cherry or strawberry
preserves
1 cup whipping cream, whipped

Line bottom of a large serving bowl with the ladyfingers and macaroons saturated in the sherry. Sprinkle with some of the almonds and pour some of the custard over almonds and lady fingers. Dot with preserves. Continue this layering process ending with the custard. Chill for several hours, top with whipped cream and serve. Serves 10-12.

For homemade boiled custard: Heat ½ gallon milk in top of a large double boiler. Beat 9 eggs; add 1½ cups sugar, a pinch of salt, and 5 heaping teaspoons cornstarch which have been blended together. Pour a small amount of hot mixture over the egg mixture. Stir well. Combine with remaining milk mixture and cook until thickened. Flavor with vanilla extract and refrigerate until thoroughly chilled. Yields 2 quarts.

Mrs. Robert S. Mattox, III
(Glenda Banks)

STRAWBERRY BAVARIAN CREAM

1 (10 ounce) package frozen
strawberries
1 cup boiling water

1 (3 ounce) package strawberry
gelatin
1 cup whipping cream, whipped

Drain berries, saving syrup. Pour boiling water over gelatin, stirring until dissolved. Add enough cold water to syrup to measure 1 cup. Stir into gelatin and chill until almost set, and then beat until foamy. Fold gelatin and strawberries into whipped cream. Pour into bowl and chill until firm. Decorate with fresh strawberries and more whipped cream.

Mrs. John A. Draughon
(Sally Hines)

HINTS

If whipping cream will not whip, add 4 drops of lemon juice to cream.

LEMON DESSERT

2 eggs, separated
½ cup sugar plus 3 tablespoons
1 teaspoon grated lemon rind
5 tablespoons lemon juice

1 cup whipping cream
1 cup graham cracker crumbs
fresh strawberries to garnish

Mix egg yolks, ½ cup sugar, lemon rind and juice. Stir and cook over boiling water until thickened. Beat egg whites with 3 table-spoons sugar until stiff. Whip cream. Fold egg whites and whipped cream into lemon mixture. Line greased mold with ½ cup graham cracker crumbs. Add lemon mixture, sprinkle remaining crumbs on top and freeze. Unmold on serving plate and garnish with fresh strawberries. Serves 8.

Mrs. W. Thompson Cullen
(Betty Hurley)

BABA au RHUM

2 packages active dry yeast
½ cup lukewarm milk
2½ cups sifted flour, divided
2 tablespoons sugar

1 teaspoon salt
2 large eggs
¼ cup melted salted butter

RUM SYRUP:
½ pound sugar cubes
1 cup water

½ cup rum

To yeast add milk and 1¼ cup flour. Work to make dough and knead on floured surface about 2-3 minutes. Place mound of dough in bowl, cover with wrap, and allow to rise ½ hour or until double in bulk. Add sugar, salt and remaining 1¼ cups flour to dough. Add eggs one at a time. Add melted butter. Knead dough carefully mixing ingredients 6-8 minutes. Cover dough. Let rest 10 minutes. Preheat oven to 425°. Butter 12 baba tins or 12 muffin tins and dust with flour. Put dough in molds filling half full. Let them rise again 20-30 minutes until dough rises just to top rim of container. Do not let them rise too high. Place in 425° oven. Drop temperature immediately to 375° and bake 15 minutes or until babas are golden. Let cool and remove from tins. To prepare syrup, combine cubed sugar and water and heat until sugar is dissolved. Bring to a boil and continue cooking at a low boil for about 6-10 minutes. Add rum and stir. Prick tops of babas with a fork. Pour sauce over slowly and let cakes absorb sauce for 30 minutes. These prepared cakes can be frozen. Yields 1 dozen.

ALICE'S BAKLAVA

2 pounds coarsely ground
   walnuts
¾ cup sugar
1 tablespoon ground cinnamon
½ teaspoon ground nutmeg

½ teaspoon ground cloves
2 cups melted butter
1 pound filo pastry
whole cloves to garnish

SYRUP:
2 cups sugar
1 cup water

1 cup honey
juice of 1 lemon

Combine the nutmeats, sugar and spices. Brush bottom of a 10½ x 15-inch pan with melted butter. Place 1 sheet of filo onto bottom of pan; brush with melted butter. Repeat this with 3 more sheets of filo. Sprinkle a handful of dry nut mixture evenly on top of this. Place 1 sheet of filo on top of nut mixture and brush with melted butter. Repeat with 2 more sheets, brushing each with melted butter. Sprinkle again with dry nut mixture. On top of this, layer 3 more sheets of filo, brushing each with melted butter. Sprinkle again with dry nut mixture. Continue until you use up all the dry mixture. You should end up with 4 or 5 sheets of filo for top. Brush with melted butter between each sheet and on top. Cut diagonally into diamonds. Place a whole clove into each diamond. Bake at 350° for 1½ hours. For syrup, combine sugar, water, honey and lemon juice in pan and boil for 10 minutes. Pour heated mixture over cooled baklava.

POTS de CRÈME au CHOCOLAT

1 cup light cream or milk
1½ pounds sweet chocolate,
   broken into small bits

4 egg yolks
3 tablespoons dark rum

Scald cream in a heavy saucepan and add chocolate. Stir constantly until chocolate is completely blended and mixture reaches the boiling point. Remove from flame. Dampen egg yolks with hot chocolate. Stir in egg yolks, approximately one at a time, beating well after each addition. Add rum a tablespoon at a time and stir well. Pour into small serving cups and chill for at least 6 hours or overnight. Serves 4.

Mrs. Thomas H. Lowe
(Maribeth Wills)

NELL'S CHESTNUT ROLL

¾ cup sifted cake flour
1 teaspoon baking powder
¼ teaspoon salt
4 eggs
¾ cup sugar

1 teaspoon vanilla extract
confectioners' sugar
shaved bitter chocolate

CHESTNUT BUTTER CREAM:
½ cup sugar
½ cup light corn syrup
3 egg yolks
1 cup softened butter
¼ cup dark rum

1 (6 ounce) cans of marrons
glacés or 2 jars of marrons
(chestnuts) in vanilla syrup,
drained

Preheat oven to 400°. Line bottom of 15 x 10 x 1-inch jelly roll pan with waxed paper. Butter the paper. Sift flour, baking powder and salt together. Beat eggs at high speed until foamy. Continue beating, adding sugar slowly until thick and doubled in bulk. Fold dry ingredients in. Fold in vanilla. Bake 12-15 minutes or until done. Turn out on a cloth sprinkled with confectioners' sugar. Cut off crisp edges of cake. Starting at *long* side, roll up the cake along with the towel. Place on cake rack to cool. When cool, unroll the cake and remove towel. Spread top of cake with half the chestnut butter cream. Reroll cake, put on serving platter and frost outside with remaining cream. Decorate with shaved chocolate. For butter cream, finely chop marrons. Cut butter in small pieces. Put egg yolks into a mixing bowl. Set aside. Combine sugar and corn syrup. Cook over medium heat, stirring constantly until mixture comes to full boil. Remove from heat. Beat egg yolks at high speed until foamy. Add syrup gradually, continuing to beat at high speed. Do not scrape the pan. Beat until mixture is cool. Beat in butter, a little at a time. Stir in rum and chestnuts. Serves 8.

CRÈME DE MENTHE MOUSSE

¼ pound marshmallows
  (16 large ones)

⅔ cup green crème de menthe
1 pint heavy cream, whipped

Place marshmallows and crème de menthe in the top of a double boiler. Stir over boiling water until the marshmallows are melted. Cool thoroughly, then fold into whipped cream. Pour into refrigerator or freezing tray and freeze until firm. Serve plain or topped with chocolate sauce, crème de cacao, or crème de menthe. Serves 8.

Mrs. Andrew G. Nichols
(Loxley Fitzpatrick)

WHITE GRAPE AND GINGER SYLLABUB

2 pounds seedless white
  grapes (6 grapes reserved,
  halved)
2 cups crushed ginger snaps
4 egg whites, stiffly beaten

*1 cup sugar
1¼ cups white wine
juice of ½ lemon
2 cups heavy cream, beaten
½ cup toasted slivered almonds

Arrange one-fourth of grapes in bottom of large-size serving bowl. Cover with one-fourth crushed ginger snaps. Repeat until grapes and ginger snaps are used up. Put beaten egg whites in medium-size bowl. Beat in one-fourth of sugar. Fold in remaining sugar. Pour egg whites over wine and lemon juice. Stir gently until well mixed. Pour cream in large mixing bowl. Beat until thick but not stiff. Fold the egg white mixture into the cream. Pour this over the grapes and ginger snaps. Chill 2 hours. Arrange the reserved grape halves on top and sprinkle with toasted almonds. Serves 6.

*The sugar should be finer than regular granulated but not confectioners' sugar. Put a cup of sugar in blender and blend for 2 or 3 seconds. Shake and repeat 3 or 4 times.

Mrs. Robert H. Jones
(Kathryn Jarvis)

GOOEY
Chocolate Lovers Dream

5 large eggs
2½ cups sugar
1 cup softened butter
2 teaspoons vanilla extract

⅔ cup flour
3 tablespoons cocoa
1¼ cups pecans

Beat whole eggs, add the sugar and continue beating in electric mixer for about 20 minutes. Add the butter, vanilla extract, flour and cocoa that have been sifted together. Remove beaters and add pecans. Put in a buttered 11 x 13-inch pan and bake 1 hour at 300°. The pan should be placed in another pan of water while it bakes. Cut in squares and serve with vanilla ice cream or whipped cream on top. Flavor whipped cream with a little bourbon for a different taste. Serves 12-14.

Mrs. Donald W. Rhame
(Alacia Lee)

PEARS IN CHOCOLATE SABAYON

3 cups water
1 cup sugar
1 (3 inch) piece lemon peel

1 cinnamon stick
6 pears, peeled

SAUCE:
3 ounces semi-sweet chocolate
¾ cup strong coffee
4 tablespoons sugar
8 egg yolks

2 tablespoons rum, cognac or
   Grand Marnier
whipped cream to garnish

In a saucepan combine water, sugar, lemon peel and cinnamon stick and bring to a simmer. After the sugar has dissolved, add peeled pears. Poach the pears over low heat until tender (the riper the pear, the shorter the cooking time). Allow the pears to cool in the syrup and refrigerate until serving time. For sauce, melt chocolate in 2 tablespoons coffee over very low heat until it is smooth. In the top of a double boiler, combine sugar and egg yolks, then add remaining coffee. Whisk mixture over simmering water until it is creamy and thick. Do not let sauce come to a boil or it will curdle. Take off heat and add chocolate, then liqueur. Drain the pears and place on a serving dish. Pour warm sauce over them. They may be garnished with whipped cream. Serves 6.

Mrs. Thomas H. Lowe
(Maribeth Wills)

RUM MOLD

24 macaroons
½ cup rum
½ cup bourbon
1 cup almonds
4 eggs, separated

⅔ cup sugar, divided
2 envelopes unflavored gelatin
   soaked in 3 tablespoons cold
   water
1 pint heavy cream, whipped

Soak macaroons in rum and bourbon. Beat eggs separately. Cook yolks in a double boiler with ⅓ cup sugar until it thickens as a custard. Add soaked gelatin to custard, stir until dissolved. Then add beaten egg whites and whipped cream to which the remainder of the sugar has been added. Fold macaroons and almonds into custard. Pour into mold and allow to set. Serves 14.

Mrs. Carr G. Dodson
(Katherine Pilcher)

CHEESECAKE
From Lindy's Restaurant, New York

CRUST:

1 cup sifted flour

¼ cup sugar

1 teaspoon grated lemon peel

½ teaspoon vanilla extract

1 egg yolk

¼ cup soft butter or margarine

FILLING:

5 (8 ounce) packages cream
cheese, softened

1¾ cups sugar

3 tablespoons flour

1½ teaspoons grated lemon
peel

1½ teaspoons grated orange
peel

¼ teaspoon vanilla extract

5 eggs

2 egg yolks

¼ cup heavy cream

For crust, combine flour, sugar, lemon peel and vanilla extract. Make a well in center, add egg yolk and butter. Mix with fingertips until dough cleans side of bowl. Form into a ball; wrap in waxed paper; refrigerate about 1 hour. Preheat oven to 400°. Grease bottom and side of a 9" springform pan. Remove side from pan. Roll one third of dough on bottom of spring-form pan; trim edge. Bake 8-10 minutes, or until golden. Meanwhile, divide rest of dough into 3 parts. Roll each part into a strip 2½ inches wide and about 10 inches long. Put together springform pan, with baked crust on bottom. Fit crust strips to side of pan, joining ends of strips to line inside of pan completely. Trim dough so it comes only ¾ way up sides. Refrigerate before filling. Preheat oven to 500°. In large electric mixer bowl, combine cream cheese, sugar, flour, lemon and orange peels and vanilla extract. Add eggs and egg yolks one at a time. Add cream. Mix thoroughly. Pour in filling and bake 10 minutes at 500°. Reduce heat to 250° and bake one hour longer. Cool in pan on wire rack. Refrigerate 3 hours or overnight. Add glaze. Serves 16-20.

STRAWBERRY GLAZE (FOR CHEESECAKE)

1 (10 ounce) package frozen,
sliced strawberries, thawed
and undrained

¼ cup sugar

1 tablespoon cornstarch

1 tablespoon lemon juice

1 quart large fresh strawberries,
washed, hulled and drained

Put thawed package frozen strawberries with their juice through coarse sieve, or blend in electric blender, to make a purée. In small saucepan, combine sugar and cornstarch, mixing well. Stir in strawberry purée. Bring to boiling, stirring, over medium heat; boil 1 minute. Mixture will be thickened and translucent. Remove from heat; cool slightly. Stir in juice; cool completely. Arrange fresh strawberries, with points up, over cooled cheesecake. Spoon glaze over strawberries.

Mrs. Bert D. Schwartz
(Edith Wasden)
Mrs. Thomas Tracy
(Jane Barrow)

PUMPKIN DESSERT

1 pound canned pumpkin
1 cup sugar
1 teaspoon ginger
1 teaspoon salt
1 teaspoon cinnamon
½ teaspoon nutmeg

1 cup chopped toasted nuts
½ gallon softened vanilla ice
  cream, divided
36 ginger snaps, halved
whipped cream

Combine pumpkin, sugar, salt and spices. Add nuts. Fold in with ice cream. Line a 9 x 13 x 2-inch pan with halved ginger snap cookies. Top with half of ice cream mixture. Repeat ginger snap layer. Add remaining ice cream mixture. Freeze 5 hours. Cut in squares to serve. Top with whipped cream. Serves 10-12.

CHOCOLATE LOG

6 egg whites (room
  temperature)
¾ cup sugar, divided
6 egg yolks

⅓ cup cocoa
1½ teaspoons vanilla extract
dash salt
confectioners' sugar

FILLING:
1½ cups whipped cream
½ cup confectioners' sugar
¼ cup cocoa

2 teaspoons instant coffee
  (optional)
1 teaspoon vanilla extract

Grease bottom of 15½ x 10½ x 1-inch jelly roll pan. Line with waxed paper; grease paper slightly. Preheat oven to 375°. Beat egg whites until soft peaks form. Add ¼ cup sugar, 2 tablespoons at a time until stiff peaks form. With same beaters, in another bowl, beat egg yolks at high speed; add remaining ½ cup sugar, 2 tablespoons at a time. Beat until mixture is very thick, about 4 minutes. At a low speed, beat in cocoa, vanilla extract and salt until smooth. With whisk, gently fold cocoa mixture into the beaten egg whites. Spread evenly in pan. Bake 15 minutes until surface springs back lightly. Sift confectioners' sugar in a 15 x 10-inch rectangle on a linen towel. Turn cake out on sugar and peel paper from cake. Roll up jelly roll fashion, towel and all. Cool seam side down on a rack at least 1 hour. For filling, combine all ingredients and beat with mixer until thick. Refrigerate. Unroll cake; spread with filling to 1-inch from edge; reroll. Place, seam side down, on plate and dust with confectioners' sugar. Refrigerate 1-2 hours. Cover loosely with foil while refrigerated. Serves 8-10.

Mrs. William W. Baxley, Jr.
(Charlene Carpenter)

BANANA FRITTERS WITH APRICOT SAUCE

2 eggs, separated
⅔ cup milk
1 tablespoon melted butter
1 tablespoon lemon juice
1½ cups flour
½ teaspoon salt

2-4 bananas cut in thirds
lengthwise
2 tablespoons lemon juice
2 tablespoons confectioners'
sugar

APRICOT SAUCE:
¾ cup strained apricot jam
¼ cup rum

water to slightly thin mixture to
mellow taste

Beat 2 yolks until thick and lemon colored; add milk, butter and lemon juice and blend well. In another bowl, mix flour with salt and stir well until blended. Fold in 2 stiffly beaten egg whites. Add milk mixture. Let batter sit for 1 hour. In meantime, slice bananas and let them sit 30 minutes in 2 tablespoons lemon juice added to confectioners' sugar. When ready to fry, drain bananas, dip in butter and drop in 360° oil. Cook until brown. To make sauce, mix ingredients and bring to a boil. Serve warm over fritters or pass to guests.

BANANAS FOSTER

3 tablespoons butter
¾ cup brown sugar
¾ teaspoon cinnamon
6 bananas (sliced lengthwise,
then halved)

1 ounce rum
1 ounce banana liqueur
1 quart vanilla ice cream

Combine butter, sugar and cinnamon in heavy skillet over low heat; cook about 5 minutes. Add bananas and cook 5 minutes, basting with sugar mixture. Add rum and liqueur; ignite rum. Pour bananas with sauce over vanilla ice cream. Serves 6.

Mrs. Wilbur I. Tucker
(Elizabeth Conner)

HINTS

To keep brown sugar light and moist, place ½ slice of bread in brown sugar box or add dried prunes to canister.

TOFFEE FONDUE

1 large package Kraft caramels
¼ cup milk
¼ cup strong black coffee
½ cup chocolate chips

apple wedges
marshmallows
angel food cake cubes or
   pound cake cubes

Place caramels, milk, coffee and chocolate in top of double boiler. Cook until melted and blended. Pour mixture in fondue pot. Spear fruits, marshmallows and cake. Dip in fondue.

CHOCOLATE FONDUE

8 squares semi-sweet chocolate
1 (15 ounce) can sweetened
   condensed milk
⅓ cup milk
dash of salt

choose one: 2 tablespoons
  instant coffee,
or ⅓ cup orange liqueur
or 4 ounces cream-filled mint
  patties
bananas or strawberries
pound cake in 1-inch squares

In saucepan, melt chocolate and stir in milks until smooth. Add salt. Heat thoroughly. Stir in choice of flavoring. Pour into fondue pot and place over heat. Fondue thickens the longer it sets up. Dip cake, bananas and strawberries into chocolate sauce. Yields 2½ cups.

CHOCOLATE LADYFINGER CAKE

2 bars German chocolate
2 tablespoons cold water
2 egg yolks
2 egg whites
3 tablespoons confectioners'
  sugar

1 (3½ ounce) can coconut
1 cup chopped nuts
ladyfingers
1 pint cream, whipped

Melt chocolate and water in double boiler. Stir in egg yolks. Beat egg whites until stiff. Mix with yolks, then blend into chocolate mixture. Add coconut and nuts. Line springform pan with ladyfingers and add chocolate mixture and repeat with layers of ladyfingers and chocolate. Top with whipped cream. Freezes well. Serves 8.

Mrs. William A. Snow, Jr.
(Jean Lamar)

EASY CHOCOLATE MOUSSE

1 (16 ounce) package semi-
sweet chocolate chips
⅔ cup sugar
⅔ cup heated milk
3 tablespoons strong brewed
coffee

3 tablespoons light Bacardi
rum
2 eggs
whipped cream

Blend all ingredients, except whipped cream, 2 or 3 minutes in blender. Chill 8 hours. Serve topped with whipped cream. Serves 4.

Mrs. Edward S. Sell, III
(Gwen Sorrell)

FLAMING BAKED ALASKA
Dramatic, delicious & fool proof

1 Box Duncan Hines Supreme
white cake mix
½ gallon vanilla ice cream
2 cups port wine

½ cup brandy
sugar to taste (enough to
sweeten egg whites)
12 egg whites

Bake cake according to directions in round pan 12 inches in diameter and 2 inches deep. Several hours before serving, place cake on round silver tray, and saturate with 2 cups port wine. Separate egg whites so they will reach room temperature. When ready to serve, heat oven to 500°, beat egg whites with enough sugar to sweeten, beating until whites are stiff. Place ½ gallon vanilla ice cream on wine-soaked cake, and completely cover with beaten egg whites. Place 2 empty egg shells on top of meringue and fill with brandy. *Place in hot (500°) oven for approximately 3 to 5 minutes, or until meringue is golden brown. Immediately serve, after igniting brandy-filled egg shells (it is essential that the brandy is placed in the egg shells *before* placing in oven. . .cold brandy will not ignite.) When placed before guests, spoon flaming brandy over Baked Alaska. Serves 12.

*The silver tray will not be harmed in this short time.

Mrs. James F. Hall
(Kathryn Terry)

ICE CREAM CAKE
Out of this world!

1st LAYER:

2 packages ladyfingers filled or unfilled

1 quart vanilla ice cream, softened

1 (6 ounce) can frozen orange juice, undiluted

2nd LAYER:

2 (10 ounce) packages frozen raspberries, drained

2 (9 ounce) cans crushed pineapple, drained

1 tablespoon frozen lemonade concentrate

3rd LAYER:

1 quart vanilla ice cream, softened

1 teaspoon almond extract

1 teaspoon rum extract

6 maraschino cherries, chopped

3 tablespoons chopped nuts

Line bottom and sides of 9-inch springform pan with ladyfingers. Mix 1 quart softened vanilla ice cream with frozen orange juice. Pour in mold and freeze. Crush raspberries (strain to remove seed). Add crushed pineapple and lemonade concentrate. Pour in mold and freeze firm. To 1 quart ice cream, add almond and rum extracts, chopped cherries, and chopped nuts. Pour over raspberry layer. Freeze overnight. Top with whipped cream. Garnish with fresh mint and fresh berries. Serves 12.

Mrs. Rufus Dorsey Sams, III
(Sidney Tucker)

GRAND MARNIER FONDUE FOR STRAWBERRIES

4 tablespoons sour cream

4 tablespoons low calorie whipped topping

2 tablespoons brown sugar

1 tablespoon Grand Marnier

2 tablespoons orange curacao

½ tablespoon dark rum

1 quart fresh strawberries

Combine sour cream and whipped topping. Blend in brown sugar, Grand Marnier, orange curacao and rum. Serve dip surrounded with fresh strawberries. Serves 4.

Mrs. Rufus Dorsey Sams, III
(Sidney Tucker)

MOCHA FUDGE DESSERT
Children love this!

1 box Famous Nabisco
  chocolate wafers, crushed
¼ cup melted butter
½ gallon coffee ice cream

1 can Hershey fudge topping
½ pint whipping cream,
  whipped
toasted almonds

Mix wafers and melted butter together. Press in a 13 x 9-inch pan and bake 8 minutes at 350°. Let cool. Layer coffee ice cream, fudge topping and whipping cream. Sprinkle with toasted almonds. Let freeze several hours before serving. Serves 8-10.

Mrs. F. Daly Smith, Jr.
(Deborah Parrish)

MARSHMALLOWS DIPPED IN CARAMEL & NUTS

2 cups brown sugar
1 cup sugar
1½ cups half and half
6 tablespoons butter

1 teaspoon vanilla extract
marshmallows
chopped pecans

Bring brown sugar, white sugar and half and half to a boil and add butter. Cook until soft ball stage is reached, remove from heat and let cool. Add vanilla extract. Beat until thick enough to coat marshmallows. Put marshmallow on ice pick and dip in caramel candy, then drop in bowl of chopped pecans and turn until the whole marshmallow is coated. Drop on buttered platter until dry.

Mrs. William H. Baskin
(Frances Solomon)

CHERI-SUISSE ROMANOFF

1 (16 ounce) jar pitted sweet
  cherries, drained
1 cup whipping cream, whipped
4 tablespoons Cheri-Suisse
  liqueur, divided

1 pint vanilla ice cream,
  softened

Drain cherries. Whip cream that has been mixed with 2 tablespoons liqueur. Fold in 1 pint softened vanilla ice cream. Fold in cherries and 2 additional tablespoons liqueur. Freeze. Serves 6.

CRÈME CARAMEL
Light, smooth, delightful

CARAMEL:

½ cup sugar

¼ cup plus 1 tablespoon water

CREME:

2 cups whole milk
½ cup half and half
½ cup minus 1 tablespoon
  sugar

1 teaspoon vanilla extract
2 eggs
2 egg yolks

Heat sugar and water over low heat stirring until sugar dissolves completely. Increase heat and boil 3 or 4 minutes until it turns golden brown. Immediately pour into heatproof casserole dish. Bring milk, half and half and sugar to a boil over moderate heat. Remove from heat and add vanilla. Let rest while you beat eggs and yolks with wire whisk until thick and pale yellow. Gradually add milk mixture to eggs, pouring through strainer. Beat while you are adding milk. *Do not use electric mixer.* Pour the mixture into large pitcher. Preheat oven to 325°. Pour the mixture through fine strainer into casserole dish on top of caramel. Place casserole dish in a pan of boiling water in lower part of oven and bake for 40 minutes. Do not allow water to simmer during cooking. Lower oven heat if it does. When done, the center of creme is firm when pressed. Remove from pan of water and allow to cool thoroughly. Chill in refrigerator 1½ to 2 hours. Run knife around edge of casserole and reverse on serving plate. The caramel is thin and you need to use a plate with curved up edges. This can be made in 6 individual custard cups using about ½ cup custard each. Cooking time can be reduced from 40 minutes when using individual cups.

Mrs. Robert H. Jones
(Kathryn Jarvis)

RASPBERRY SHERBET

2 cups sugar
juice of 8 lemons
grated rind of 3 lemons
1½ quarts milk

1 (13 ounce) can evaporated
  milk
1 (10 ounce) package frozen
  raspberries

Dissolve sugar in lemon juice and add rind, milk and evaporated milk. Stir in thawed raspberries. Freeze in electric freezer. Yields 3 quarts.

RASPBERRY BOMBE

2 tablespoons kirsch
½ cup chopped walnuts
¼ cup chopped maraschino
  cherries

1½ cups sifted confectioners'
  sugar
1 pint cream, whipped
1 quart raspberry sherbet

Mix kirsch, walnuts, cherries, and sugar with whipped cream and line a 1½ quart mold with three-fourths of mixture. Freeze until firm. Place softened sherbet in hollow in center. Cover with remaining cream mixture and cover with waxed paper. Freeze at least 3 hours or up to a week ahead. Place hot water in dish, submerge mold and unmold on chilled platter. Serves 8-10.

Mrs. William W. Baxley, Jr.
(Charlene Carpenter)

MACADAMIA ICE CREAM

3 egg yolks
¾ cup sugar
2½ cups hot milk
1 teaspoon vanilla extract

2 cups heavy cream, whipped
¾ cup rum
¾ cup chopped macadamia
  nuts

In double boiler, beat yolks with sugar until light colored. Stir in hot milk. Stir over heat until mixture thickens. Remove pan from heat. Strain custard, stir in vanilla extract, and let mixture cool. Fold in heavy cream that has been whipped. Freeze mixture in ice cream freezer. When mixture is almost frozen, add rum and nuts. Freeze until firm.

JANE'S CHOCOLATE ICE CREAM DESSERT

1 cup flour
¼ cup oatmeal
¼ cup brown sugar
½ cup chopped nuts

1 (12 ounce) jar butterscotch
  topping, divided
½ cup butter (no margarine)
½ gallon chocolate ice cream

Combine flour, oatmeal, brown sugar and nuts. Melt butter in 13 x 9-inch pan. Spread flour mixture on top. Stir to blend. Bake at 400° for 10 to 15 minutes. Stir several times to keep from burning on bottom. Cool. Spread one-half into pan. Dribble one-half of the topping over the crumbs. Pack ice cream over topping and then add the rest of the topping and crumbs. Freeze. Serves 8-10.

Mrs. Ralph G. Newton, Jr.
(Harriet Adams)

COFFEE ICE CREAM

5 eggs
3 tablespoons flour
3 cups sugar
1 tablespoon vanilla extract

dash salt
3 cups strong, cold coffee
6 cups half and half

Mix eggs, flour, sugar, vanilla extract, and salt in blender until thoroughly mixed. Pour into ice cream freezer and add coffee and half and half. Stir until blended. Churn according to manufacturer's directions for your churn. Yields 4 quarts.

Mrs. F. Kennedy Hall
(Ann Kite)

PEPPERMINT FREEZE

2 cups vanilla wafer crumbs
¼ cup melted butter
2 cups confectioners' sugar
½ cup softened butter
2 (1 ounce) squares
  unsweetened chocolate,
  melted and cooled

1 teaspoon vanilla extract
3 egg yolks, beaten
3 egg whites, stiffly beaten
1 quart peppermint ice cream,
  softened
1 cup chopped pecans

Combine crumbs and melted butter, press firmly and evenly in bottom of 13 x 9 x 2-inch baking pan. Cream sugar and softened butter, until light and fluffy. Add chocolate, vanilla and egg yolks beating well. Fold whites into chocolate mixture and spread in pan. Spread ice cream over chocolate mixture. Sprinkle with nuts. Lightly press nuts into ice cream. Freeze 3-4 hours. Serves 10-12.

ORANGE ICE CREAM

2 pints vanilla ice cream,
  softened
2 (6 ounce) cans frozen orange
  juice concentrate, melted

2 ounces Grand Marnier

Mix and place ingredients in freezer. Do not let mixture get too hard. Serve in parfait or sherbet glasses. Serves 8.

Mrs. Agnes Domingos
(Agnes Burdett)

HOMEMADE SHERBET TRIPLE DELIGHT
Tastes churn-made

2 cups buttermilk
½ cup sugar
½ cup light corn syrup
½ cup fresh orange juice
⅓ cup fresh lemon juice
  (approximately 3 lemons)

1 (8 ounce) can crushed
  pineapple, undrained
1 teaspoon grated orange rind
1 teaspoon grated lemon rind

In a large bowl stir together the buttermilk and sugar until the sugar is dissolved. Whisk in the corn syrup, orange juice, and lemon juice until blended. Stir in the pineapple, orange rind and lemon rind. Turn into an 8 x 8 x 2-inch metal cake pan. Freeze until firm around the edges. Turn into a bowl and beat out until uniformly smooth; return to pan and freeze until entirely firm. Cover tightly. At serving time, let stand in refrigerator or at room temperature to soften slightly before serving in squares or scoops. Serves 8.

Mrs. Thomas F. Richardson
(Mary Anne Berg)

FRENCH VANILLA ICE CREAM

1 quart light cream
1 cup heavy cream
3 cups milk
1½ cups sugar

¼ teaspoon salt
12 egg yolks, well-beaten
2 tablespoons vanilla extract

In a double boiler combine light cream, heavy cream and milk. Over a direct moderate flame or medium heat, bring mixture to the boiling point, but do not boil. Add sugar and salt, stirring until sugar dissolves. Place mixture over simmering water. Do not let water touch top section of boiler. Stir a little of the hot cream mixture into the beaten egg yolks. Slowly stir the yolks into the cream mixture in top section of the double boiler. Cook, stirring constantly, until mixture just begins to thicken slightly. It should have the consistency of heavy cream. Remove from flame. Stir in vanilla extract. Chill to refrigerator temperature. Freeze following freezer directions.

Mrs. Robert W. Stribling
(Ginger Meadows)

BUTTER PECAN ICE CREAM

2 cups brown sugar
1 cup water
¼ teaspoon salt
4 eggs, beaten
4 tablespoons butter

2 cups milk
1 tablespoon vanilla extract
2 cups whipping cream,
    whipped
1 cup chopped pecans

In double boiler combine first 3 ingredients and cook until sugar melts. Add eggs and continue stirring until mixture thickens. Stir in butter, cool; add milk and vanilla extract. Beat whipping cream and fold into mixture. Stir in pecans. Freeze in ice cream freezer. Yields ½ gallon.

CHOCOLATE ICE CREAM

5 quarts milk
10 large eggs
6 cups sugar, divided
1 cup flour
8 ounces unsweetened
    chocolate

3 cups hot water
1 quart whipping cream
2 tablespoons vanilla extract

Scald milk. Whip eggs thoroughly. Add 5 cups sugar and beat, then add flour to eggs and sugar. Add a little scalded milk to mixture. Slowly pour mixture into the scalded milk, stirring constantly. Melt chocolate with 3 cups hot water and while milk is cooling, add 1 cup sugar to chocolate. When custard is done, add a small amount to chocolate mixture. Stir all ingredients together. When cold, add 1 quart whipping cream and 2 tablespoons vanilla extract. Freeze in ice cream freezer.

LEMON EGG SAUCE

1 cup sugar
4 egg yolks, beaten
4 tablespoons margarine
juice of 2 lemons

½ cup boiling water
sherry to taste (optional)

In double boiler combine all ingredients, adding water slowly. Cook until thickened. Serve hot. Add sherry if desired. Good on sponge, spice, prune cakes or ginger bread.

VARIATION: Mix in a double boiler: 1 whole egg, 3 egg yolks, ½ cup sugar, ½ cup Grand Marnier, and 1 teaspoon grated orange peel. Heat until thickened. Try served over fresh fruit. Serves 6.

Mrs. Sidney B. McNair
(Katherine Alfriend)

BLACK CHERRY RUM SAUCE

1 cup canned Bing cherry juice
3 tablespoons sugar
1 tablespoon cornstarch
2 tablespoons cold water

½ teaspoon lemon juice
2 cups canned Bing cherries,
  halved
¼ cup rum

Heat cherry juice. Add sugar and cornstarch, which has been dissolved in 2 tablespoons cold water. Cook 10 minutes. Cool. While warm, add lemon juice, cherries and rum. Chill. Serve over cake or ice cream.

VARIATION: Mix 1 cup dark cherry preserves with ¼ cup rum and ½ cup chopped walnuts. Serve cold over ice cream.

BUTTERSCOTCH ICE CREAM SAUCE

1½ cups packed brown sugar
¼ cup butter
⅔ cup white corn syrup

¾ cup evaporated milk

Combine brown sugar, butter and corn syrup in heavy saucepan over medium heat; stir until butter is melted and ingredients are blended. Bring to a boil, cook to soft-boil stage or 235° on candy thermometer. Remove from heat; cool slightly. Add evaporated milk slowly, stirring until blended. Store in refrigerator. Yields 2 cups.

Mrs. Albert S. Hatcher, III
(Deryl Howington)

CHOCOLATE SAUCE

½ cup butter
2¼ cups confectioners' sugar

⅔ cup evaporated milk
6 squares semi-sweet chocolate

Mix butter and confectioners' sugar in top of double boiler, add evaporated milk and chocolate and cook over hot water for 30 minutes. Do not stir while cooking. Remove from heat and beat. You may store in refrigerator and reheat as needed. If you wish to have a thinner sauce, add cream. (Do not add water.) Yields 1½ pints.

Mrs. Leo B. Huckabee, Jr.
(Randall Adams)

PICKLES,
RELISHES
AND
JELLIES

PEAR CHUTNEY
Excellent with meats and curry dishes

5 pounds sugar, divided
4 oranges, peeled, cored, and sliced
2 large ginger roots, peeled and sliced
1 (2 ounce) box white mustard seed
1 pound pecan pieces or halves
1 teaspoon salt
1 teaspoon cloves
1 tablespoon cinnamon
1 teaspoon allspice
1½ quarts cider vinegar, divided
29 pears, peeled, cored, and chopped
2 (15 ounce) boxes raisins
1 cinnamon stick in each jar before sealing

Part 1: Cook the following ingredients together for ½ hour: 2½ pounds sugar, oranges (use juice and cut up pulp and rind, cut very thin), ginger roots, mustard seed, pecans, salt, cloves, cinnamon, allspice, and ½ quart vinegar.

Part II: To the first mixture which was cooked ½ hour, add the pears, 2½ pounds sugar, 1 quart vinegar and the raisins. Do not overcook, as the juice is always a little short. (One additional cup vinegar can be added to insure enough liquid.) Cook slowly until fairly thick and pears are darkened, about 4½-5 hours. Seal in sterilized jars with 1 stick of cinnamon. Process in hot bath 10 minutes. Yields 8 quarts.

Mrs. Robert T. Thetford
(Elizabeth Goodwyn)

MINCEMEAT

2 pints lean beef
1 pint ground suet
2 pints raisins
1 pint chopped citron
3 pints chopped, unpeeled apples
4 pints sugar
1 pint molasses
1 pint cider vinegar
1 tablespoon ground cloves
2 tablespoons ground cinnamon
1 tablespoon ground nutmeg
salt to taste

Cut beef in 2-inch cubes and cook until tender. Remove and grind meat. Grind suet, raisins and citron. Set aside. Chop apples and add to prepared meat, suet, raisins and citron. Add other ingredients. Mix well and cook 4-5 hours at 200 - 300° or until apples are done. Remove mincemeat to jars. Cover and refrigerate for 2 - 3 weeks.

ARTICHOKE PICKLES

8 pounds Jerusalem artichokes
1 cup salt
1 gallon vinegar
red pepper pods
2 quarts cider vinegar

8 cups sugar
2 teaspoons whole cloves
1 teaspoon whole allspice
1 stick cinnamon, broken into
  small pieces

Clean well 8 pounds artichokes, scrubbing with a brush. Soak over-night in clear water. The next morning, add 1 cup of salt to 1 gallon of vinegar and heat to boiling. Add a few pods of red pepper. While hot, pour vinegar over the artichokes, which have been placed in a stone jar or enameled container. Let stand 24 hours. Next day, throw away the first vinegar and make a new vinegar by combining cider vinegar, sugar and spices. Bring mixture to a boil. Pour over artichokes. Let stand until next day. Pickles are ready to seal in hot, sterilized jars. (The vinegar is the preservative since the mixture is put up cold.)

Mrs. Leo B. Huckabee
(Jane Odom)

ICED GREEN TOMATO PICKLE

7 pounds green tomatoes,
  sliced thin, (no pink or pale
  green)
3 cups slaked lime
1 gallon water
2 quarts cider vinegar
5 pounds sugar

1 teaspoon cloves
1 teaspoon ginger
1 teaspoon allspice
1 teaspoon celery seed
1 teaspoon mace
1 teaspoon cinnamon

First day: Soak in an enamel container, sliced tomatoes for 24 hours in lime water (a mixture made from mixing 3 cups slaked lime to 1 gallon water). Second day: Change water every 4 hours to clean lime off tomatoes. Make a syrup of cider vinegar, sugar, cloves, ginger, allspice, celery seed, mace, and cinnamon. Cook about 10 minutes, then pour over drained tomatoes and let stand overnight. Third day: Cook tomatoes in syrup for 1 hour over medium heat almost to boiling point. Pack tomatoes in hot, sterilized jars, add syrup and seal. Yields 7 pints.

Mrs. Donald D. Comer
(Harriet Fincher)

PAULINE DUNWODY'S WATERMELON RIND PICKLES

watermelon rind
  (from 2 quarts fruit)
1 teaspoon soda
2 tablespoons alum
1 tablespoon ginger

vinegar
3 pounds sugar
¼ cup whole cloves
¼ cup stick cinnamon

Pare rind from 2 quarts of fruit and cover with water. Add soda. Let mixture stand overnight. Next morning, drain and cover with water to which alum has been added. Boil 10 minutes. Cover again with cold water. Add ginger and boil for 15 minutes. Drain. Measure water and record amount; then discard water. Measure as much vinegar as you had water. To each quart of vinegar add 3 pounds sugar, ¼ cup whole cloves, and ¼ cup stick cinnamon. Add fruit and boil until clear (about 45 minutes or to 222°). Process and seal in hot, sterilized jars. Yields 9 (½-pint) jars.

Mrs. J. Everett Flournoy
(Adele Warnock)

DILL PICKLES

2 quarts water
1 quart cider vinegar
¼ cup salt
2 cloves garlic

1 or more flowers of fresh dill
2 whole cloves
6 whole peppercorns
cucumbers

Boil water, vinegar and salt. Pack each of 6 hot quart jars with garlic, dill, cloves, peppercorns, and cucumbers (may be sliced or left whole if small enough). Pour hot liquid over cucumbers and seal. Let pickles cure for 5 days to reach best flavor before eating.

Mrs. William E. Hollis
(Allee Gardiner)

PICKLED CHERRIES

2 quarts large sweet cherries
¼ cup sugar
2 dozen whole cloves

one (3-inch) stick cinnamon
2½ cups vinegar

Wash and stem cherries. Set aside. Mix sugar, spices (tied in a bag), and vinegar. Cook 5 minutes. Add cherries and cook until tender. Remove from heat and let mixture stand overnight. Next day remove spices. Drain syrup from cherries. Pack cherries in hot, sterilized jars. Boil syrup rapidly until it has thickened. Pour hot syrup over cherries. Adjust lids and process. Yields 2½ pints.

SWEET AND SOUR APPLE RELISH
Good with pork

1 large onion, chopped
1 large tomato, chopped
¼ cup raisins
4 tablespoons wine vinegar
¼ teaspoon cinnamon
¼ teaspoon cloves

1 teaspoon ginger
1 teaspoon dry mustard
1 (10 ounce) jar red currant jelly
4 tablespoons butter
8 firm apples, sliced

Mix all ingredients together, except apples. Cook in a saucepan 20 minutes. Add apples and cook 10 minutes. Seal in sterilized jars.

"END OF THE GARDEN" RELISH

1 cup chopped cucumber
1 cup chopped sweet pepper
1 cup chopped cabbage
1 cup chopped onions
1 cup chopped green tomatoes
salt
1 cup chopped carrots
1 cup green string beans, cut in
  small pieces

2 tablespoons mustard seed
1 tablespoon celery seed
1 cup chopped celery
2 cups vinegar
2 cups sugar
2 tablespoons turmeric

Soak cucumbers, peppers, cabbage, onions, and tomatoes in water overnight. (½ cup salt to 2 quarts water) Drain. Cook carrots and beans in boiling water until tender. Drain. Mix soaked and cooked vegetables with remaining ingredients and boil 10 - 15 minutes. Pack in hot, sterilized jars and seal.

CHOW-CHOW RELISH

12½ pounds green tomatoes
12½ pounds green and red
  peppers
½ medium head cabbage,
  chopped

4 pods hot pepper
10 large onions, chopped
½ cup salt
8 cups sugar
3 pints vinegar

Grind all vegetables together using fine blender blade. Boil ingredients for 2 hours. Seal in hot, sterilized jars. Yields 22 pints.

Mrs. William E. Hollis
(Allee Gardiner)

DAMSON PLUM PRESERVES
Good on vanilla ice cream

2 quarts Damson plums	1½ oranges
4½ cups sugar	3 cups seeded raisins
1½ lemons	1½ cups chopped nuts

Wash plums, cover with water and soak until tender. Remove seeds and chop. Measure 6 cups plum pulp. Add sugar, juice and grated rind of fruits. Add raisins. Cook until thickened mixture is transparent. Add nuts. Process in sterilized jars and cover with paraffin. Yields 12 (6 ounce) jars.

APRICOT-PINEAPPLE PRESERVES

1 cup crushed, canned pineapple	1½ cups sugar juice of one lemon
1 cup dried apricots, softened	¼ cup liquid pectin

Cook fruit, sugar, and juice to boiling point. Boil 1 minute. Add pectin. Stir mixture well. Cook until thickened and pour into hot, sterilized jars.

FIG-STRAWBERRY JAM

3 cups peeled, mashed figs	3 cups sugar
2 (3 ounce) packages strawberry gelatin	

In a saucepan, bring all ingredients to a boil over medium heat and cook 3 minutes. Seal in hot, sterilized jars and cover with paraffin.

BRANDIED APRICOT JELLY

1½ cups apricot nectar	2 tablespoons fresh lemon juice
3½ cups sugar	
¾ cup brandy	6 tablespoons liquid fruit pectin

Combine apricot nectar, sugar, brandy and lemon juice in a saucepan. Bring to a boil and cook 2 minutes stirring constantly. Remove from heat and stir in pectin. Mix well. Skim off any foam. Pour jelly into hot, sterilized jars and seal with paraffin. Yields 4 cups.

GRAPE CONSERVE

8 cups Concord grapes
½ cup water
2 oranges, peeled,
   reserving peel
6 cups sugar

¼ teaspoon salt
1 cup seedless raisins
1 cup chopped walnuts or
   pecans

Separate skins and pulps of grapes. Put skins in a saucepan and add ½ cup water. Cook on low heat for 20 minutes. Then work mixture through a sieve. Mix pulp with cooked grape skins. Peel oranges and remove membrane. Slice and put through a food chopper. Add sugar, salt, orange and peel to cooked grapes. Add raisins and simmer mixture until thickened. Add nuts. Pour mixture in hot, sterilized jar.

BLUEBERRY CONSERVE

4 cups sugar
2 cups water
½ unpeeled lemon, thinly
   sliced
½ unpeeled orange, thinly
   sliced

½ cup seedless raisins
1 quart fresh blueberries,
   washed and stemmed

Combine sugar and water and bring to a boil. Add lemon and orange slices and raisins. Simmer 5 minutes. Add blueberries and cook rapidly 20 minutes or until thickened, stirring frequently to prevent sticking. Pour into hot, sterilized jars and seal. Yields 10 (½-pint) jars.

BRANDIED FRUIT

10½ cups sugar
3 quarts water
½ cup orange liqueur
¼ cup brandy
rind of 3 lemons, grated
3 fresh peaches, halved and
   peeled

3 fresh nectarines, halved and
   peeled
3 fresh pears, halved and
   peeled
3 bunches of seedless green
   grapes, stemmed
3 whole fresh plums

In a large skillet, combine sugar and water. Stir over medium heat and bring mixture to a boil. Boil for 7 minutes and remove mixture from heat. Stir in liqueur, brandy and lemon rind. Arrange fruit, evenly distributed, in hot, sterilized jars. Pour heated syrup over fruit. Screw jar tops on and process in hot water bath for 25-30 minutes. Remove jars from bath and tighten lids. Yields 3 quart jars.

SWEET PICKLED FIGS

5 quarts ripe firm figs
4 cups water
2 cups sugar
4 cups sugar
2 cups vinegar

1 tablespoon whole cloves
1 tablespoon ground mace
1 teaspoon whole allspice
1 (2 inch) stick cinnamon

Scald figs in soda bath allowing 1 cup soda to 6 quarts boiling water. Drain and rinse. Cook figs in a syrup of 4 cups water and 2 cups sugar. When figs are tender, add 4 cups sugar, 2 cups vinegar, whole spices tied in cheesecloth bag, and mace. Cook figs until they are transparent and allow figs to stand in syrup overnight. Next day pack in hot, sterilized jars, cover with syrup, seal and process 15 minutes.

CRANBERRY CRUNCH

2 (12 ounce) bags fresh
  cranberries
1 cup sugar
1 (12 ounce) jar orange
  marmalade

rind of 1 orange, grated
4 ounces crystallized ginger
1 cup chopped nuts

Combine cranberries and sugar. Place in oblong pyrex baking dish and seal with aluminum foil. Bake at 350° for 25 minutes. Let cool and add remaining ingredients. Pour mixture in jars and refrigerate. Keeps for 3-4 weeks in refrigerator.

Mrs. Bruce J. Bishop
(Eleanor Richardson)

CRANBERRY NUT SAUCE

1 quart fresh cranberries
½ cup orange juice
¼ cup brandy or Benedictine
  liqueur

2 cups sugar
½ cups coarsely chopped
  walnuts

Combine cranberries, orange juice and liqueur in saucepan. Cover and cook about 7 minutes. When skins burst, add sugar and mix thoroughly. Cool. Stir in walnuts and serve as a side dish. Keep in refrigerator and serve cold. Serves 8.

Mrs. Toof A. Boone, Jr.
(Sylvia Wyllys)

APPLE JELLY A LA MICROWAVE

3½ pounds apples, washed,
   cored and cut in eighths
3½ cups water

3 cups sugar or ¾ cup sugar
   for each 1 cup of juice
2 tablespoons lemon juice

Place apples and water in a 4-quart casserole. Cook in microwave covered, full power, 20 minutes or until apples are tender. Strain apples and liquid through cheesecloth. There should be 4 cups of juice. Add sugar and lemon juice. Cook, full power, 35 minutes or until jellying point is reached. Pour into hot, sterilized jars and cool. Refrigerate.

ORANGE MARMALADE

1 quart water
4 large oranges
juice of 2 grapefruits

1 lemon
5 pounds sugar

Put water in saucepan on low heat and add juice of fruit. Grind orange and lemon peel. Cook in juice 20 minutes until tender. Add sugar, stir often, until thickened. Seal in hot, sterilized jars. Yields 5-6 pints.

Mrs. C. Hall Farmer
(Eugenia Lowe)

"HOT" PEPPER JELLY
Very hot, but easy

1½ cups banana peppers
   (5 or 6)
¼ - ½ cup hot peppers
   (20 small red or green)
1½ cups vinegar

6½ cups sugar
1 bottle Certo
red or green food coloring
   (optional)

Blend peppers and vinegar in blender. Pour mixture into a saucepan and add sugar. Boil 3-4 minutes. Add Certo and boil 1 minute. Set aside for 5 minutes. Strain into large bowl through colander and add red or green food coloring. Stir well and seal in hot, sterilized jars. Yields 6 (½-pint) jars.

Mrs. Donald Beaty
(Ann Chandler)

CRÈME DE MENTHE JELLY

2½ cups sugar	1 cup water
1 cup green crème de menthe	6 tablespoons liquid fruit pectin

Bring sugar, crème de menthe, and water to a boil. Stir until sugar is dissolved. Add pectin and boil 1 more minute. Remove from heat and skim off any foam. Pour jelly in hot, sterilized jars. Seal with paraffin. Yields 4 cups.

MRS. HAPP'S CATSUP
Hot

1 gallon peeled, chopped and drained tomatoes	1 teaspoon cinnamon
3 tablespoons salt	½ teaspoon cloves
1 tablespoon cayenne pepper	1 tablespoon dry mustard
1 teaspoon mace	2 large onions, chopped
1 teaspoon allspice	1 quart apple vinegar
	8 ounces brown sugar

Simmer all ingredients in a saucepan for 4 hours, stirring often. Put up in sterilized ½-pint jars, seal and place in a hot water bath for 20 minutes. Yields 8 (½-pint) jars.

Best if allowed to sit for a week. Refrigerate after opening.

Mrs. John H. Puryear
(Erin Crandall)

MUSTARD

½ cup wine vinegar	2 eggs, beaten
½ cup Burgundy wine	1 cup sugar
1 cup dry mustard	½ teaspoon salt

Stir vinegar, wine and mustard together and allow to stand overnight. The next day, beat the eggs and sugar together until creamy. Add sugar-egg mixture to vinegar, wine and mustard. Stir in salt. Store mixture in an air tight container in the refrigerator.

HINTS

Ground spices darken the appearance of pickles.

To deodorize jars, pour in a solution of dry mustard and water.

TABLE OF SUBSTITUTIONS

Instead of:	Use:
BAKING POWDER 1 teaspoon baking powder	¼ teaspoon baking soda **plus** ½ teaspoon cream of tartar
BREAD CRUMBS 1 cup bread crumbs	¾ cup cracker crumbs
BROTH 1 cup chicken or beef broth	1 bouillon cube or 1 teaspoon powdered broth or 1 envelope powdered broth base dissolved in 1 cup boiling water
BUTTER (OR MARGARINE) 1 cup butter or margarine (for shortening)	1 cup shortening with ½ teaspoon salt
CHOCOLATE 1 square (1-ounce) unsweetened chocolate	3 tablespoons cocoa **plus** 1 tablespoon butter or margarine
6 ounces semi-sweet chocolate	2 ounces unsweetened chocolate **plus** 7 tablespoons sugar and 2 tablespoons fat
CORNSTARCH 1 tablespoon cornstarch (for thickening)	2 tablespoons all-purpose flour
CORN SYRUP 1 cup corn syrup	¾ cup sugar **plus** ¼ cup water
CREAM 1 cup light cream	⅞ cup milk **plus** 3 tablespoons butter
1 cup heavy cream	¾ cup milk **plus** ⅓ cup butter
GARLIC 1 clove fresh garlic	1 teaspoon garlic salt or ⅛ teaspoon garlic powder
FLOUR 1 tablespoon flour (for thickening)	½ tablespoon cornstarch or ½ tablespoon arrowroot starch or 1 tablespoon granulated tapioca
1 cup all-purpose flour	1 cup **plus** 2 tablespoons cake flour or Up to ½ cup bran, whole wheat flour, or corn meal **plus** enough all purpose flour to equal 1 cup
1 cup cake flour	1 cup **minus** 2 tablespoons all-purpose flour
1 cup self-rising flour	1 cup all-purpose flour **plus** 1 teaspoon baking powder and ½ teaspoon salt

TABLE OF SUBSTITUTIONS

Instead of:	Use:
HONEY	
1 cup honey	1¼ cups sugar **plus** ¼ cup liquid or 1 cup molasses
MILK	
1 cup sour milk or 1 cup buttermilk	1 tablespoon vinegar or lemon juice or 1¾ teaspoons cream of tartar **plus** homogenized milk to equal 1 cup (let stand 5 minutes)
1 cup sweet milk (homogenized)	1 cup sour milk or buttermilk **plus** ½ teaspoon baking soda
1 cup whole milk	¼ cup powdered skim milk **plus** 2 tablespoons butter and 1 cup water or 4 teaspoons powdered whole milk **plus** 1 cup water or ½ cup evaporated milk **plus** ½ cup water or 1 cup milk **plus** 2 tablespoons butter or margarine
MUSTARD	
1 tablespoon prepared mustard	1 teaspoon dry mustard
MUSHROOMS	
1 pound fresh mushrooms	6 ounces canned mushrooms
ONION	
2 teaspoons minced onion	1 teaspoon onion powder
SOUR CREAM	
1 cup commercial sour cream	1 tablespoon lemon juice **plus** evaporated milk to make 1 cup.
TOMATOES (canned)	
1 cup canned tomatoes	1⅓ cups fresh, cut-up tomatoes, simmered 10 minutes
1 cup tomato juice	½ cup tomato sauce **plus** ½ cup water
1 cup tomato purée	1 (6 oz.) can tomato paste **plus** 1 can water
YOGURT	
1 cup yogurt	1 cup buttermilk or sour milk

GRACIOUS GOODNESS
P.O. Box 935
Waycross, Georgia 31502

Please send me _____ copies of **GRACIOUS GOODNESS!** at $14.95
plus $2.00 postage and handling, or 3 for $41.85 plus $3.00 postage.
Georgia residents add 6% sales tax.

Enclosed is my check or money order for $ _____

Name _____

Address_____

City _____ State _____ Zip _____

GRACIOUS GOODNESS
P.O. Box 935
Waycross, Georgia 31502

Please send me _____ copies of **GRACIOUS GOODNESS!** at $14.95
plus $2.00 postage and handling, or 3 for $41.85 plus $3.00 postage.
Georgia residents add 6% sales tax.

Enclosed is my check or money order for $ _____

Name _____

Address_____

City _____ State _____ Zip _____

GRACIOUS GOODNESS
P.O. Box 935
Waycross, Georgia 31502

Please send me _____ copies of **GRACIOUS GOODNESS!** at $14.95
plus $2.00 postage and handling, or 3 for $41.85 plus $3.00 postage.
Georgia residents add 6% sales tax.

Enclosed is my check or money order for $ _____

Name _____

Address_____

City _____ State _____ Zip _____

Re-Order Additional Copies

Names and addresses of bookstores, gift shops, etc.
in your area would be appreciated.

_____

_____

_____

_____

_____

_____

Names and addresses of bookstores, gift shops, etc.
in your area would be appreciated.

_____

_____

_____

_____

_____

_____

Names and addresses of bookstores, gift shops, etc.
in your area would be appreciated.

_____

_____

_____

_____

_____

_____